TABLE OF CONTENTS

United Nations Interregional Crime
and Justice Research Institute

PATHWAYS TO THE MANAGEMENT OF MENTALLY-ILL OFFENDERS IN THE CRIMINAL JUSTICE SYSTEM

Edited by

Adelmo Manna
Ryosuke Kurosawa
Koichi Hamai

Publication No. 48
Rome, December 1993

©

**United Nations Interregional Crime
and Justice Research Institute**

Director: Ugo Leone

| United Nations Publication |
| Sales No. E.93.III.N.1 |

ISBN 9 290 78022 4

Text revision
Anne Baroni
Oksanna Hatalak

Publication layout & graphics
Roberto Gaudenzi

ACKNOWLEDGEMENTS

This book would not have been possible without the enthusiastic involvement of many people. In a sense it stands as the result of a truly collective commitment.

The work of our contributors is the core of this study and for its unique insights we are grateful to each of them.

Our appreciation goes to Dr. Anna Alvazzi del Frate for her assistance and suggestions in the revision of the drafts of the project. Special gratitude goes to Anne Baroni and Oksanna Hatalak for decoding and typing various versions of the manuscript.

PREFACE

Mentally-ill offenders present a challenge to the criminal justice system since they raise fundamental issues regarding normality/abnormality of both criminal behaviour and the individuals concerned, as well as the concept of criminal responsibility. Unfortunately, the present lack of information in this field, especially in developing countries, does not allow for an adequate analysis of the problems posed by mentally-ill offenders in the context of the criminal justice system.

Therefore, the United Nations Interregional Crime and Justice Research Institute (UNICRI) launched a project entitled 'Pathways to the Management of Mentally-ill Offenders in the Criminal Justice System'. The project was initially divided into three stages, the first of which was to involve a survey to review experiences in the management of the mentally-ill within the criminal justice system; the second was to take the form of a thorough comparative inquiry into the actual features and functioning of the systems created for these offenders in various countries; and the third aimed to provide guidelines for the improvement of the management of the mentally-ill within the criminal justice system.

This volume is the result of the first stage of the project, which attempts to present the realities and problems experienced when treating mentally-ill offenders within the criminal justice system. UNICRI plans to launch the second stage, in preparation for the third stage, by initiating a field study whereby the staff and management of institutions treating mentally-ill offenders, and the offenders themselves, will be visited and interviewed.

The main body of this volume is made up of the national reports prepared by the experts from the countries participating in this project. The countries include the following: Canada, Egypt, England & Wales, Germany, Italy, Japan, Nigeria, Peru, Sweden and Thailand.

The findings have produced several important thought-provoking issues regarding mentally-ill offenders, especially the conflict between safety in the community and the question of the human rights of offenders, which we plan to explore in the next stage of the project.

I would like to express my sincere gratitude to all those who collaborated in the preparation of this publication.

Ugo Leone
Director

Rome, December 1993

iv

EDITORS' INTRODUCTORY NOTES

The problems related to individuals who are suffering from a mental illness are of great concern to the socio-medical sciences. The programmes for the management of the mentally-ill encounter enormous difficulties in terms of their implementation in both the developed and developing world.

The overall picture becomes even bleaker in the case of mentally-ill offenders and the way they are dealt with by the criminal justice systems, which are very often unprepared and unable to cope with socio-medical problems. In many cases, the criminal justice system lacks the necessary skills, instruments and even facilities to deal with the mentally-ill offender. As a consequence, if not properly treated, these individuals may be subjected to increased personal suffering and psycho-physical deterioration and may possibly become a danger to society in general.

In the past, the United Nations dealt with the problem of the mentally-ill offender by means of specific provisions contained in the Standard Minimum Rules for the Treatment of Prisoners of 31 July 1957. Provisions 82-83 of the Rules read as follows:

No. 82:

1) Persons who are found to be insane shall not be detained in prisons and arrangements shall be made to remove them to mental institutions as soon as possible.

2) Prisoners who suffer from mental disease or abnormalities shall be observed and treated in specialised institutions under medical management.

3) During their stay in prison, such prisoners shall be placed under the special supervision of a medical officer.

4) The medical or psychiatric service of the penal institution shall provide for the psychiatric treatment of all other prisoners who are in need of such treatment.

No. 83 :

...it is desirable that steps should be taken, by arrangement with the appropriate agencies, to ensure, if necessary, the continuation of psychiatric treatment after release and the provision of social-psychiatric aftercare.

Another worthy United Nations contribution to the management of this enormous and complex problem is represented by the 'Principles, guidelines and guarantees for the protection of persons detained on the grounds of mental ill health or suffering from mental disorders' (United Nations Report, prepared by EIA Daes, Special Rapporteur of the Sub-Commission on the Prevention of Discrimination and the Protection of Minorities, New York, 1986). The Report represents 'a contribution to (a) the protection of the fundamental freedoms, human and legal rights of persons who are mentally ill or suffering from mental disorder; (b) the abolition of psychiatric abuses; (c) the promotion of mental health and medical practices and, (d) the improvement of mental care and mental institutions'.

There is still a very limited amount of reliable information available in this field, in particular from developing countries, which causes difficulty when trying to analyse the many problems posed by the mentally-ill offender in the context of the criminal justice system.

Project issues *

The problems related to the social and judicial management of the phenomena of the association between mental disorders and criminal behaviour in both the clinical and legal spheres are considered the most classical subjects of penal interest. The various changes that have

---

* The project proposal was prepared jointly by UNICRI Senior Scientific Consultants Professors Francesco Bruno and Adelmo Manna.

2

taken place in recent years, both in the scientific and cultural domains, have greatly influenced the perception and management of the problems concerning the social processing of the mentally-infirm, both inside and outside the criminal justice system. The mere existence, rapidity and sometimes contradictory directions of such changes have rendered more difficult, and often obsolete, the analysis and evaluation of developments in this field in different national and cultural environments. As a result, apart from a few commendable exceptions (Council of Europe, 1986 and ISISC, 1987), there has been a lack of objective valid and reliable information. In addition to this, the variety and heterogeneity of the systems adopted in various countries of the world, as well as their equally inconsistent enforcement, have made comparative research excessively complex and reduced the possibilities of international technical co-operation.

The concept of imputability tends to override the legal and normative aspects of responsibility and overshadows others of a psycho-pathological nature related to mental disturbances.

The concept of dangerousness, on the contrary, tends to be empirical in nature and is not sufficiently explained, either in absolute terms or in relation to the treatment and sanctioning effects with which it is inevitably associated.

Finally, treatment appears as a hybrid which combines, under a single phenomenology, the affliction of the sentence with society's concern for its own security and the patients' right to health and therapy.

Added to these problems are those specifically related with the efficiency and functioning of the criminal justice system and others that stem from the crisis that has affected psychology in recent years. This crisis is the result of the proliferation of ideological-philosophical theories over scientific ones, as well as the domination of socio-political aspects over clinical and technical ones which distinguish the psychic and behavioural sciences in every social system.

The importance of this research project appears evident, therefore, and the newly-gained knowledge will facilitate the policy-maker in identifying the new legal, evaluative and treatment options to be carried out in the framework of a more general process of penal reform. At the same time, new phenomena, such as AIDS, drugs, suicide, abnormal violent behaviour, etc. and the evolution of the neurobiological and behavioural sciences should be taken into consideration.

The project is divided into three phases: the first phase involved a comparative analysis of the treatment of mentally-ill offenders in the different legislative systems; the second phase should take the form of a thorough comparative inquiry into the actual features and functioning of the systems created for these offenders in various countries; and the third phase aims to provide guidelines on the most appropriate treatment for mentally-ill offenders which can then be offered to national governments for reflection and further development.

Phase 1: An analysis of comparative law

The first phase of the project - an analysis of comparative law - examines the two main stages of the legal treatment of mentally-ill offenders. The first stage involves the judicial decision on the responsibility of the offender who is found guilty for an offence; the second concerns the type of sanctions or security measures applied in those cases where it is established that the offender represents a danger to society. An intermediary stage exists between the other two, during which the offender is processed by means of technical, diagnostic and prognostic methods during the psychiatric examination.

The first part of the analysis involves the study of a series of rules which are of considerable interest given the novelty and originality of the solutions adopted. In particular, some systems - like that existing in Sweden - are taken into consideration because they have eliminated the distinction between imputability and non-imputability, with the aim of ascertaining responsibility without, however, renouncing differentiated treatment once treatment is decided upon.

Another particularly interesting system is the German one which, in 1975, underwent important innovations. These involved the radical modification of the section regarding imputability - which is considered as an element of penal responsibility - by including 'deep distance of conscience' and 'grave psychical anomaly' among the causes of imputability. The restrictive legal interpretation, however, has greatly reduced the number of offenders who are recognised as being afflicted by such llnesses.

As far as treatment is concerned, reference can be made once again to the German system, which introduced the so-called 'socio-therapy institutions'. These were set up for the treatment and care of psychopathic patients and were recently modified to become an alternative measure to detention.

The analysis includes other systems, each with special features, from Europe, the Arab region, Africa, Asia and Latin America.

Phase 2: Field studies

The field studies should constitute the second phase of the research project, i.e. the comparison of the actual features and operational processes of the systems dealing with mentally-ill offenders adopted by various countries.

Various methodological approaches will be used when carrying out these studies, which should allow for the evaluation of the numerous aspects of a complex, multi-faceted reality. The aim of the study is to observe the actual functioning of penal control and health mechanisms in order to discover both the positive and negative elements. The following instruments will be utilised:

-   a series of guided interviews, with the use of questionnaires, related to the basic functioning of the system. The questionnaires will be standardised in order to collect homogeneous and comparable replies, and interviews will be carried out by carefully selected experts in each country;

- a report on the positive and negative aspects of the systems in each country. In the preparation of the report, each expert will follow the outlines provided by the international research group so as to guarantee a certain degree of comparability;

- a comparative pilot study on sentences for offences committed by mentally-ill offenders;

- a comparative pilot study on the examinations to evaluate the imputability of the patient. For both pilot studies, appropriate analysis graphs will be drawn up;

- a series of illustrated examples to be tested on the operators working in the field of the treatment of mentally-ill offenders; the replies to these examples will permit an evaluation of the operators' perceptions of the problems related to the efficiency of the system.

Phase 3: Guidelines

In conclusion, some reference parameters which will be essential for the policy-maker, will be drawn up from the data collected from the above-mentioned analyses. These parameters will be related to the efficiency of the system, its effectiveness in preventing recidivism, and its success in the treatment of the patient.

As clearly indicated in the Preface, this book is the result of the first phase of the project. The main body of this publication is composed of the national reports which were prepared by the national experts. A summary report has also been prepared in which the original national reports are re-classified into subject matter, and an attempt has been made to reflect the main ideas of the original reports without referring to details concerning the Articles of the Criminal (Penal) Law (Codes) which exist in each country. This was done in order to present the main concepts and differences which prevail in the countries concerned.

One of the main purposes of this project was to present the problems in treating mentally-ill offenders within the criminal justice system in the selected countries, in both the developed and the developing world, in order to provide suggestions and proposals for the formulation of policies regarding the management of mentally-ill persons in the criminal justice system. We hope this publication provides some new insights into this area and will stimulate further research and improvements in policies.

CANADA
Donald K. Piragoff*

RESPONSIBILITY

According to Sections 13 and 26 of the Criminal Code of Canada, children under the age of 12 years are not responsible under the criminal law, nor are persons who, at the time they committed a criminal act or omission, were 'suffering from a mental disorder that rendered the person incapable of appreciating the nature and quality of the act or omission or of knowing that it was wrong'.

In Canada, there is no concept of diminished responsibility in the sense of a specific defence as in the United Kingdom. However, evidence of the type of abnormality of mind required to establish the defence of diminished responsibility would, in certain circumstances, be sufficient to reduce murder to manslaughter in Canada, and would be taken into account by the judge in sentencing for offences where there is no mandatory sentence. For offenders aged between 12 and 18 years, the Young Offenders Act prescribes a maximum penalty of three years, which is based in part on the belief that young persons, because of their immaturity, are not fully responsible for their criminal acts or omissions.

Although children under the age of 12 years cannot be convicted under the criminal law, they may be subject to some form of supervision and control by 'social welfare' authorities. As regards those above 12 who are found not criminally responsible on account of a mental disorder, they are detained in a secure hospital until a review board concludes that they no longer constitute a danger to the public.

---

*   General Counsel, Criminal Law Policy Section, Department of Justice, Ottawa, Ontario, Canada. This report was prepared in March 1992.

The criminal law does not prescribe any particular procedure for dealing with borderline cases, and this is therefore left to the discretion of those administering the law.

Although the criminal law makes no special provision for such specific cases as neuroses, psychopathic disorder, emotional distress and irresistible impulse, nevertheless, in relation to psychopaths, the Supreme Court of Canada has interpreted Section 16 of the Criminal Code in such a way that the defence of mental disorder would not normally be available to them.

DANGEROUSNESS

Part XXXIV of the Criminal Code deals with 'dangerous offenders'. It provides that, in order to impose the status of 'dangerous offender' on an offender, an application to that effect (approved by the Attorney General) must be made to the court after the offender has been convicted, but before s/he has been sentenced. The court may make such an order if it is satisfied that the offence for which the offender has been convicted is a 'serious personal injury offence' (defined as an offence involving violence against another person, or a conduct endangering or likely to endanger the life or safety of another person or inflicting or likely to inflict severe psychological damage upon another person and for which the offender may be sentenced to imprisonment for ten years or more, or an attempt to commit an offence involving sexual assault under prescribed sections of the Criminal Code). It also has to be satisfied that the offender constitutes a threat to the life, safety or physical or mental well-being of other persons, on the basis of evidence establishing:

a) a pattern of repetitive behaviour by the offender, of which the offence for which s/he has been convicted forms a part, showing a failure to restrain her/his behaviour and a likelihood of her/his causing death or injury to other persons, or inflicting severe psychological damage on other persons, through failure in the future to restrain her/his behaviour;

b) a pattern of persistent aggressive behaviour by the offender, of which the offence for which s/he has been convicted forms a part, showing a substantial degree of indifference on the part of the offender with respect to the reasonably foreseeable consequences to other persons of her/his behaviour; or

c) any behaviour by the offender, associated with the offence for which s/he has been convicted, that is of such a brutal nature as to compel the conclusion that her/his future behaviour is unlikely to be inhibited by normal standards of behavioural restraint.

Where the serious personal injury offence is a sexual one, the court may make a dangerous offender order if it is satisfied with the evidence that the offender, by her/his conduct in any sexual matter including that involved in the commission of the offence for which s/he has been convicted, has shown a failure to control her/his sexual impulses and that there is a likelihood of her/his causing injury, pain or other evil to other persons in the future through failure to control her/his sexual impulses.

If the court is satisfied that the offender is a dangerous offender, it may impose a sentence of detention in a penitentiary for an indeterminate period *in lieu* of any other sentence that might be imposed for the offence for which the offender has been convicted.

Similar provisions are now included in Sections 672.65 and 672.66 of the Criminal Code regarding 'dangerous mentally disordered accused'. These deal with the accused person who is charged with a serious personal injury offence and who is found by the court to be not criminally responsible on account of mental disorder. However, these provisions will not be put into force until the new 'capping' provisions (described further on) are brought into effect.

PSYCHIATRIC EXAMINATIONS

Section 672.11 of the Criminal Code empowers the court to order an assessment of the mental condition of the accused if it has reasonable grounds to believe that such evidence is necessary to determine:

a) whether the accused is unfit to stand trial;

b) whether the accused was, at the time of the commission of the alleged offence, suffering from a mental disorder so as to be exempt from criminal responsibility;

c) whether the balance of the mind of the accused was disturbed at the time of the commission of the alleged offence, where the accused is a female charged with an offence arising out of the death of her newly-born child;

d) the appropriate disposition to be made, where a verdict of 'not criminally responsible' on account of mental disorder or 'unfit to stand trial' has been rendered in respect of the accused; or

e) whether an order should be made, under Sub-section 736.11(1), to detain the accused in a treatment facility, if the accused has been convicted for the offence.

Paragraph (e) of Section 672.11 will not come into force until the 'hospital order' scheme, established under Section 736.11 of the Criminal Code, is brought into effect.

In addition to the above provisions, the Common Law permits expert psychiatric evidence to be given on any matter relevant to the case. However, the evidence of an expert opinion may be excluded if the court is satisfied that the matter upon which the expert opinion is expressed falls within common knowledge, and therefore would not be helpful to the finder of fact, whether judge or jury.

If the evidence is relevant, and the testimony from an expert psychiatrist or psychologist would be helpful, then psychiatric and psychological tests are conducted on the accused and presented before the court. However, in criminal cases, decisions as to responsibility and dangerousness are based on legal rather than psychiatric criteria. Evidence given by a psychiatrist is therefore considered by the court in the context of determining whether the legal criteria are met.

SANCTIONS

Two categories of measures are applied to mentally-ill offenders. The first category deals with the mentally-ill offender who has been convicted and has been sentenced to a term of imprisonment. In this case, the measures applicable, from both health and security standpoints, are determined by the prison authorities. As a general rule, however, the offender cannot be given treatment for a medical or psychiatric problem without her/his consent. The second category deals with the mentally-ill accused who has been found either unfit to stand trial or not criminally responsible on account of mental disorder. In these cases, the accused is put into a secure hospital rather than a prison. As in the case of the first category, the general rule is that no treatment can be given without consent, but there is a specific exception with respect to treatment designed to render the accused fit to stand trial. The court may make a treatment order if it is satisfied that:

a) without treatment, the accused is likely to remain unfit to stand trial;

b) with the prescribed treatment the accused is likely to be rendered fit to stand trial within 60 days;

c) the risk of harm to the accused from the treatment is not disproportionate to the benefit anticipated to be derived from it; and

d) the treatment is the least restrictive and the least intrusive treatment that could, in the circumstances, be specified to render the accused fit to stand trial (Criminal Code, Section 672.59).

There are also two exceptions to the general rule against involuntary treatment. First, the Common Law permits a doctor to administer treatment without the consent of the patient if lack of consent would put the latter's life in danger. Secondly, persons in either of the above-mentioned categories may be committed as involuntary patients under provincial mental health legislation. In some provinces, involuntary patients may be treated without their consent.

REFORMS

A major reform on mentally-ill offenders was introduced in Canada in February 1992, which aims to modernise and streamline the legislation, and to increase the protection of the rights of the mentally-disordered accused, while at the same time assuring the maintenance of adequate protection for the safety of the public. In particular, the objectives of the reform are to:

- modernise the terminology used throughout the legislation;

- change the verdict of 'not guilty on account of insanity' to 'not criminally responsible on account of mental disorder';

- protect the accused against the use of statements s/he made during a court-ordered psychiatric assessment;

- clarify the criteria for determining whether an accused is unfit to stand trial on account of mental disorder;

- establish legal authority for the court to order the treatment required to render the accused fit to stand trial;

- require the establishment of review boards to conduct regular reviews of mentally-disordered accused being held under the authority of the criminal law as being either unfit to stand trial or not criminally responsible;

- set out procedural rules to be followed by the review boards and the dispositions the boards may make;

- replace the current system of potentially indeterminate detention for those found either unfit to stand trial or not criminally responsible on account of mental disorder with a 'capping' system, so that the mentally-disordered accused cannot be held significantly longer under the authority of the criminal law than if s/he had been convicted of the offence charged;

- introduce provisions parallel to the Dangerous Offender Provisions which will be applicable to those found not criminally responsible on account of mental disorder;

- introduce appeal provisions with respect to decisions of review boards;

- set up a procedure for determining the placement and supervision of 'dual status' offenders who have both an outstanding prison sentence and an order for custody as mentally-disordered accused;

- create a 'hospital order' scheme which gives the trial judge the power to order that an offender who has just been sentenced by the judge to a term of imprisonment shall serve up to the first 60 days of her/his sentence in a hospital (if both the hospital and the offender consent to the order);

- introduce consequential amendments with respect to young offenders and persons tried under military law, to assure that procedures with respect to them are compatible with those applicable to adult offenders under the criminal law.

Two of the above-mentioned provisions have not yet been enforced. The provisions dealing with 'capping' and the new 'dangerous mentally-disordered accused' will come into enforcement when the provinces have had a reasonable length of time to make any necessary modifications to their mental health legislation. The 'hospital order' provisions will not take effect nationally until some pilot projects have been conducted to determine likely utilisation rates and costs.

STATISTICS

Statistics related to the number of mentally-ill offenders treated by the Canadian criminal justice system are presented in Annex 1.

THE CANADIAN DATA BASE:
PATIENTS HELD ON LIEUTENANT-GOVERNORS'
WARRANTS*

*Sheilagh Hodgins** & Christopher D Webster****

Persons in Canada found legally unfit to stand trial (UFST) or not guilty by reason of insanity (NGRI) are usually held responsible to hospital administrators under warrants of the Lieutenant Governor[1]. While on warrant they come within the purview of boards of review. These boards are constituted under the Criminal Code as amended for the purpose in 1968. The legal and administrative procedures surrounding warrants have been described fully elsewhere[2]. These warrants, and the provincially-constituted boards which administer them, have been the subject of considerable contention[3] and even a recent challenge to the highest court[4]. Although there has been strong support for the existing arrangement[5], there have also been persistent demands for the reformation of the Code's pertinent Sections[6]. The most vigorous, and perhaps the most powerfully articulated criticism came a decade and a half ago in the form of a report by the Law Reform Commission of Canada[7]. This report was followed subsequently by a Department of Justice study under the Mental Disorder Project[8]. These two documents, together with many large

*   The authors gratefully acknowledge the co-operation and help received from the chairs and staff, former and present, of the Lieutenant Governors' Boards of Review. Several officials of the Canadian Department of Justice contributed substantially to the success of this venture, the late David Alford, John Fleischman, Gilbert Sharpe, David Solberg, Bernard Starkman and Ed Tollefson. Jean Paquet is thanked for all his painstaking and thoughtful compilation of the data. All the staff at the Centre de Recherche Philippe Pinel contributed in numerous ways to the completion of this report. We sincerely thank them.

**   Director of Research, Institut Philippe Pinel de Montréal, Montreal, Canada.

***   Head, Psychology Department, Clarke Institute of Psychiatry, Toronto, Canada.

cross-provincial consultation exercises, resulted in a bill presented to Parliament in 1986[9]. That bill died on the order paper following a change in the federal government. Although a study of the complex legal and administrative issues continued subsequent to the demise of the proposed legislation, it was the Supreme court case of Swain which has now energised the present production of revised legislation[10]. The Supreme Court demanded reform by early November 1991. This deadline was later extended to early February 1992 at which time Bill C-30 passed into law. Most provisions were proclaimed with a few, including the so-called 'capping' conditions, held over for the future. Under the WLG provisions, as they stood for many years, a person deemed UFST or NGRI was held indefinitely. Although each case had to be considered by the Lieutenant Governor's Review Board within six months of a warrant application and at least annually thereafter, patients had no automatic right to release once stipulated criteria had been met, and no form of regular appeal against board rulings. Indeed, the recent Swain case turned on a man being subject to secure hospitalisation as NGRI after having demonstrated his competence to live on bail productively and amicably in the community. The new legislation, when fully in force, aims to correct these and other long-noted difficulties.

Anticipating some kind of eventual reform of the law, the Department of Justice heeded strong calls from the authors of the Law Reform Commission Report and the Mental Disorder Project to secure data on the then-existing warrant system. Both reports noted that it is hard, if not impossible, to form new law and procedure without some means of measuring the effects of existing procedures. The Department funded a feasibility report[11], preliminary study[12] and subsequently a major project. The project, conducted by the present authors, systematically compiled data on each and every warrant case in Canada over a three-year period. The data were collected by the various board offices in each province. At the end of each year, copies of various specially-prepared forms were submitted to the first author. Data were then consolidated for each province and also amassed to yield an overall account of patients across the country. Reports containing data in tabular form were filed at the end of each data-collection year[13]. The data base is designed to allow the study of the expected changes in the law. Responsibility for the system has now shifted to the Centre for Criminal Justice Statistics.

The data over three years are the most systematic and comprehensive yet collected in Canada. With two exceptions[14], previous surveys have been limited to particular provinces[15]. Both previous attempts to complete cross-Canada information, though valuable, were markedly limited by the fact that the boards themselves supplied information from idiosyncratic systems ill-designed for research purposes. It was difficult to obtain rigour and detail. The present data are important because they: (i) are systematic and dependable; (ii) allow study over a consecutive three-year time span; and (iii) provide the necessary base-line data against which it will be possible in the future to consider the effects of the new legal reforms.

How many warrant patients are there in Canada?

The Quinsey and Boyd[16] survey published in 1977 yielded a total of 677 warrant patients. Several years later, Webster, Phillips and Stermac[17] obtained a figure of 867 for 1983. The present survey yielded a figure of 1 007 on 1 March 1988. The figure rose to 1 120 on 1 March 1989 and to 1 156 on 1 March 1990. It is clear that, with an increase of about 35 cases each year, there has been a slow but steady expansion of the system over time. Although it is hard to predict with any certainty, it seems unlikely that this trend will be slowed or halted over the next few years. Indeed, it appears highly probable that there will be a growth in numbers of 'accused' persons held under hospital authority as UFST and what will now be known as 'not criminally responsible on account of mental disorder' (NCRMD). There is also the point that the new law allows the provisions to be applied against persons accused of summary conviction offences.

What has been the 'turnover' in warrants?

There are two ways of being detained under warrant. Patients have been found UFST or NGRI. As would be expected, the turnover is higher in the former category than the latter. This is because a certain proportion of the unfit cases came to be seen as fit by the time of a first board review (conducted within six months of the court finding) or a subsequent review (held at least annually). Of the 1 007 LGW patients under warrant on 1 March 1988, 91 per cent were there as a result of NGRI status and the remaining 9 per cent as UFST. During the 1988 year (1 March 1988 to 28 February 1989) 309 warrants were issued. Only 140 (45 per cent) were NGRI; almost the complete balance, 168, were UFS (54 per cent). The same pattern holds for warrants fully vacated during the year. Of the 251 warrants vacated during 1988 in Canada, 247 were UFST cases (59 per cent) and 103 were NGRI patients (41 per cent). Figures for 1989 and 1990 reflect approximately the same relative proportion of NGRI and UFST cases entering and leaving the system. It seems that, to some extent, the previous Criminal Code unfitness provisions allowed persons to receive seemingly necessary pre-trial, brief psychiatric treatment. Some follow-up research is needed to determine how the courts disposed of these UFST cases and how those decisions were affected by the seriousness of the index charges (i.e. to find out the proportion of cases in which charges were dropped; to find out the extent to which eventual sentences were withheld in consideration of restricted liberty while under warrant). A study of cohort of UFST cases in Quebec found that the charges were dropped against 47 per cent of them once they were judged fit to stand trial[18].

What kinds of psychiatric disorders do these patients suffer from and how serious are their index crimes?

Most patients (64 per cent) who received a WLG were diagnosed as suffering from schizophrenia. Another 7 or 8 per cent were said to present affect disorders, and approximately 10 per cent with personality disorders. The remaining patients had widely varying diagnoses. The distribution of diagnoses was very stable over the three years of the project. The provincial differences were also stable. Quebec had the lowest percentage of patients diagnosed as schizophrenic, at about 54 per cent, and British Columbia had the highest, at about 85 per cent. Diagnoses were similar for men and women and for those found UFST and NGRI.

Just over 30 per cent of the WLG patients had allegedly committed homicide. Another 17 per cent attempted murder, another 24 per cent and fewer than 7 per cent committed sexual assault. Adding these figures suggest that three quarters of WLG patients were put on warrant as a result of interpersonal aggression. About 10 per cent of the patients were under warrant for minor offences. The alleged offences varied considerably across provinces, but most patients were under warrant for serious violence directed towards others. This conclusion applies to both men and women. Generally, far fewer of those found UFST as compared to those NGRI were alleged to have committed serious violent offences. The relatively few personality-disordered patients were distinguished by their history of violence; 50 per cent were alleged to have killed; 15 per cent to have tried to kill; 16 per cent to have assaulted another person and 9 per cent to have sexually assaulted.

How long did the patients spend on warrant until full vacation and what proportion of the time was spent in hospital?

Patients found UFST were hospitalised on average for 9.3 months (SD=24.2), and held on warrant on average for 8.6 months (SD=20.7) (on average, one month lapsed between the boards' declaration that they were fit to return to trial and the actual trial). The time on warrant varied considerably from one province to another. For example, warrants of unfitness vacated between 1 March 1990 and 28 February 1991 had been in place on average, in Quebec for 7 months, in Ontario for 10 months and in Saskatchewan for 32 months.

Patients found NGRI were hospitalised, on average, for 53.0 months (SD=51.4), and held on warrant on average for 78.2 months (SD=67.4). As with UFST cases, time on warrant varied considerably from one province to another. For example, warrants of insanity vacated between 1 March 1990 and 28 February 1991 had been in place, on average, in Quebec for 49 months, in Ontario for 130 months and in British Columbia for 136 months. These provincial differences in length of warrants were stable over the three years of the project, and have probably existed, at least since the early 1970s. The differences appear to be due, in part, to differences in characteristics of the patients put under warrant and, in part, to board policy.

On what factors do the provinces differ with respect to warrant patients?

Although there were similarities across provinces in terms of patients' characteristics such as age (mean = 40.0 years), gender (89 per cent male and 60 per cent incidence of previous robbery charges), there were also some marked differences. False conclusions are easy to draw from the cross-provincial data. Numbers of warrant patients in 1988 ranged from 7 (Newfoundland) to 386 (Ontario) and, in 1990, from 3 (Prince Edward Island) to 457 (Quebec). Obviously, provinces with only a few cases can skew the overall impression. Ontario and Quebec, each with over 400 cases in 1990, allow for robust comparisons. Quebec's warrant system grew over the three-year span, whereas Ontario's did not. Quebec, with a rise from 345 in 1988 to 457 in 1990, accounted on its own for the bulk of the increase noted in point 1 above. Ontario's increase was inconsequential, from 386 to 403 over the same period.

Relative to Quebec, Ontario was a more heavily criminalised population. Exactly half of the 1990 Ontario cases had been convicted previously of criminal offences. The comparable figure for Quebec was 32 per cent. At 13 per cent, Ontario warrant patients had nearly doubled Quebec's previous convictions for sexual aggression (7 per cent). With respect to the index offence, Ontario's population at 39 per cent had doubled Quebec's homicide rate of 19 per cent, figures which held up with respect to attempted murder (20.6 per cent versus 10.3 per cent. Almost all (87 per cent) the patients put on warrant in Quebec had previously been hospitalised and 72 per cent of them depended on welfare payments as their sole source of income. By contrast, in Ontario 70 per cent of the patients had previously been hospitalised and only 21 per cent had received social assistance. Patients in Quebec, according to the 1990 data which are essentially similar to those for the two previous years, were slightly more apt to be diagnosed as suffering from schizophrenia or other psychotic or paranoid conditions (73 per cent) than comparable patients in Ontario (70 per cent). The number of cases of mental retardation, though not high overall across the country (6.5 per cent), was highest in Quebec at 10 per cent versus 4.5 per cent in Ontario. The most notable difference diagnostically between Ontario and Quebec came in the use of personality disorder as a primary ascription with the condition being attributed in 18 per cent of the cases in the former and only 4 per cent in the latter. Ontario traditionally has been the province with the highest proportion of personality disorders. It would appear, though, that this trend is decreasing in Ontario. Webster, Phillips and Stermac[19] found a figure of 27 per cent in 1983. This figure dropped to 22.5 per cent in 1988 to 20 in 1989 and to 18 per cent in 1990. In 1990, only 1.6 per cent of the new warrant cases in Ontario had a primary diagnosis of personality disorder. In a very general way, it is probably fair to say that the Quebec Board is being held responsible for a group of chronic patients with major mental disorders who live in the community on welfare. Only one out of three had committed a violent offence. The Ontario Board, in contrast, is responsible for persons with major mental disorders, many of whom are homeless, have no source of income and are repeatedly in and out of hospitals and jails.

The fact that Quebec and Ontario have, over the years, inducted apparently different kinds of patients make it unsurprising that in 1990, fully a quarter (27 per cent) of Quebec's warrant patients were cared for under the auspices of general hospitals. The comparable figure for Ontario was 2 per cent. Both of these large provinces held a little over a quarter of their warrant population in maximum security hospitals (26 per cent in Ontario and 29 per cent in Quebec). Of incidental note is the fact that, over the three study years, there was a slight drop in the use of security hospitals with data from all provinces combined (42 per cent in 1988, 40 per cent in 1989 and 38 per cent in 1990). Whether or not there will continue to be small-magnitude decreases over time, remains to be seen.

Quebec boasted the shortest mean length of time on warrant (excluding PEI with its three cases). With UFST and NGRI warrants combined, its average in 1990 was 50 months. This compares to Ontario's 95 and British Columbia's 94. Figures for the two preceding years were similar. We compared the length of warrants for schizophrenic patients in Ontario, in Quebec and in the other provinces who were alleged to have committed homicide. In Ontario, these cases were held on average for 167.0 months (SD=53.5), in Quebec for 90.2 months (SD=43.1) and in the other provinces, for 145.9 months (SD=53.6) ($F_{(2,29)}=4.77, p=02$).

It would appear that, generally, Quebec and Ontario employ the warrant system differently. The Ontario patients have a strong criminal background, commit more serious index offences, less often suffer from a major mental disorder, and spend longer on warrant than the Quebec counterparts. In attempting to explain these differences, it must be remembered that provinces organise their health and social services in radically different fashions. That a large proportion of Quebec patients receive care and supervision from general hospitals reflects the fact that these institutions are equipped to carry out the role. That some 30 per cent of warrant patients in Saskatchewan end up being housed in the Correctional Service of Canada's Regional Psychiatric Centre has to do with the fact that the facility, though not designed for unconvicted persons, is available and other resources are not.

What is the relationship between diagnosis and crime and length of detention?

The relationship between diagnosis and crime and the length of detention remains unclear. The variables we have studied do not successfully predict length of hospitalisation or time on warrant. Multiple regression statistics were calculated separately for men and women to identify the predictors of length of hospitalisation and time on warrant. The predictors entered in the analyses were history of employment, previous criminal convictions, previous sentence to a correctional facility, previous conviction for a violent offence, previous psychiatric hospitalisation, whether in treatment at time of the index offence, severity of the index office, treatment in a maximum security hospital while under current warrant, diagnosis of intellectual deficiency and diagnosis of personality disorder. The regression equation calculated to predict length of hospitalisation among male patients produced an R^2 of .11 ($F=14.21$, $2=.0002$). The same equation for female patients produced an R^2 of .24 ($F=6.50$, $p=02$). In both these analyses, only one predictor, severity of the alleged offence, had a statistically significant beta weight. The regression equation calculated to predict time on warrant for male patients produced an R^2 of .11 ($F=10.53$, $p=002$). The same equation for female patients produced an R^2 of 19 ($F=4.47$, $p=.05$). Again, in both the analyses for male and female patients, only one predictor - the severity of the alleged offence - had a statistically significant beta weight.

While the predictors of time in hospital and time on warrant continue to elude us, a number of facts have emerged from our analyses. For both men and women the most important variable, among those we studied, influencing length of hospitalisation and time on warrant, was the severity of the alleged index offence. Among patients found NGRI, the men spent, on average, 17 more months on warrant than the women. Yet the percentages of men and women alleged to have committed homicide, attempted murder, and assault are similar. Among patients found NGRI, those with a diagnosis of schizophrenia are held on warrant, on average, 11 months longer than those with personality disorders. The length of unfitness warrants are similar for both genders and across diagnostic categories.

Were there any marked changes in the characteristics of the WLG population over the three-year period?

The answer to this question is no. Trend analyses conducted on all the principal variables indicated that the system was very stable over the three year study period. Neither characteristics of the patients' nor the boards' decision-making practices changed appreciably over the study years.

Have the boards met their statutory obligations?

The project allowed for the collection of limited data on decision-making at the board level. Between 1 March 1990 and 28 February 1991, the boards heard 1 233 persons. In all, 1 504 hearings were conducted. Seventy nine per cent had a single hearing. Twenty per cent had two hearings. One per cent had three or more hearings. The average number of hearings was 1.2 per patient. Although the old provisions did not require that the patient attend his or her hearing, this did occur in over 9 out of 10 cases. Quebec had the lowest attendance rate but even it reached 80 per cent. Provinces showed considerable variability in the extent to which their warrant patients were represented by lawyers. Alone among the three provinces with the largest warrant populations, Ontario had a lawyer-representation rate of 78 per cent with Quebec and British Columbia at 7 per cent and 5 per cent respectively. Support at the hearing from wives, husbands, family members and other persons also varied considerably. Ontario had a rate of 34 per cent, Quebec of 22 per cent and British Columbia of 5.5 per cent. The most common board recommendation in Ontario, one given in 77 per cent of cases, was that of hospitalisation in the same institution; the most common recommendation in Quebec was that permission be granted for the patient to live outside the hospital (33 per cent). Only in 22 per cent of cases did the Quebec Board recommend hospitalisation at the same institution. Quebec's second most frequent recommendation was warrant vacation at 21 per cent. This contrasts with Ontario's 9 per cent and the cross-country average of 13 per cent. Board recommendations were accepted by the Lieutenant Governor or provincial cabinet in 98 per cent of the cases across Canada.

Discussion

The present study is largely descriptive. It provides simple but important data concerning a large group of persons held for mental health reasons under Criminal Code authority. The Code provisions in effect at the time of data collection were in some cases imprecise. This meant that procedural variations among provinces were considerable which, in turn, complicated the task of amassing and analysing information. The amendments, not all of which have taken effect, are aimed at ensuring that, relative to the previous state of affairs, warrant patients have: (a) improved procedural protection at hearings; (b) reduced the risk of being held in jails pending hospital placements; (c) increased likelihood of securing complete release from warrant at the earliest realistic date. These and other changes, arising partly as a result of successive protracted studies and partly from Swain, are apparently intended to guard the accused's interests (e.g. the Crown will have to demonstrate that it continues to have a case against the UFST person; the NGRU patient will have to be released outright or into civil authority at the end of the cap; lengths of remand times for the purpose of psychiatric assessment are decreased). The total warrant population could shrink over time.

Although it is possible that there will be a reduction in the size of warrant population before the year 2000, it is also possible that the opposite will occur. The present data should help determine whether in fact the new provisions will create an expansion of the warrant system. This might come about because prosecutors will come to make extensive use of the 'dangerous mentally-disordered accused' framework (transferred with relatively minor alternations from Parts XXIV of the Code). Once a person has been found 'dangerous' by the court in a special hearing it may, if experience under Part XXIV is any guide[20], become almost impossible later for that individual to find release from indeterminate detention. Some persons who would otherwise be capped at 10 years may, in other words, be moved as a result of the added deliberate court decision into a particular high risk category. Once in that category they may be less likely than formerly to be able to secure partial or full vacation. There is also the point that the actual rather than intended effect of introducing the two year and ten year caps will be to have the boards come to see themselves as 'authorised' to hold individuals to the maximum. The mere stipulation of upper bounds may mean that persons on warrant will reach those limits (i.e. that boards will be less inclined than formerly to recommend releases at one year, at five years, etc.). Also, there is a distinct possibility that more persons than previously will be found UFST. The defence bar, knowing that the onus is on the Crown to ensure that there is in fact a case against the accused, and that there is to be a two year cap for summary offences, may be less inclined than previously to employ stratagems aimed at averting transfer from the criminal justice to the mental health system.

We avoided speculation during the course of the study years. Not only did we not know what changes to the Code would be introduced but we had no actual knowledge as to when they would take effect. As it turns out, Parliament's timing was ideal as far as the overall project is concerned. With three years of data collection in hand, it will now, with only slight modifications to the data collection system, be possible to gauge quite well the effects of this new and important legislation.

REFERENCES

1   RC Turner, 'Warrants of the Lieutenant-Governor', *Canadian Journal of Psychiatry*, 1987, vol. 32, pp. 337-341.

2   M Schiffer, *Mental Disorder and the Criminal Trial Process*, Butterworths, Toronto, 1987.

3   H Savage & C McKague, *Mental Health Law in Canada*, Butterworths, Toronto, 1987.

4   RV Swain, *63 C.C.C.* (third edition), 1991, p. 193.

5   EL Haines, *The Ontario Lieutenant-Governor's Board of Review*, (third edition), Queen's Printer, Ontario, 1984.

6   KB Jobson, 'Commitment and Release of the Mentally-ill under Criminal Law', *Criminal Law Quarterly*, 1969, vol. 11, pp. 186-203.

7   EP Hartt, *Mental Disorder in the Criminal Process*, Law Reform Commission of Canada, Ottawa, 1976, pp. 36-40.

8   G Sharpe, *Criminal Law Review, Final Report*, (Mental Disorder Project), Department of Justice, Canada, September 1985.

9   The Minister of Justice, *Proposed amendments to the Criminal Code (mental disorder)*, first session, Thirty-third Parliament 33-34-35, Elizabeth II, 1984-85-86, pp. 16-32.

10 Bill C-30, *An Act to amend the Criminal Code (mental disorder) and to amend the National Defence Act and the Young Offenders Act in Consequence Thereof*, third session, Thirty-fourth Parliament, 40 Elizabeth II, 21 November 1991.

11 CD Webster, S Hodgins, MS Phillips & L Stermac, *Feasibility of Establishing a Canadian Data Base for Forensic Patients under Warrants of the Lieutenant-Governor*, report submitted to the Department of Justice, Canada, 1985.

12 S de St Croix & CD Webster, 'Patients on Warrants of the Lieutenant Governor of Alberta: A Statistical Summary with Comments on Treatment and Release Procedures', *Canadian Journal of Psychiatry*, 1988, vol. 33, pp. 14-22.

13 S Hodgins, SD Webster, J Pacquet & E Zellerer, *Canadian Database: Patients held on Lieutenant-Governors' Warrants*, Year 1 Annual Report, January 1990; S Hodgins, CD Webster & J Pacquet, *Canadian Database: Patients held on Lieutenant-Governors' Warrants*, Year 2 Annual Report, September 1990; S Hodgins, CD Webster & J Paquet, *Canadian Database: Patients held on Lieutenant-Governors' Warrants*, Year 3 Annual Report, August 1991.

14 VL Quinsey and B Boyd, 'An Assessment of the Characteristics and Dangerousness of Patients held on Warrants of the Lieutenant-Governor', *Crime and Justice*, 1977, vol. 4, pp. 268-274; CD Webster, MS Phillips & L Stermac, 'Persons held on Warrants of the Lieutenant Governor in Canada', *Canada's Mental Health,* 1985, no. 33, pp. 28-32.

15 S de St Croix *et al.,* 1988, *op. cit.*; S Hodgins, 'Men found unfit to Stand Trial and/or not guilty by Reason of Insanity: Recidivism', *Canadian Journal of Criminology,* 1987, no. 29, pp. 51-70; MS Phillips, T Landau & C Osbourne, *Persons discharged from Warrants of the Lieutenant-Governor,* 1987, no. 32. pp. 343-350.

16 VL Quinsey *et al.,* 1977, *op. cit.*

17 CD Webster *et al.,* 1985, *op. cit.*

18 S Hodgins & J Hébert, 'Les personnes avant reçu un mandat du Leutenant-Gouverneur au Québec de 1973 à 1975: Une étude de leur récidive criminelle', *Cahier de Recherche de l'Institut Philippe Pinel de Montréal,* 1982, no. 2.

19 CD Webster *et al.,* 1985, *op. cit.*

20 CD Webster, BM Dickens & S Addario, *Constructing Dangerousness: Scientific, Legal and Policy Implications,* Centre of Criminology, University of Toronto, Toronto, 1985.

EGYPT
Naguib Hosni*

INTRODUCTION

Egyptian criminal law is based on the principle of 'freedom of choice' that is, the offender is considered responsible and free to choose between right and wrong. If the offender readily and knowingly commits an act or omission that threatens the public interests, and behaves in a way which is contrary to the obligations and constraints of the law, s/he is punished accordingly.

If the principle of 'freedom of choice' is the basis for responsibility, then the necessary and logical consequence is the following: if a person does not enjoy this 'freedom' at the time s/he commits the act or omission, such a person would not be responsible or punished for her/his conduct. The law implies by 'freedom of choice', the ability of the offender to determine the way in which s/he behaves. It is presumed that this behaviour is the product of free choice.

The freedom referred to is not absolute, and is obviously restricted by certain factors that are beyond the control of the person concerned. These factors leave a certain degree of freedom. If the offender, as determined by law, does not enjoy such freedom, due to uncontrollable factors s/he is not considered responsible for her/his conduct. It is not difficult, therefore, to explain why the law considers the principle of 'freedom of choice' as the basis for responsibility. Responsibility is considered legal blame directed at the offender by the law. Such blame is not possible unless the offender is, at the time of the action or omission, able to choose between right and wrong.

---

* Former President of the University of Cairo and former Dean of the Faculty of Law of the University of Cairo, Cairo, Egypt. This report was prepared in November 1991.

The presupposition of freedom of choice is 'discernment', that is the ability to comprehend the nature of the act and to foresee its relevant legal effects. In other words, 'discernment' means the possibility and capacity to understand what harm and danger the act would produce to society as a whole and to individuals.

RESPONSIBILITY

Egyptian criminal law is based upon the clear and precise distinction between offenders who are 'criminally responsible' and those who are considered to be 'criminally irresponsible'. It determines the rules and takes into consideration the interests of the general public. The rule that distinguishes the responsible from the irresponsible is that the former is subject to punishment whereas the latter is not punishable, but is only subject to measures of security.

Section 61 of the Egyptian Penal Code states that 'no penalty is inflicted upon someone who, in a state of necessity, commits an offence to preserve her/himself or others from gross danger to the person, if it is impossible for her/him to avoid it by any other means'. Section 62 of the Code states that 'no person shall be liable to punishment for any act committed at a time when s/he had lost consciousness and freedom of choice, for reasons of insanity, mental infirmity or intoxication caused by intoxicants administered to her/him against her/his will or without her/his knowledge'.

In order to apply these definitions, the court must examine the state of the accused, in order to see if s/he was in possession of discernment and freedom of choice at the time of the act, or has lost one or both of them. The court should proceed by placing the accused under medical examination, in order to verify whether s/he is sane or mentally-ill, and, at the same time, to verify whether the illness causes her/him to lose her/his discernment and/or freedom of choice, so that s/he is not responsible for the actions and hence is not liable to punishment. In principle, since the court has no competence over the technical and medical contents of the report, it has to accept the conclusions presented therein. Nevertheless, if the court is not convinced of the findings contained in the report, or thinks that it contains

30

contradictions in parts, it has the authority to reject it and to nominate another expert to carry out another examination and submit a new report. The accused also has the right to question the report of the official expert chosen by the court and to demand the nomination of another expert. In this way, the court may have to compare several reports and choose one which it considers correct and decisive.

Diminished responsibility

The Egyptian Penal Code does not include any provisions for diminished responsibility. This is explained by the fact that the Egyptian Penal Code was influenced by the jurisprudence of the classical school, which provided an abstract and absolute concept of the notion of criminal responsibility: thus, responsibility either exists in a normal and complete form or does not exist at all. Hence, there is no half-way between the two forms and the offender is either responsible or irresponsible. An offender who fails to prove her/his irresponsibility as a form of defence is considered to be completely normal and responsible for her/his actions. This means that an offender of 'diminished responsibility' is completely responsible for her/his acts, as a normal person, as long as there no proof of irresponsibility in her/his favour. As a result of this legislative silence, when a case of diminished responsibility is submitted to an Egyptian court, it must be considered as a case of normal responsibility. In other words, an offender suffering from diminished responsibility cannot be treated as a non-responsible person.

The justification for this rule is that such an offender cannot prove in her/his defence the conditions for her/his irresponsibility, namely, the loss of consciousness and/or freedom of choice. However, the court can apply in her/his favour the system of 'mitigated circumstances', which is the only legal method available to deal with offenders with diminished responsibility that allows a balance to be established between the capacity of the offender to appreciate her/his responsibility and the full penalty.

If it is proved beyond doubt to the court that the offender is 'non-responsible' for her/his acts, then s/he must be declared innocent and go unpunished. This is applied regardless of the seriousness of the offence, (i.e. whether it is a felony, a misdemeanour or a contravention) and whether it is intentional or unintentional.

After the court has acquitted the offender, it must then ensure that s/he is moved to a place of security if it has been proved that s/he is a danger to society, or that s/he may commit another similar or more dangerous offence. According to Section 342 of the Egyptian Criminal Procedure Code, if a person accused of a felony or a misdemeanor is acquitted because s/he is mentally insane, the court should ensure that s/he is detained in an institution specialised in the treatment of mental illnesses until the authorities decide to release her/him. Although this measure deprives the offender of her/his liberty, it is obviously a security measure taken to protect society against a dangerous individual. Thus, despite the gravity of the fact that the offender is deprived of her/his liberty, this measure is still not regarded as a punishment since there is no legal reason for punishment if the offender is not responsible for the action.

This security measure can only be applied by the public prosecutor or the court if it is proved to them that the mentally-ill offender has committed an offence. If this is not the case, then the administrative authority is the only competent body to deal with the matter.

If the accused develops a mental disorder after judgement has been passed against her/him, then the problem arises as to whether this sentence should be served. According to Section 478 of the Criminal Procedure Code: 'If the accused receives a sentence that deprives her/him of freedom, then the execution of the sentence should be postponed until s/he has been cured. The public prosecutor could place her/him in a mental institution set up specifically for this purpose and the amount of time spent in the institution should be deducted from the length of the sentence passed against the offender'. Legislation distinguishes between sentences that can be suspended and those that cannot. Thus, sentences that deprive the offender of her/his freedom can be suspended until s/he has been cured, whereas sentences that are of a financial nature, such as fines or confiscation, cannot be suspended even if the offender is suffering from a mental illness.

Treatment of borderline cases

In the Egyptian criminal justice system, the term 'borderline case' refers to the 'half insane' or 'half responsible' criminal. Thus, according to the Egyptian legislation: 'Although the capacity for responsibility exists, it is not complete and normal, because such a capacity requires a stable and healthy condition and, consequently, requires normal "discernment and freedom of choice". In accordance with this rule, mitigated sentences are to be imposed on those offenders who are considered "borderline cases". The court has the legal discretional power to apply this mitigation through the "system of mitigated circumstances".

The rule is justified by the principle that the harshness of the sentence should be appropriate to the capacity of discernment and freedom of choice, and if it is proved to the court that the offender is 'half responsible' and at the same time a danger to society, then suitable measures of security will be taken by the court.

Since the court is not considered competent in medical matters, the task of carrying out psychological and mental examinations in order to determine and diagnose mentally-ill offenders is assigned to experts specialised in psychiatric diseases. The examinations can take place both before the preliminary investigations and/or during the trial. If they are carried out during the preliminary investigations, they determine the latter's decisions. If the investigations are conducted during the trial, then the results determine whether the court should acquit the offender; or consider her/him to be fully responsible; or, finally, to pronounce a mitigated sentence if it is proved that s/he is 'half insane'. As mentioned above, if the competent authorities are not convinced by the expert's report, a new expert can be appointed to re-examine the case. In the same way, if the offender does not agree with the conclusion of the report, s/he can ask for the nomination of a 'consultative expert', at her/his own expense.

Neurosis

Neurosis means abnormal activity of the nervous system. This type of illness diminishes the control of the nervous system, and causes disorders in the connection between that system and the centres of orientation in the brain and other parts of the body. As such, it has to be taken into consideration in legal cases. The neurotic illnesses that are of concern to both the Doctrine and Practice of Egyptian Jurisprudence are the following:

Epilepsy: epilepsy takes the form of a stroke during which the patient looses consciousness and her/his memory. S/he is exposed to irresistible impulses during the period preceding the stroke, which could be the reason for committing the offence. There is also another kind of epilepsy which is called 'psychological epilepsy', which manifests no physical symptoms but only produces psychological effects which could induce the patient to commit an offence. People suffering from epilepsy may be completely or partially non-responsible, depending on whether its effects destroy the faculties of discernment and freedom of choice in a partial or total manner;

Hysteria: this involves an imbalance in the nervous system and a disturbance in the emotions and desires. Hysteria does not abolish discernment but it weakens control over willpower. However, it does not exclude responsibility since it cannot be considered as a form of insanity, but can only be described as a cause for diminished responsibility;

Neurasthenia: neurasthenia is a weakness in the nervous system, which causes the loss of control over the body and over one's behaviour. It also causes an inability to perform normal physical tasks and diminishes the power of the patient to resist impulses to commit an offence. A person suffering from neurasthenia is not considered insane, but only lacks the control over her/his will and, as a consequence, is considered 'half insane';

Psychopathy: psychopathy means an abnormality of the personality and a deficiency in some of its elements which can reflect upon the behaviour of the individual. It also involves a deficiency and disorder in moral and social values. Psychopaths take a hostile attitude towards most of the values which normal people have, and do not hesitate to contradict them. In this regard, there appears to be a close relationship between criminality and psychopathic disorder. According to the Doctrine and Practice of Egyptian Jurisprudence, psychopathic disorder is not considered as a mental or neurotic illness and therefore cannot be used as a case for irresponsibility. Due to its effects on the personality and the related social and moral values, it may be a cause of diminished responsibility and therefore mitigation of punishment could be applied for offenders with this type of personality defect;

Emotional distress: emotional distress does not necessarily reveal a mental or neurotic illness, but can be considered as a symptom of psychological illness. Despite the fact that the terms 'insanity or mental infirmity' are mentioned in Section 62 of the Egyptian Penal Code, a wide interpretation can be given for 'mental infirmity', so as to include all illnesses which may cause a reduction in the faculties of discernment or freedom of choice. According to this definition, all psychological illnesses may affect the capacity for criminal responsibility, as much as they affect discernment and freedom of choice. The elimination of one or both of these would result in the loss of responsibility. If the effect is only a diminution of one or both of these faculties, this would lead to diminished responsibility and hence a reduced penalty. It can be concluded, from the above concept, that if the feeling of distress produces no psychological consequences, then full responsibility remains and normal punishment is administered, unless the court, for other reasons, and within its own discretionary powers, mitigates the punishment;

Irresistible impulse: this is considered an aspect of mental, neurotic or psychological illness. Accordingly, it may be included in the definition of 'mental infirmity', as in Section 62 of the Penal Code. Its effect on responsibility depends upon its effect on discernment and freedom of choice, as previously pointed out. In addition, 'irresistible impulse' could be included in the concept of constraint which is exempt from responsibility as stated in Section 62 of the Penal Code. The Doctrine and Practice of Egyptian Jurisprudence state that the source of constraint could be either an internal or external force. An internal force could be an illness which creates an impulse which is very difficult or even impossible to resist. This means that the final consequence of 'irresistible impulse' is the exclusion of freedom of choice and the exemption from responsibility.

DANGEROUSNESS

Since the Egyptian Penal Code does not provide a definition of the term 'dangerousness', it does not determine its elements or specify the means to prove it. The Egyptian Doctrine identifies dangerousness as 'criminal dangerousness' or 'the dangerous state of the offender', and defines it as the probability of the offender committing another offence in the future. This definition means that criminal dangerousness is a mere 'probability'; it is a kind of expectation or prospect of what might happen in the future, if the offence were committed again by the same person. Jurisprudence endorses the rules laid down by the Doctine for this concept.

Criteria in determining dangerousness

Criminal dangerousness is a psychological state. The law identifies it by means of two kinds of criminological factors: those which refer to the gravity of the offence and those which refer to a criminal tendency. The first type of factor consists of two categories: elements related to the actual commission of the offence and elements connected with the mental and psychological state of the offender.

The draft of the Egyptian Penal Code of 1958 provided the means to prove criminal dangerousness by stating that: 'The state of criminal dangerousness of the offender to society is revealed by the circumstances and motives of the offence and by the circumstances, background and morality of the offender which reveals that there is a serious probability of her/his committing another offence'.

The law establishes a relationship between criminal dangerousness and the principle of legality. A previous offence is a necessary pre-condition to guarantee respect of the principle of legality. Therefore, according to this principle, it is not possible to inflict punishment or a measure of security on a person unless a criminal act has been committed. This basic principle in the field of incrimination is now accepted by most constitutions in the modern world. The same principle must also be applied when dealing with measures of security. The court is therefore not allowed to seek proof of the dangerousness of a person in order to inflict a security measure on her/him, unless it is proved that s/he previously committed an offence. Although measures of security aim at protecting society as a whole against dangerous offenders, the protection of individual freedom should not be overlooked, and would surely be threatened if the application of a measure of security were not related to an act that is defined by law as criminal. If an offence has not been committed, the legal way to deal with the offender's dangerousness is to take social measures, such as social supervision or assistance, which are not a form of penalty or criminal sanction.

Treatment of dangerous offenders

The protection of society is ensured by inflicting measures of security which are proportionate to the type and degree of criminal dangerousness. This means that different kinds of measures are applied according to the degree and type of dangerousness. For example, the Egyptian law has established a number of rehabilitation and correctional measures for juveniles and those who exhibit anti-social behaviour. It also provides special measures for mentally-ill offenders, whereby they are treated in special institutions and, in the case of habitual offenders, placed in a correctional institution. Other measures are also envisaged, such as police control, confiscation and the deprivation of some rights. The Egyptian Penal Code does not consider measures of security as an independent and autonomous legal category, but as variables in a series of measures that are applied according to the type of offender.

Several legal consequences have resulted from the subordination of measures of security to the principle of legality, the most important of which are as follows:

- a security measure can only be legally inflicted on a person. Measures are also applied according to the principle of 'judicial competence', which means that it is not permitted to inflict a measure on a person unless s/he has been found guilty, and during the execution of the measure, the offender is under strict judicial supervision, in order to guarantee the correct and appropriate execution of the measures;

- measures of security are characterised by their indefinite duration; they must continue to be applied until the criminal dangerousness disappears.

Diagnosis of dangerousness

It is in the court's power to affirm that the offender is criminally dangerous, to specify the nature and extent of this dangerousness and to decide on the type of security measure to be applied. The court has a legal obligation to protect the individual's liberty and in order to guarantee this protection, requires proof of the criminal dangerousness of the offender before applying a security measure. This proof must be of a technical nature, and can take the form of an expert's report, following a medical, psychological or social examination.

PSYCHIATRIC EXAMINATIONS

The role and function of a mental and psychological examination in the criminal procedure is that of 'judiciary expertise'. The court cannot take any decision on the responsibility of the offender unless it has sufficient information on her/his discernment and freedom of choice and their effects on this responsibility, i.e. whether the offender is free from any mental, neurotic or psychological disease, or any abnormal condition which could affect these faculties. Although the court is not obliged to nominate an expert and has the authority to examine the case itself, the opinion of an expert is usually requested. The Egyptian Court of Cassation has decided that: 'If the matter is of a purely technical nature, so that the legal culture and knowledge would not be sufficient to settle the matter, then the court's refusal to nominate an expert is contrary to the logical and scientific methods of research, in which case its judgement is to be considered invalid'.

The court is not obliged to accept the conclusions of the report, but can adopt all or part of it, or even refuse it completely. Egyptian jurisprudence accepts that 'the court is the supreme expert'. Therefore, the expert's report is considered as evidence and is submitted for examination by the court who will evaluate its validity. Since it is the court that nominates the experts and supervises their work, and therefore has confidence in their capacity, it usually accepts the conclusions presented in their reports.

A criminological examination involves probing into the different criminological aspects of an offender's personality in order to acquire enough information concerning her/his capacity for responsibility. The examination is carried out by a group of specialists, each of which examines a particular aspect of the offender's personality. The most important are the mental, psychological and the empirical examination. The results of the various examinations are then evaluated and the criminological data are set out in a report which is considered an important element of the 'file of the offender's personality', for presentation to the court during the trial.

The evaluation of psychiatric/psychological tests in the criminal procedure

Although the Egyptian legislation does not envisage provisions on the use of psychiatric and psychological tests in the criminal procedure, neither does it prevent the competent authorities from carrying them out. Given their technical nature, the decision on the appropriateness of carrying out the tests is left to the competent experts, whose decision is based on their technical knowledge and experience. If the experts decide to carry out the tests, the results of their report will be taken into consideration by the court when making a decision.

The relationship between the judicial decision and psychiatric examinations

The psychiatric and psychological examinations represent the medical and technical expertise that are at the basis of the court's decision regarding the level of responsibility and freedom of choice of the offender. If both of them exist, s/he is declared fully responsible and hence is liable to normal punishment. On the contrary, if at least one of them does not exist, the offender is considered incapable and no punishment should be inflicted upon her/him. Finally, if the results of the examination show diminished discernment or diminished freedom of choice, then the level of responsibility is considered to be diminished, and the offender should receive a mitigated form of punishment.

The psychiatric and psychological examinations are also considered the technical basis of the decision related to the criminal dangerousness of the offender. Dangerousness is 'the likelihood of committing another offence', and this likelihood is measured according to the offender's mental and psychological health. Consequently, if the offender is still suffering from the mental illness that affected her/him upon the commission of the first offence, this could cause her/him to commit another offence. Therefore, the criminal dangerousness of the offender is based on this illness, and it is the role of the experts - by means of the above-mentioned examination - to determine the gravity of the illness and its influence on the offender's behaviour. Though the expert's report is not obligatory, it is usually accepted by the court given its technical nature.

SANCTIONS

Mentally-ill offenders can be divided into two categories:

a) offenders whose illness has abolished their capacity for discernment and/or freedom of choice are classified as 'insane';

b) offenders whose illness has only diminished their level of discernment and/or freedom of choice are classified as 'half insane'.

Offenders in the first category are not punished, whereas those in the second category receive a mitigated form of punishment. This distinction is based upon a legal principle which establishes a proportional relationship between the capacity for responsibility and the punishment to be inflicted.

If it is proved that the mentally-ill offender, whether fully or half insane, is a danger to society, then measures of security are applied. However, proof of insanity alone is not sufficient for the application of these measures; it must also be proved that the offender represents a danger to society. These measures take the form of commitment to a specialised institution. In Egypt, there is only one type of institution for both insane and half insane offenders. The two types of patients are placed in different sections of the institution according to the type of illness and the degree of dangerousness.

The relationship between traditional criminal sanctions in Egypt and measures of security such as the German vicarial system or the cumulative system in Italy is quite straightforward. The court cannot punish a mentally-ill offender but can only inflict a security measure on her/him.

The Egyptian Penal Code does not contain any provisions concerning half insane offenders and therefore, in these cases, the court applies a mitigated sentence. Usually, this type of offender will carry out the sentence in a ward of the prison hospital set up especially for mentally-ill offenders, where s/he will receive the appropriate medical care.

Egyptian mental hospitals use the most up-to-date methods in the treatment of mentally-ill offenders. These methods have produced significant results in that they have brought about the 'social recovery', i.e. the elimination of the criminal dangerousness of many of the patients.

REFORMS

A draft for the reform of the Egyptian Penal Code was prepared in 1966. It contains new regulations on the responsibility of mentally-ill offenders, as well as on the types of punishment and measures of security foreseen in these cases.

Section 32 of the draft for the reform of the Penal Code states that: 'No responsibility should be placed on someone who, at the moment of the commission of the criminal act, was without the faculties of discernment and freedom of choice'. This Section is concerned with the 'insane offender'. As mentioned earlier, mental insanity eliminating discernment and the freedom of choice, leads to the exclusion of the capacity for criminal responsibility. As in the case of the half insane offender suffering from an illness which has diminished her/his discernment and freedom of choice, Section 34 of the draft for the reform of the Penal Code states that: 'If a person, at the time of committing the offence, has partial discernment or freedom of choice because of her/his illness, s/he should receive a mitigated sentence or be put in an institution for treatment'.

With respect to measures of security, Section 50 of the draft for the reform of the Penal Code states that: 'If the offence was committed by an insane person, or a person with an unbalanced mind or a mental or psychological weakness which reduces her/his ability to control her/his behaviour, the court should place her/him in an institution for treatment'. Section 51 added that the same measure should be taken if - as mentioned in Section 50 - the illness appeared during the preparatory instruction or after the final decision. The two Sections deal with the offender affected by an illness which has eliminated her/his discernment or freedom of choice. Section 57 of the draft considers the mentally-ill offender to be socially dangerous 'if medical observation proves that s/he is completely unable to control her/his actions and could be a threat to her/his own safety and that of others'.

As for the half insane, Section 34 of the draft states that such an offender should receive a mitigated sentence or be placed in an institution for treatment, while Sections 105 and 106 deal with confinement in this institution. Section 105 states that the offender who is sentenced to confinement in a mental institution should be sent to a medical establishment specialised in this type of illness, where s/he will receive the medical treatment and care indicated by the state. The presiding judge must ensure that the offender does not remain in this institution for longer than a year, and that medical reports are submitted regularly to the judge during this period, who can decide to release the offender if her/his condition improves. Section 106 of the draft states that it is not possible for an offender to remain in an institution for treatment for more than five years for a misdemeanour, and more than ten years for a felony.

The reform aimed at up-dating the rules concerning mentally-ill offenders in the present Egyptian Penal Code, which is of a traditional character and is similar to the French Penal Code of 1810. It was implemented in 1937, when only a few minor changes were made to the previous Penal Code of 1904. At that time, the institution of measures of security and the theory of criminal dangerousness were unknown; the concept of the half insane offender had not yet been formulated and no distinction had been made between this and other kinds of offenders. The aim of the draft for the reform of the Penal Code was to formulate new rules concerning mentally-ill offenders that took into account the most modern theories in law and medicine, and to bring the Egyptian legislation to the same level as other modern Penal Codes.

ENGLAND & WALES
Nigel Shanks*

RESPONSIBILITY

The distinction between responsibility and non-responsibility is dealt with in the Criminal Procedure (Insanity) Act of 1964, amended by the Criminal Procedure (Insanity and Unfitness to Plead) Act of 1991, although only a very few cases are dealt with under this legislation, the average being approximately six cases per year up to 1991.

Mentally-disordered persons are not convicted for a criminal act if, at the moment it was committed, they were in such a state of disorder that they could not be held criminally responsible. In such cases, the offenders are not guilty by reason of insanity.

Similarly, those persons whose mental disorder is such that they cannot be tried, are deemed unfit to plead. This would occur if the persons were unable to understand the nature of the plea or the course of court proceedings, or to instruct counsel.

Various forms of treatment are envisaged for non-responsible offenders. They may receive an order to be admitted into a hospital for treatment, or an order to be placed under the guardianship of the Social Services. Another option is a probation order on condition that they receive social supervision and treatment and, finally, they may receive absolute discharge.

Diminished responsibility

Although the concept of diminished responsibility is recognised by the criminal justice system, the degree of mental health of the offender

---

*   Head, C3 Division, Mental Health Section, Home Office, London, England. This report was prepared in March 1992.

45

before, during and after the offence(s) is usually taken into consideration in relation to the classification of the offence (i.e. reducing an offence from murder to manslaughter) rather than the mental health aspects.

No specific measures exist to differentiate the salient issues in borderline cases: the extent of mental disorder is taken into account and the content of medical recommendations weighed before determining the final disposal.

Upon the request of the court, a psychiatric and psychological examination is carried out by consultant forensic psychiatrists or general psychiatrists, one of whom must be approved under Section 12 of the Mental Health Act of 1983. The patient is visited in prison or hospital, or even at court, and the practitioner submits written or oral evidence.

The treatment of mentally-ill offenders in the criminal justice system

Section 1(2) of the Mental Health Act of 1983 defines four categories of mental disorder. *Mental disorder* means mental illness, arrested or incomplete development of the mind, psychopathic disorder and any other disorder or disability of the mind. *Severe mental impairment* means a state of arrested or incomplete development of the mind which includes a severe impairment of intelligence and social functioning and is associated with abnormally aggressive or seriously irresponsible conduct. *Mental impairment* means a state of arrested or incomplete development of the mind which includes a significant impairment of intelligence and social functioning, and is associated with abnormally aggressive or seriously irresponsible conduct. *Psychopathic disorder* means a persistent disorder or disability of mind (whether or not it includes a significant impairment of intelligence) which results in abnormally aggressive or seriously irresponsible conduct. Neuroses, emotional distress and irresistible impulse are a matter for clinical judgement.

DANGEROUSNESS

The concept of dangerousness exists in the criminal justice system and is determined by the following criteria: the nature of the offence, the antecedents of the offenders, and the risk of their committing further offences if discharged.

Treatment of dangerous offenders

If a court is convinced that an offender is a danger to the general public, it can make restriction orders, under Section 42 of the 1983 Act, when directing the admission of dangerous offenders (by Section 37) to hospital. The Home Secretary may make restriction directions under Section 49, agreeing to the transfer of sentenced (Section 47) or un-sentenced prisoners (Section 48) to hospital.

A three-tier security system exists in England and Wales which operates as follows: high-risk offenders are sent to one of three special hospitals - Broadmore, Ashworth or Rampton - where conditions are of maximum security. Medium-risk offenders are sent to one of the twenty-three regional Secure Units. These Units provide beds for 600 patients in medium secure conditions, and it is planned to increase this number by a further 100 beds. Finally, there is provision for 35 000 mentally-ill and mentally-handicapped patients in the local hospitals, some 2 000 beds of which are in locked wards.

PSYCHIATRIC EXAMINATIONS

As mentioned earlier, the court may request that an offender undergoes psychiatric and psychological examinations, so that it can use the results of the forensic report to investigate relevant aspects of the background of the offender and to decide upon an appropriate disposal. The court may alternatively or additionally call for reports from the Social Services, which are prepared by community psychiatric nurses or approved social workers. The function of psychiatric examinations in the criminal justice procedure, therefore, is to identify and analyse the behaviour and mental state of the patient, particularly in relation to the offence and previous history, whenever this is relevant.

The use of criminological examinations is not foreseen in England and Wales.

SANCTIONS

The 1983 Mental Health Act envisages the following sanctions and security measures in the case of mentally-ill offenders:

a) under Section 135 of the Mental Health Act, the police can enter premises on the issue of a warrant by a Justice of the Peace or, under Section 136, can remove persons from a place of public access to a place of safety, i.e. a police station, prison or hospital. These measures could be applied, for example, on persons who appear to be suffering from mental disorder within the meaning of the Act and who are in immediate need of care and control. This action would be in the interests of the person and would also ensure the safety of others. Detention can last for up to 72 hours, during which the person is assessed in the place of safety by a psychiatrist and an approved social worker;

b) under Sections 2 and 3 of the Act, the police or a magistrate's court can order the admission of mentally-ill offenders into a hospital for treatment; and under Section 7, they can be placed under the guardianship of the Social Services or receive informal support in the community, again through the Social Services;

c) magistrates' and crown courts can make arrangements for bail on condition that the offender receives hospital treatment;

d) the Crown Prosecution Service can discontinue cases where mental health interests outweigh the interests of justice, when proceedings might have an adverse effect, or when the public interest is not served since the offence is not likely to be repeated;

e) some magistrates' courts have a duty psychiatrist scheme, whereby a designated psychiatrist attends court and interviews mentally-disordered defendants. Offenders may be diverted from the court or a diagnosis may be made available to the court by the visiting psychiatrist;

f) under Section 35 of the Act, instead of receiving bail, the magistrates' court (summary convictions) and crown courts may order that offenders be remanded to hospital, and that a medical report be obtained on their mental condition;

g) magistrates' (for summary offences) and crown courts can order the offender to be detained in hospital for a limited or indefinite period, under Section 37 of the Act. With the restriction order the power to grant leave of absence, transfer, discharge or recall to hospital cannot be exercised without the consent of the Home Secretary;

h) magistrates' and crown courts can place the offender under the guardianship of local Social Services under Section 37;

i) magistrates' and crown courts can also make a probation order, on the condition that the offender receives treatment, under Section 3 of the Powers of Criminal Courts Act of 1973;

j) magistrates' and crown courts can also, of course, decide on absolute or conditional discharge;

k) under Section 36, a crown court can remand an accused person to hospital for treatment instead of prison;

l) the provisions of the Criminal Procedure (Insanity and Unfitness to Plead) Act of 1991 can be used, as described in the section on responsibility/non-responsibility;

m) under Sections 47 and 48, the Prison Medical Service can arrange for the transfer of prisoners to hospital through the Home Office.

It is Home Office policy to encourage co-operation between agencies to ensure that mentally-disordered persons are not prosecuted where this is not required by the public interest. Diversion policy allows courts to choose alternative options throughout each state of the criminal justice process.

A prison sentence may be appropriate for persons who are currently mentally stable or who have recovered from mental disorder sufficiently, provided the Prison Medical Service has facilities to meet the patients' needs. However, it is Home Office policy to transfer mentally-disordered offenders whenever mental illness is of a nature or degree that warrants detention in hospital for medical treatment, and in the cases of psychopathic disorder and mental impairment, such treatment is likely to alleviate or prevent a deterioration of the condition.

Role and function of the traditional criminal psychiatric hospitals in the criminal justice system

As mentioned in the section dealing with dangerous offenders, crown courts can make restriction orders when directing admission to hospital, when they are satisfied that this is necessary for the protection of the public. At present, there are no plans to change the current three-tier security pattern, but it has been recognised that there is a need for an increase in medium security placements (by 100 beds in the first instance). An extension of hospital facilities for patients who are on course for entry into the community is also currently planned.

The alternatives to lower security hospitals comprise hostel facilities and flat (apartment) clusters of single-person accommodation. These are normally reserved for conditionally discharged categories who are able to cope in a community. The provision of this accommodation is dependent upon its availability from the Social Services.

REFORMS

At present, no plans for reform concerning mentally-ill offenders in the criminal justice system are envisaged. Nevertheless, services for mentally-ill offenders are being reviewed by the Home Office and the

Department of Health, and this may lead to the discussion of recommendations for changes or amendments to the law.

STATISTICS

Home Office Statistics of mentally-ill offenders in England and Wales (1989 and 1990) are presented in Annex 1.

STATISTICS OF
MENTALLY DISORDERED OFFENDERS,
ENGLAND AND WALES 1989 AND 1990[*]

MAIN POINTS

The main points that are described in this Bulletin are:

- the number of mentally-disordered offenders admitted to hospitals with restrictions on discharge under the 1959 and 1983 Mental Health Acts was 519 in 1990, some 85 per cent higher than in 1980 (paragraph 3);

- there was a large increase in 1990 in the number of patients admitted on transfer from Prison Service Establishments (paragraph 5);

- the number of patients transferred from Prison Service Establishments before sentence, doubled from 98 to 180 between 1989 and 1990, whilst after sentence the number rose from 119 to 145 (paragraph 5);

- total discharges and disposals were 52 per cent higher in 1990 than in 1980, but discharges into the community were 9 per cent lower in 1990 than in 1980 (paragraph 13);

- the population detained in hospital in 1990 rose to 1 964 patients; this figure was higher than in any of the previous ten years (paragraph 2);

---

[*] This excerpt of issue 29/91 of the Home Office Statistical Bulletin was prepared by the Probation Section, Statistics Division 2, Research and Statistics Department, Home Office, London, England. For further information contact: Ms. Cheryl Morgan, SD Division, Home Office Research and Statistics Department, 50 Queen Anne's Gate, London SW1H 9AT, England.

- the proportion of the total population detained in the special hospitals as opposed to the other hospitals fell from 66 per cent to 60 per cent between 1980 and 1990 (paragraph 2).

INTRODUCTION

This report provides information about mentally-disturbed offenders who are detained in, or discharged from hospital and are subject to restrictions on discharge, under Part III of the Mental Health Act of 1983 or the Criminal Procedure (Insanity) Act 1964[1]. Table 11 shows the number of transfers from Prison Service Establishments to hospital of persons without special restrictions on discharge. Table 12 presents the number of persons made subject to hospital orders, again without special restrictions on discharge and by type of offence, between 1979 and 1989.

POPULATION AND ADMISSION OF RESTRICTED PATIENTS BY TYPE OF HOSPITAL
(see Tables 1 to 9)

On 31 December 1990, the number of restricted patients detained in psychiatric hospitals rose to 1 964[2]. This figure was 4 per cent higher than in 1989 and some 16 per cent higher than the 1985 low of 1692. Both Table 1 and Figure 1 show that, in recent years, there have been larger increases in the population in the other hospitals than in the three special hospitals (which are intended for patients who require conditions of special security)8[3]. This trend continued in both 1989 and 1990 so that, between 1988 and 1989, the population in the special hospitals increased by only 1 per cent before falling again in 1990. Conversely, between 1988 and 1990, the population in the other hospitals increased by 13 per cent from 694 to 786. Figure 1 shows the falling population of detained patients in all hospitals until 1985, followed by a continued upturn; most growth occurred in the other hospitals.

Although around 60 per cent of patients in hospital subject to special restrictions discharge were in the special hospitals, admissions to such hospitals accounted for just 24 per cent of patients in 1990

Figure 1: Patients detained in hospital on 31 December who were subject to special restrictions on discharge, by type of hospital, sex and year

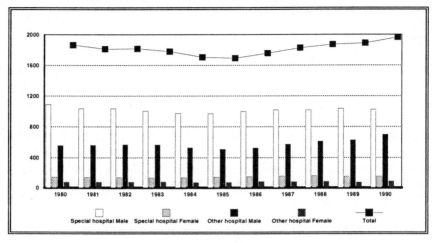

Figure 2: Patients admitted to hospital subject to special restrictions on discharge, by type of hospital, sex and year

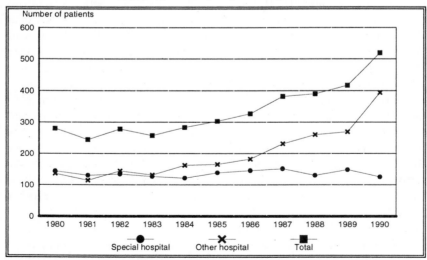

(compared to 51 per cent in 1980 and 43 per cent in 1984). Between 1983 and 1990, admissions to hospital of patients subject to special restrictions on discharge more than doubled from 257 to 519 patients. Particularly in 1990, most of the increase was amongst those admitted to the other hospitals (Figure 2). The increase in admissions to the other hospitals was small, at 3 per cent, between 1988 and 1989, but the increase between 1989 and 1990 was 46 per cent. In 1990, the figure of 394 patients admitted to the other hospitals was over four times the number in 1990 - this was the lowest number of admissions since 1984. Only 11 per cent of all admissions in 1989, and 13 per cent in 1990, were women; the proportion of females has always been small at between 10 and 15 per cent.

On 31 December 1990, 45 per cent of patients detained in hospital were aged between 21 and 39 years, and 35 per cent were aged between 40 and 59 years. The corresponding figures for 1988 were 52 and 38 per cent.

Legal category (see Table 3)

In 1980, of all patients admitted to hospital subject to special restrictions on discharge, 42 per cent were admitted as a result of a court order, 34 per cent were transferred from prison, 9 per cent had been recalled and 14 per cent were unfit to plead. In 1985, the corresponding figures were 38, 41, 12 and 8 per cent, and 26, 63, 8 and 4 per cent by 1990. Since 1983, there has been a steady increase of admissions to hospital from the Prison Service Establishments *after* sentence, from 70 patients in 1983 to 145 patients in 1990. These increases reflect government initiatives. Further information about the sentenced population was published in a report by Professor John Gunn, Dr. Tony Maden and Dr. Mark Swinton entitled 'Mentally-Disordered Prisoners'. This suggested that up to 38 per cent of sentenced prisoners had some psychological problem. Not only has there been an increase in transfers *after* sentence, but between 1989 and 1990 the number of patients admitted to hospital, on transfer from a Prison Service Establishments sentence virtually doubled from 98 to a total of 180 patients (or 35 per cent of all admissions in 1990).

Figure 3: Patients admitted to hospital subject to special restrictions on discharge, by legal category and year

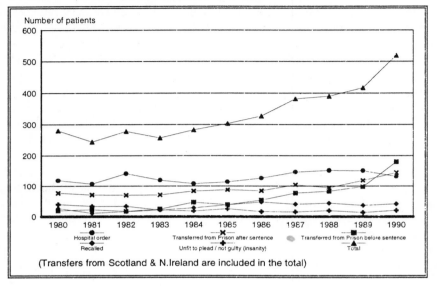

(Transfers from Scotland & N.Ireland are included in the total)

Type of mental disorder (see Tables 4 and 5 and Figure 4)

As in previous years, by far the largest number of patients detained in hospital in both 1989 and 1990 were diagnosed as having a mental illness. In 1990, this disorder accounted for 67 per cent of illnesses. A further 22 per cent were considered to have a psychopathic disorder and 8 per cent had some form of mental impairment. The size of the population classified as having mental illness has been increasing slowly over the years; this has been reflected in the admission figures. In 1980, 77 per cent of patients admitted into hospital were described as having a mental illness, but in 1990 the corresponding proportion was 85 per cent. In 1990, patients with psychopathic disorders, who tend to be in hospital for longer periods, accounted for 8 per cent of all admissions.

The number of restricted patients admitted to hospital suffering from mental illness rose further in both 1989 and 1990, after falling

56

back slightly from the peak in 1987. Between 1980 and 1990, the figure more than doubled from 215 to 442 patients. There was little change in total admissions for psychopathic disorders - in 1980 the number of patients totalled 40, whilst in 1990 the figure was 42 (although the figures varied between a low of 33 and a peak of 58 patients in the intervening years). As a proportion of total admissions, those classed as having a mental impairment continued to fall from 9 per cent in 1980 to 6 per cent in 1987, and to under 3 per cent in 1990.

Figure 4: **Admissions to hospital of patients subject to special restrictions on discharge, type of mental disorder and year**

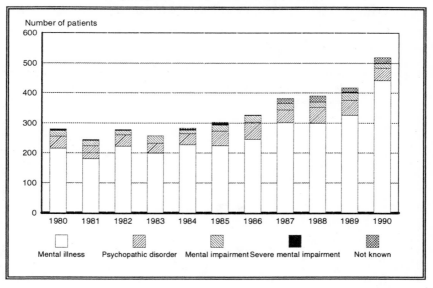

Type of offence (see Tables 6 and 8 and Figure 5)

Of the admissions in 1989 and 1990 the largest group of patients had committed acts of violence against the person. In 1989, violence against the person accounted for 47 per cent of admissions (a little lower than in previous years), but by 1990 the proportion had again risen to 50 per cent. Although patients admitted for homicide continued to increase from 1988 to a new peak in 1990, the largest increase in admissions was for other offences of violence against the person.

The number of patients admitted with special restrictions who had committed sexual offences fluctuated between 1980 and 1989, but in the most recent years (1987 to 1990), their numbers have gradually risen. The total number of such patients was still relatively small in 1990 at 41, as was the number of those who were admitted with restrictions on discharge for robbery. The number of patients admitted for robbery has grown steadily from just 9 patients in 1980, to 25 in 1986, and 39 in 1990. Those admitted for arson have also increased in the last three years. The rise in admissions for summary offences may be partly due to the reclassification of some triable either way offences as summarised by the Criminal Justice Act 1988.

Figure 5: **Patients admitted to hospital subject to special restrictions on discharge, by selected offences and years**

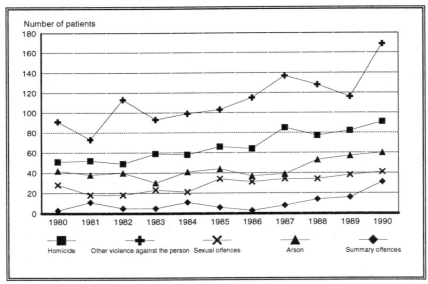

On 31 December 1990, of the 1 964 patients who were detained in hospital and subject to special restrictions on discharge, 63 per cent (as

in 1988) had committed acts of violence against the person. Of these, 63 per cent (i.e. 533 patients) had been placed in hospital for homicide. Twelve per cent of the restricted population had committed sexual offences in 1990 and 14 per cent were arsonists; these proportions showed little annual variation. Of those who were diagnosed as suffering from a mental illness, around 70 per cent had committed violence against the person, 8 per cent sexual offences and 11 per cent some form of criminal damage (mainly arson). For patients with psychopathic disorders, the corresponding figures were 50, 16 and 26 per cent respectively, whilst for those with some form of mental impairment, they were 42, 48 and 24 per cent.

Age and offence (see Table 7)

When offence is matched with age, in terms of absolute numbers, persons aged between 21 and 39 years who have been admitted to hospital for violence against the person outnumber those aged between 40 and 59, but proportionately more of the older age group had committed violence against the person in 1990 than in the younger age group. Of those aged between 21 and 39, 40 per cent had been committed to hospital for violence against the person, 12 per cent for criminal damage, 9 per cent for robbery and 8 per cent for sexual offences. For those aged between 40 and 59, the percentages were 57 for violence against the person, 17 for criminal damage, 2 for robbery and under 5 for sexual offences. With the exceptions of violence against the person and criminal damage, figures for 1990 were all very small for all age groups, except those aged between 21 and 39.

Period in hospital (see Table 9 and Figure 6)

In 1990, 33 per cent of patients with special restrictions on discharge had been in hospital for under 2 years, 17 per cent had been in hospital for between 2 and 5 years and 31 per cent had remained for over 11 years. There were differences between the hospitals, in that in 1990, as in previous years in the three 'special hospitals', only 25 per cent of patients had been detained for less than 2 years, whereas in the other hospitals the proportion was 46 per cent. Figure 6 shows that the proportion detained for over 2 years was considerably lower in the other hospitals, but even in these hospitals, 30 per cent had been detained for 11 years or more, which is similar to the 'special hospitals' figures.

Figure 6: **Patients detained in hospital by period spent in hospital since original committal or last recall, type of hospital and sex, 1990**

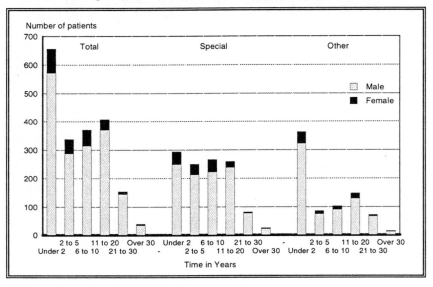

DISCHARGES AND DISPOSALS OF RESTRICTED PATIENTS
(see Table 10 and Figure 7)

In 1989, 400 patients were discharged or disposed of. This figure rose to 444 patients in 1990, which was 66 per cent higher than the corresponding figure of 293 patients for 1980. Within the total, only 37 per cent were discharged into the community in 1990, compared to 49 per cent in 1989, 56 per cent in 1985 and 61 per cent in 1980. The reason for the fall in proportions discharged into the community is due to the large increase in admissions in 1990 (and to a lesser extent in 1989), particularly of unsentenced prisoners, from Prison Service Establishments, many of whom on discharge, were returned to custody. Seventeen per cent of all disposals in 1990 were due to patients being returned to custody to resume sentence. In 1980, only 7 per cent of patients disposed of were returned to custody. A conditional discharge may either be authorised by the Home Secretary or ordered by a Mental Health Review Tribunal[4]. Although, in the preceding two years, the number of discharges had been fairly similar via the two routes, in 1989 and 1990 there were substantially more conditional discharges by tribunal than those authorised by the Home Secretary. The total number of conditional discharges increased by a third between 1988 and 1989 to number 165, before falling back in 1990 to 128. Total discharges into the community peaked at 196 in 1989 before falling back to 163 in 1990.

Figure 7: Discharges and disposals of patients subject to restrictions on discharge, by type of discharge or disposal and year

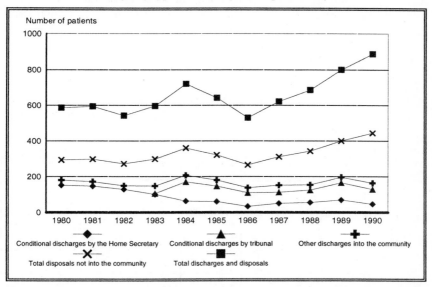

In 1989, 204 patients ceased to be subject to restrictions although they were not discharged into the community. By 1990, this figure had increased to 281. In 1990, around 22 per cent of the patients who had their restrictions removed, remained in hospital. Comparable figures

for 1980 were 10 and 16 per cent. Of the remainder who were no longer subject to restrictions, 16 patients (or 4 per cent) had died in 1989 and 26 patients (or 6 per cent) had done so in 1990. Most patients were transferred from 'special hospitals' to the other hospitals prior to discharge.

ADMISSION OF UNRESTRICTED PATIENTS
(see Tables 11 and 12)

In 1989, of the 760 patients admitted to hospital under hospital order who were not subject to restrictions upon discharge, almost 30 per cent had committed violence against the person (Table 12). After violence against the person, the most common offences were criminal damage (14 per cent), summary offences (19 per cent) and theft and handling stolen goods (12 per cent). Each year, in addition to the restricted offenders shown in Table 3, some offenders are transferred from Prison Service Establishments without restrictions on discharge[5].

Table 1: **Patients detained in hospital on 31 December who were subject to special restrictions on discharge, by type of hospital, sex and year**[1]

England and Wales   Number of patients

Type of hospital	Sex	1980	1981	1982	1983	1984	1985	1986	1987	1988	1989	1990
Special hospital	Male	1 088	1 035	1 034	1 002	972	969	999	1 018	1 016	1 036	1 024
	Female	144	141	138	134	136	144	151	158	162	153	154
	Total	1 232	1 176	1 172	1 136	1 108	1 113	1 150	1 176	1 178	1 189	1 178
Other hospital	Male	556	560	567	565	527	508	525	572	611	627	698
	Female	76	76	77	79	70	71	82	79	83	73	88
	Total	632	636	644	644	597	579	607	651	694	700	786
Total	Male	1 644	1 595	1 601	1 567	1 499	1 477	1 524	1 590	1 627	1 663	1 722
	Female	220	217	215	213	206	215	233	237	245	226	242
	Total	1 864	1 812	1 816	1 780	1 705	1 692	1 757	1 827	1 872	1 889	1 964

(1) Excludes those patients known not to have been resident in hospital on 31 December and includes only once those patients detained under more than one order.

Table 2: **Patients admitted to hospital subject to special restric-tions on discharge, by type of hospital, sex and year**

England and Wales   Number of patients

Type of hospital	Sex	1980	1981	1982	1983	1984	1985	1986	1987	1988	1989	1990
Special hospital	Male	117	114	121	112	103	121	123	130	115	129	102
	Female	27	16	13	14	18	17	22	21	15	19	23
	Total	144	130	134	126	121	138	145	151	130	148	125
Other hospital	Male	120	99	129	117	149	137	156	204	227	242	348
	Female	16	15	15	14	13	28	26	27	33	27	46
	Total	136	114	144	131	162	165	182	231	260	269	394
Total	Male	237	213	250	229	252	258	279	334	342	371	450
	Female	43	31	28	28	31	45	48	48	48	46	69
	Total	280	244	278	257	283	303	327	382	390	417	519

Table 3: **Patients admitted to hospital subject to special restrictions on discharge, by legal category[1] and year**

England and Wales   Number of patients

Legal category (1)	1980	1981	1982	1983	1984	1985	1986	1987	1988	1989	1990
Hospital order with restriction order	119	107	142	120	108	114	127	147	152	151	133
Transferred from Prison Service Establishment after sentence	76	70	69	70	83	87	84	104	94	119	145
Transferred from Prison Service Establishment before sentence	19	22	17	24	46	38	53	76	82	98	180
Recalled after conditional discharge	26	11	16	21	28	38	47	40	43	36	41
Transferred from Scotland, Northern Ireland, Channel Islands or Isle of Man	1	1	1	1	-	1	-	-	-	-	-
Unfit to plead or not guilty by reason of insanity	39	33	33	21	18	25	16	15	19	13	20
Total	280	244	278	257	283	303	327	382	390	417	519

(1) See Note 1 for details of section of Acts.

Table 4:   **Patients detained in hospital on 31 December who were subject to special restrictions on discharge, by type of mental order[1], age and sex**

England and Wales 1990   Number of Patients

Mental category	Total			Age on 31 December 1990									
				Under 17		17-20		21-39		40-59		60 and over	
	T	M	F	M	F	M	F	M	F	M	F	M	F
Mental illness	1310	1177	133	-	-	19	3	637	77	429	39	92	14
Psychopathic disorder	425	337	88	-	-	18	8	192	62	111	18	16	-
Mental impairment	162	143	19	-	-	3	-	76	12	57	6	7	1
Severe mental impairment	35	35	-	-	-	1	-	16	-	16	-	2	-
Not known	32	30	2	-	-	1	-	19	1	9	1	1	-
Total	1964	1722	242	-	-	42	11	940	152	622	64	118	15

(1) See Note 6 for classification of mental disorder[6].

Table 5:   **Patients admitted to hospital subject to restrictions on discharge, by type of mental disorder[1] and year**

England and Wales   Number of patients

Type of mental disorder	1980	1981	1982	1983	1984	1985	1986	1987	1988	1989	1990
Mental illness	215	180	222	199	227	224	245	301	299	326	442
Psychopathic disorder	40	43	38	33	37	49	58	43	54	50	42
Mental impairment (2)	19	18	15	25	12	20	22	22	17	24	15
Severe mental impairment (3)	6	3	3	-	3	7	2	-	-	3	-
Not known	-	-	-	-	4	3	-	16	20	14	20
Total	280	244	278	257	283	303	327	382	390	417	519

(1) See Note 6 for classification of mental disorder.
(2) 'Subnormality' for patients admitted up to 30 September 1983.
(3) 'Severe subnormality' for patients admitted up to 30 September 1983.

Table 6: **Patients admitted to hospital subject to special restrictions on discharge, by offence[1] and year**

England and Wales   Number of patients

Offence (1)	1980	1981	1982	1983	1984	1985	1986	1987	1988	1989	1990
Violence against the person:											
Homicide	51	52	49	59	58	66	64	85	77	82	91
Other	91	73	113	93	99	103	115	137	128	116	169
Sexual offences	28	18	18	23	21	34	31	34	34	38	41
Burglary	21	16	20	14	22	17	15	25	23	33˜	33
Robbery	9	9	8	9	7	10	25	32	34	30	39
Theft and handling stolen goods	14	9	9	11	13	10	15	6	13	17	20
Fraud and forgery	8	8	3	2	2	1	4	-	-	4	2
Criminal damage:											
Arson	42	38	40	30	41	44	37	39	53	57	60
Other	9	8	10	6	3	3	8	8	3	10	5
Other indictable offences	4	1	1	4	4	4	7	4	6	9	16
Summary offences	3	11	5	5	11	6	3	8	14	16	31
Total	280	244[2]	278[3]	257[2]	283[3]	303[4]	327[5]	382[6]	390[7]	417[7]	519[8]

(1) The offence categories are shown in Appendix 5 of Criminal Statistics, England and Wales 1989.
(2) Includes 1 civil prisoner.
(3) Includes 2 civil prisoners.
(4) Includes 4 civil prisoners and 2 persons detained under the Immigration Act of 1971.
(5) Includes 1 civil prisoner and 2 persons detained under the Immigration Act of 1971.
(6) Includes 2 civil prisoners and 2 persons detained under the Immigration Act of 1971.
(7) Includes 3 civil prisoners and 2 persons detained under the Immigration Act of 1971.
(8) Includes 3 civil prisoners and 5 persons detained under the Immigration Act of 1971.

Table 7: **Patients admitted to hospital subject to special restrictions on discharge, by offence and age**

England and Wales   Number of patients

Offence	Total	Under 17	17-20	21-39	40-59	60 plus
Violence against the person:						
Homicide	91	-	1	66	18	6
Other	169	-	14	121	30	4
Sexual offences	41	-	4	31	4	2
Burglary	33	-	4	26	3	-
Robbery	39	-	3	34	2	-
Theft and handling stolen goods	20	-	2	16	2	-
Fraud and forgery	2	-	-	1	1	-
Criminal damage:						
Arson	64	-	7	42	13	2
Other	5	-	-	4	1	-
Other indictable offences	16	-	3	8	5	-
Summary offences	31	-	3	25	3	-
Total	519[1]	-	41	380[2]	84[3]	14

(1) Includes 3 civil prisoners and 5 persons detained under the Immigration Act of 1971.
(2) Includes 2 civil prisoners and 4 persons detained under the Immigration Act of 1971.
(3) Includes 1 civil prisoner and 1 person detained under the Immigration Act of 1971.

Table 8: **Patients detained in hospital on 31 December who were subject to special restrictions on discharge, by offence[1] and type of mental disorder[2]**

England and Wales   Number of patients

Offence	Mental illness	Psychopathic disorder	Mental impairment	Severe mental impairment	Not known	Total
Violence against the person:						
Homicide	398	95	29	5	6	533
Other	515	117	39	10	16	697
Sexual offence	108	67	44	11	4	234
Burglary	43	10	4	1	1	59
Robbery	51	10	2	-	1	64
Theft and handling stolen goods	18	4	1	-	-	23
Fraud and forgery	2	-	-	-	-	2
Criminal damage:						
Arson	123	99	36	6	3	267
Other	16	12	5	1	-	34
Other indictable offences	18	5	1	-	1	25
Summary offences	18	6	1	1	-	26
Total	1310	425	162	35	32	1964

(1) The offence categories are shown in Appendix 5 of Criminal Statistics, England and Wales 1989.

(2) See Note 6 for classification of mental disorder.

Table 9: Patients detained in hospital on 31 December who were subject to special restrictions on discharge, by period spent in hospital since original committal or last recall, type of hospital[1] and sex

England and Wales

Number of patients

Period since original committal or last recall	Total			Type of hospital					
				Special			Other		
	T	M	F	T	M	F	T	M	F
Under 2 yrs	656	572	84	294	250	44	362	322	40
2 to 5 yrs	337	288	49	251	213	38	86	75	11
6 to 10 yrs	370	314	56	267	223	44	103	91	12
11 to 20 yrs	408	369	39	260	239	21	148	130	18
21 to 30 yrs	154	145	9	82	78	4	72	67	5
Over 30 yrs	39	34	5	25	22	3	14	12	2
Total	1964	1722	242	1179	1025	154	785	697	88

(1) Patients may not have spent their entire period of detention in the type of hospital under which they are shown.

Table 10: Discharges and disposals of patients subject to special restrictions on discharge, by type of discharge or disposal and year

England and Wales

Number of patients

Type of discharge	1980	1981	1982	1983	1984	1985	1986	1987	1988	1989	1990
Discharges into the community:											
- Discharged conditionally under a warrant issued by the Home Secretary	151	146	128	100	63	60	33	50	55(1)	69	46
- Discharged conditionally by tribunal	-	-	-	5	107	86	76	62	69	96	82
- Other discharges into the community	29	25	20	42	37	34	28	39	29	31	35
Total discharges into the community	180	171	148	147	207	180	137	151	153	196	163
Disposals not into the community:											
- Remained in hospital; no longer subject to restriction	30	56	47	72	55	52	46	46	46	64	62
- Returned to custody to resume sentence	21	18	22	18	31	31	21	36	50	46	77
- Died	28	25	19	23	23	20	14	18	15	16	26
- Other	34	27	35	38	44	38	47	60	79	78	116
Total disposals not into the community	113	126	123	151	153	141	128	160	190	204	281
Total discharges and disposals	293	297	271	298	360	321	265	311	343	400	444

(1) A further 4 conditional discharges were authorised under a warrant issued by the Home Secretary but are not included in this Table. The patients were originally released from hospital by Mental Health Tribunals in 1986 (3 absolutely and 1 conditionally) but following Judicial Review, such authorities for discharge were set aside.

Table 11: Admissions to hospital from Prison Service Establishments of patients with and without special restriction on discharge before (S48) and after sentence (S47) 1980 to 1990

England and Wales   Number of patients

Type of discharge	1980	1981	1982	1983	1984	1985	1986	1987	1988	1989	1990
Section 47											
Restricted	76	70	69	70	83	87	84	104	94	119	145
Unrestricted	11	16	16	21	25	13	23	26	27	11	11
Total:	87	86	85	91	108	100	107	130	121	130	156
Section 48											
Restricted	19	22	17	24	46	38	53	76	82	98	180
Unrestricted	0	0	1	0	1	3	0	2	3	2	1
Total:	19	22	18	24	47	41	53	78	85	100	181
Total Restricted	95	92	86	94	129	125	137	180	176	217	310
Unrestricted	10	16	17	21	26	16	23	28	30	13	12
Total	106	108	103	115	155	141	160	208	206	230	337

Table 12: Persons made subject to hospital orders without restriction[1] on discharge by offence and year

England and Wales   Number of patients

Offence	1979	1980	1981	1982	1983	1984	1985	1986	1987	1988	1989
Violence against the person: Homicide Other	125	139	144	135	134	206	197	204	169	211	110
Sexual offences	23	31	25	21	22	24	30	26	35	46	49
Burglary	46	52	59	55	44	57	58	54	66	65	63
Robbery	6	8	7	8	12	10	7	10	16	17	21
Theft and handling of stolen goods	107	109	108	88	109	138	132	103	102	103	93
Fraud and forgery	27	42	35	22	23	35	28	21	14	22	28
Criminal damage: Arson Other	58	66	74	77	98	104	125	104	124	135	105
Other indictable offences	24	26	15	11	21	27	36	26	33	36	30
Summary offences	135	115	134	109	114	130	121	117	124	115	147
Total:	551	588	600	526	577	731	734	665	683	750	756

(1) Section 37(1) and Section 37(3) patients. (These figures are from the Criminal Statistics).

NOTES

1   The provisions of the two Mental Health Acts are similar; where two references are made below to sections or parts, the first relates to the 1959 Act and the second to the 1983 Act. They provide for:

   i)   the admission to hospital by the court of a person convicted of an offence (Section 60(1)/37(1));

   ii)   the admission, under certain circumstances, of a person who the court is satisfied committed the act or made the ommission charged of, and in respect of whom it made a hospital order without convicting her/him (Section 60(2)/37(3));

   iii)   the transfer to hospital by the Home Secretary of prisoners serving sentence in a Prison Service Establishment (Section 72/47). Under Sections 64/41 (for hospital orders) and 74/49 (for transfers) these patients may also be made subject to restrictions which have the effect of requiring the Home Secretary's consent on all matters related to absence, transfer or, except where directed by a Mental Health Review Tribunal, discharge;

   iv)   the transfer to a hospital from a Prison Service Establishment of an unsentenced or untried defendant in criminal proceedings by the Home Secretary (Section 73/48). In this case, restrictions are mandatory. Civil prisoners and persons detained under the Immigration Act 1971 may also be admitted under this section;

   v)   under Section 66(3)/42(3), the Home Secretary may recall to hospital a patient subject to a restriction order who had previously been conditionally discharged from hospital;

   vi)   Part VI of either Act enables patients to be transferred from one part of the United Kingdom, Channel Islands or the Isle of Man to another. Those transferred to England and Wales are treated as if they had been admitted to hospital under the Act, so that some of them will, in effect, be subject to hospital and restriction orders;

   vii)   Section 5(1) of the Criminal Procedure (Insanity) Act 1964 allows juries to return a special verdict of 'not guilty by reason of insanity' or to find a defendant 'unfit to plead'; in both cases restrictions are automatic;

   viii) patients who have been ordered to be detained during Her Majesty's Pleasure and who, under Section 71/46 of the main Acts, may be admitted to hospital subject to restrictions.

2   Transfer of patients between hospitals in England and Wales are not counted as admissions, but any transfer of a patient from or to a hospital outside England and Wales is counted as an admission or discharge respectively. It is possible for a patient to be admitted to, or discharged from, hospitals more than once during a year; each event has been included in the relevant tables. In the population tables,

however, a patient is counted once only. A few patients may be held under more than one order or warrant and these are counted only in the population tables. Similarly, patients who are in prison but have current detention in hospital orders are not counted in the population tables.

3   There were four 'special hospitals' - Broadmoor, Moss Side and Park Lane - until 18 February 1990. On that date, Moss Side and Park Lane merged to become Ashworth. Under the Mental Health Act 1983 (or earlier legislation) the special hospitals are intended to detain patients who, in the opinion of the Secretary of State for Health, require treatment under conditions of special security because of their dangerousness, violent or criminal propensities. The term 'other hospital' refers to other psychiatric hospitals in England and Wales which admit mentally-disordered offenders; these hospitals, unlike the specials, also admit informal patients.

4   The powers of the Mental Health Review Tribunals were extended by Part V of the Mental Health Act 1983. The Tribunals may now be required to review the cases of certain patients held under hospital orders or transfer directions and must review the case of any restricted patient whose case has not been considered in the last three years. These tribunals have power, *inter alia*, to direct the absolute or conditional discharge of such patients in certain specific circumstances.

5   Tables 1-10 cover patients who have been admitted to hospital subject to restriction orders and directions under the Mental Health Acts. Such patients may not be discharged or transferred without the consent of the Home Secretary or a Mental Health Review Tribunal. Tables 11 and 12 cover certain mentally-ill offenders whose discharge or transfer is not subject to a restriction - those receiving a hospital order from a court and those transferred from a Prison Service Establishment. As the Home Office has no occasion to monitor the movements of unrestricted patients after their admission, only admission figures have been included in this Bulletin.

6   The Mental Health (Amendment) Act 1982 replaced the term 'subnormality' used in the Mental Health Act 1959 by 'mental impairment' and covered a narrower range of patients. The provisions of the Act covering psychopathic disorder were also redrafted but this did not appear to have any effect on the admission of such patients. In the Tables showing category of mental disorder any patient with other forms of mental disorder, in addition to mental illness, are included under 'mental illness'. Similarly, those with subnormality, severe subnormality, mental impairment or severe mental impairment in addition to psychopathic disorder are shown under 'psychopathic disorder'.

GERMANY
*Helmut Kury**

RESPONSIBILITY

The German Criminal Code makes a distinction between responsibility and non-responsibility. Thus, paragraph 1, Article 51 of the 1934 Penal Code originally provided three criteria for non-responsibility: interruption of consciousness, mental disorder and feeblemindedness.

The corresponding Article concerning non-responsibility in the revised version of the Penal Code of 1 January 1975 is Article 20 which deals with 'lack of criminal capacity because of mental disorder'. As regards non-responsibility it states: 'A person is not criminally responsible if at the time of the act, because of a psychotic or similar serious mental disorder, or a profound interruption of consciousness, or due to feeblemindedness or any other type of serious abnormality, s/he is incapable of understanding the wrongfulness of her/his conduct or of acting in accordance with this understanding'. The Penal Code then summarises the criteria of non-responsibility as: a psychotic or similar serious mental disorder; a profound interruption of consciousness; feeblemindedness; and any other type of serious mental abnormality. This last criterion was included in the Penal Code after the reform of 1975.

Children under the age of 14 years are also regarded as non-responsible (Article 19), whereas the responsibility of juveniles between 14 and 18 years is decided on an individual basis (Article 3 of the Juvenile Court Act). People over 18 years of age are normally considered by the Penal Code as being responsible. Responsibility is

---

* Head, Department of Victimology, Max-Planck-Institute for Foreign and International Criminal Law, Freiburg im Breisgau, Germany. This report was prepared in March 1992.

defined as the capacity to understand the wrongfulness of one's conduct and act in accordance with this understanding[1].

Diminished responsibility

The concept of diminished responsibility appears in Article 21 of the Penal Code as 'diminished capacity'. If, at the time of the offence, the capacity of the perpetrator to understand the wrongfulness of the act or to act in accordance with this understanding is substantially diminished, due to the existence of one of the criteria listed in Article 20, the punishment shall be reduced in accordance with the provisions cited in Article 49.

Treatment of non-responsible offenders

The treatment of 'non-responsible' offenders is defined in Articles 61 *et seq.*, and depends on the causes leading to non-responsibility. The German criminal justice system deals with non-responsible offenders within the 'measures of rehabilitation and security' in one of the following ways:

- commitment to a mental health institution;
- commitment to an institution for the treatment of chemical dependency;
- commitment to a custodial institution;
- supervision of conduct;
- withdrawal of driver's licence;
- prohibition to practice a profession.

Article 62 of the Penal Code highlights the principle of proportionality, by stating that: 'A measure of rehabilitation and security may not be ordered if it would be disproportionate to the offender's past crimes and anticipated criminal behaviour, as well as to the amount of danger which s/he poses to society' (p. 77 *et seq.*). If a person commits an unlawful act at a time when s/he lacked criminal capacity (Article 20), 'the court shall order her/his commitment to a mental institution if a total evaluation of the offender and her/his offence indicates that serious unlawful acts are to be expected of her/him because of her/his condition and that s/he therefore represents a danger to society' (p. 78, Article 63 of the Penal Code). Article 64, p. 78, of the Penal Code states:

1. If a person has the propensity for taking alcoholic beverages or other intoxicants to excess and commits an unlawful act, either while intoxicated or because the act is associated with her/his propensity and for which s/he is convicted, or escapes conviction only because her/his lack of criminal capacity has been proved or not excluded, the court shall order her/his commitment to an institution for the treatment of chemical dependency if a danger exists that, because of her/his propensity, s/he will commit serious unlawful acts.

2. No such order shall be made if there is no likelihood of success of the withdrawal treatment.

Treatment of borderline cases

Kernberg has defined 'borderline' as a specific, stable, pathological organisation of personality, the pathology of which differs from that of neuroses, psychopathic disorders and psychoses[2]. It does not represent a transitory state between neurosis and psychosis.

The concept of borderline as a personality defect is still rather new, and its inclusion in the psychiatric examination and diagnosis is in the early stages. Therefore, the effects of this definition on the diagnosis of responsibility still remains to be seen. As a rule, it can be said that the diagnosis of a borderline personality alone does not mention anything about the responsibility or non-responsibility of an offender in relation to a certain offence. The criteria for the examination of psychopathic disorders and neuroses have to be applied accordingly[3].

Psychiatric/psychological diagnosis of borderline cases

In general, the same instruments are used in the diagnosis of borderline cases that are applied in clinical psychiatry or psychology, and any variations in the methodology or contents of the examination are related to the judicial framework.

The psychiatric or psychological interview represents the main instrument for diagnosing borderline cases. The results drawn from the interview are then usually integrated by a series of psychological tests and by a psychiatric examination using standard methods. A physical and neurological check-up are also carried out.

The different stages of the psychiatric-psychological examination are described below, while Table 1 describes one of the possible ways to structure an examination. Although the succession of topics may vary, the form and contents are more or less the same throughout Germany[4].

I   The forensic-psychiatric interview (anamnesis)

i) *Specific anamnesis:*

- actual lapse (offence);
- psychological, somatic and social problems, life-circumstances (changes in one's life), original conflict situation, recurrence of the delinquent behaviour.

ii) *Biographical anamnesis:*

- family characteristics;
- childhood and youth;
- sexual anamnesis;
- social anamnesis;
- present social situation;
- forensic anamnesis.

iii) *Medical anamnesis:*

- anamnesis of family disease;
- anamnesis of the offender;

- present state of health.

II *Standardised psychiatric instruments of examination*

- German version of the 'Standardised Interview Schedule for Psychiatric Present State Examination' (PSE);
- standardised scales for physical and psychological disorders (such as anxiety, depression and paranoid symptoms).

III *Psychological test*

The application of psychological tests is recommended for various reasons. Usually, the following tests are applied:

- an intelligence test (mainly the 'Hamburg Wechsler Intelligenztest' (HAWI);
- tests for specific mental (psychic) functions (such as the 'Benton Test' for the ability to use visual memory and the 'D2-Test' for level of concentration);
- personality inventories (personality-questionnaires): 'Eysenck-Persönlichkeits-Inventar' (personality-inventory), 'Freiburger Persönlichkeits-Inventar', 'Giessen-Test', 'MMPI Saarbrücken'.

IV *Physical examination*

- description of the general state of health;
- general physical check-up;
- examination of the neurological status.

Treatment of mentally-ill offenders

Rasch gives a schematic description of the psychiatric-psychological diagnoses of the psychological characteristics of Articles 20 and 21 of the Penal Code; this is shown in Table 1[5].

Table 1: Psychiatric-psychological diagnoses of psychological characteristics of Articles 20 and 21 of the Penal Code

Legal term	Psychiatric-psychological diagnoses
Serious mental disorder	**Exogenous psychoses or changes of personality caused by** brain diseases brain infections hormonal disturbances poisoning alcoholism etc. **Endogenous psychoses** schizophrenia paranoia affective psychoses **Feeblemindedness by known genesis**
Profound interruption of consciousness	affective irritability fright over fatigue exhaustion
Feeblemindedness	**Intellectual feeblemindedness by unknown genesis** feeblemindedness oligophreny debility imbecility idiocy
Any other type of serious mental abnormality	**Disturbances of personality development** psychopathic disorder abnormal personality **neuroses** **abnormal psychopathological personality development** alcoholism drug-addiction

In a case where a criminal act is due to a neurotic disturbance which caused the person to become 'incapable of understanding the wrongfulness of her/his conduct or of acting in accordance with this understanding' (Article 20), the offender will not be considered responsible for the offence. If the neurotic disturbance diminishes the offender's capacity to understand the wrongfulness of the conduct or to act in accordance with this understanding, the court may apply Article 21 of the Penal Code.

As a rule, a person suffering from neurosis is classified as 'suffering from a serious mental abnormality', which is one of the four categories that allow for the application of Article 20 or 21.

A psychopathic personality development might be characterised by an 'abnormal personality' trait, such as paranoia, hysteria, asthenia, irritability, schizophrenia or anti-social behaviour. It might also be manifested by sexual misconduct, sexual perversion, alcoholism and/or drug addiction. Psychopaths are also included in the category of 'serious mental abnormality' and, accordingly, Articles 20 or 21 may be applied to these cases.

Emotional distress, like affective irritability, fright, over fatigue or exhaustion, belongs to the category of 'profound interruption of consciousness', which allows for the application of Articles 20 or 21.

'Irresistible impulse' belongs to the category of affective disturbances, and may be sexually or non-sexually motivated. The term 'irresistible impulse' means an explosion of repressed emotions which have slowly accumulated and escalated, and applies particularly to psychopaths. Since individual characteristics hardly appear, it is also referred to as 'primitive reactions'[6]. From a forensic point of view, when these primitive reactions are determined by a 'profound interruption of consciousness', they are generally dealt with by Articles 20 and 21.

DANGEROUSNESS

The concept of dangerousness exists in German criminal law and is determined by the criteria listed in Articles 63 and 64 below, which also determine the treatment to be applied to dangerous offenders.

Thus, according to these Articles, any offender who, at the moment of the commission of the offence, lacked criminal capacity or possessed only diminished capacity, and who is likely to commit other offences in the future, is considered to be dangerous, and should be admitted into a psychiatric hospital or institution for the treatment of chemical dependency.

Treatment of dangerous mentally-ill offenders

The treatment of offenders who are determined to be dangerous is catered for by Articles 63 and 64, under 'measures of rehabilitation and security'.

Article 63 (under the heading 'Committal to a mental health institution') states that:

If someone commits an unlawful act at a time when s/he lacked criminal capacity (Article 20), or possessed only diminished capacity (Article 21), the court shall order her/his commitment to a mental health institution if a total evaluation of the offender and the offence indicates that, given her/his condition, it is likely that s/he will commit serious unlawful offences again in the future, and that s/he therefore represents a threat to society.

Article 64 (under 'Committal to an institution for the treatment of chemical dependency') states:

1. If a person has the propensity for taking alcoholic beverages or other intoxicants to excess, and commits an unlawful act, either while intoxicated or because the act is associated with this propensity and for which s/he is convicted, or escapes conviction only because her/his lack of criminal capacity has been proved or is not excluded, the court shall order her/his committal to an institution for the treatment of chemical dependency if a danger exists that, because of her/his propensity, s/he will commit serious unlawful acts.

2. No such order shall be made if there is no likelihood of success of the withdrawal treatment.

Diagnosis of dangerousness

If, following the psychiatric-psychological examination mentioned above, the offenders are diagnosed as being non-responsible or as having diminished responsibility, a prognosis is given of the likely development of their mental condition. The classification of the offenders as being dangerous is then based on this prognosis.

The criminal justice system demands 'a total evaluation of the offender and the offence committed'[7]. This evaluation takes the form of a prognosis, which is based on the knowledge of human nature, professional experience and the individual ethical beliefs of the examiner or judge respectively[8]. Kaiser points out that, although this method cannot provide objective criteria for a prognosis, it is still widely used[9].

The clinical or empirical individual prognosis is based upon an extensive examination of the offender by means of exploration and observation, including psycho-diagnostical tests. The evaluation of the collected data for the prognosis of dangerousness must be carried out by psychiatric-psychological experts who also have a great deal of criminological knowledge of, and experience with offenders[10]. In fact, Schöch concludes that only those psychologists and psychiatrists who have sufficient criminological experience should carry out this task[11].

PSYCHIATRIC EXAMINATIONS

The Code of Criminal Procedure provides only a fragmentary regulation of those cases which require a psychiatric/psychological examination. For the main procedure, according to Article 246a of the Criminal Penal Code, it is prescribed that a medical expert *is to be heard* if there is a possibility that the accused is to be committed to a mental health institution, to an institution for the treatment of chemical dependency, or to an institution of protective custody. According to Articles 80a and 414 of the Code, an expert *should be consulted,* under the same circumstances, during the investigation. According to Article 81 of the Code, *it is permissible,* after an expert and the lawyer of the accused have been heard, to commit the accused to a mental health institution, if this appears necessary for the expert to provide an opinion on the mental and psychic state of mind of the offender.

According to the present law, the court alone must make a final decision and, in fact, the Federal Supreme Court refers to the expert as the 'assistant' of the judge. Kaufmann rightly objects that this title does not reflect the real relationship between the court and the 'assistants', and Schreiber proposes that the expert should be called the 'independent assistant' in the decision-making process[12]. Nevertheless, this does not alter the fact that, from an effective and legal point of view, the judge alone, according to the conception of her/his function, is responsible for the final decision[13].

The Federal Supreme Court states very clearly, in its widely cited federal principle, that: 'the expert is an assistant of the judge. S/he is obliged to deliver the court the kind of data that can only be obtained by an expert's observation. S/he must handle the scientific means which make an evaluation possible. Furthermore, the expert is neither permitted nor able to take the considerations on which a judgement is based off the judge's shoulders'. However, notwithstanding the emphasis on the judge's freedom to make a final decision, the professional standing and specific knowledge of the experts have placed them in a rather powerful and influential position, which is hardly in accordance with the law[14].

Criminological examination

The 'criminological' or forensic examination is part of the general psychiatric analysis. This part of the examination is sometimes left to the end and contains questions concerning the offence and the circumstances related to it. The accused usually know that they will be asked about these facts and are, therefore, well prepared to answer the questions; they obviously provide a version of the event that will represent the best form of defence for themselves. Although omissions or contradictions in the stories of the accused will be questioned by the expert, their versions are usually accepted.

The description of the event on the part of the accused is of important diagnostical value; repression, minimisation, denial or a blunt description are characteristic ways of dealing with conflicts. Baer notes that there is no need to confront the accused by means of interview techniques that expose their weaknesses and contradictions during their self-description[15]. On the other hand, it is important to know why some facts are ommitted or misrepresented. An expert should respect this fact and mention it when expressing an opinion on its diagnostical value.

The evaluation of psychiatric/psychological tests in the criminal procedure

Lienert defines a psychological test as 'a scientific method for the assessment of one or more defined characteristics of personality which aims at quantitative information about the degree of manifestation of the characteristics in question'[16].

Schraml notes that psychological tests contribute in various ways to the clinical differential diagnosis[17]. Their results might have a persuasive, complementary, reinforcing and occasionally, even determining character. This might also be true in the field of forensic-psychiatric-psychological diagnoses; although they are usually applied to complement or reinforce the information that has been gathered during the examination, their results sometimes open new, hitherto unexplored, pathways.

The psychiatric examination is mainly based on the biographical data of the investigation, known as the qualitative data. These data aim at assessing the person from a longitudinal section. A great deal of the clinical psychological examination is based on the data from psychological tests, which are called 'quantitative data' and are considered to be highly objective, at least those of a standardised form. The information gained from these tests shows the personality in a cross-section which should be representative for the longitudinal section. Despite the diversity of these two methods, they must produce results which support one another.

Barbey notes three basic reasons for a test-psychological examination:

1) since the results of the psychiatric interview are not usually sufficiently validated, they are considered as being rather subjective. Therefore, the examiner attempts to be objective and completes the interview results by carrying out psychological tests;

2) from the judge's point of view, the results of the examination become more comprehensible and hence facilitate the task of understanding and evaluating the expert's opinion.

3) the application of tests is considered to be positive for both the offender and the other persons present in court, such as the judge, attorney and lawyer, in the sense that a 'real examination' has taken place[18].

However, the value of psychological tests should not be exaggerated since they can be subjected to various influences, as is the case with interview results. It is also important to be aware that the test results present a picture of the offender's personality at the time of the examination. Göppinger mentioned that only limited conclusions on the personality of the offender at the time of the act can be drawn from those results[19]. And these are the conclusions that the judge is interested in. The same problem exists for the psychological tests, since the psychiatric interview also permits insufficient conclusions in relation to the time of the offence. A further argument against the application of a psychological test-result within the forensic examination refers to the fact that the tests in general are valid only for normal psychological conditions, whereas they would not differentiate in psychopathological peculiarities. This objection is only partially correct. Of course, psychiatric diagnoses are not always dependent upon psychological tests. Psychic disturbances of a psychopathological nature are diagnosed on the basis of an interview. In the field of forensic problems, very often it is not the endogenous psychosis or the brain-organic disturbance which creates difficulties for the examiner, but the neuroses and personality disturbances which are also far more numerous than the former ones. In these cases, psychological tests allow for a better understanding of the offender's personality. The expert can provide a general evaluation of the offender's personality and, possibly, what type of demands the offender may be able to fulfill. But in addition, brain-organic disturbances can also be verified by test-psychological means, so that further clinical examinations may be carried out.

Test-psychological personality diagnoses should also be carried out by a clinical psychologist. Whenever complex questions arise with respect to the offender's personality, a forensic psychologist should be consulted. Often s/he will be the only person responsible for an examination and to provide an expert opinion, since her/his profession also allows her/him to carry out interviews and analyse them with respect to a specific question. To a limited extent, a psychiatrist can learn how to apply simple tests in order to widen her/his diagnostical instruments. However, psychological tests demand the familiarity of the examiner with the test-theoretical preconditions, with the construction, carrying out, analysis, interpretation and possible sources of faults of the tests. It is necessary to obtain the consent of the offender before carrying out the tests.

Relationship between the judicial decision and psychiatric examinations

Kaiser points out that, in general, according to Article 63 of the German Penal Code, the court appoints an expert to provide an opinion in cases of offenders who are being considered for committal to a mental health institution. Kaiser also claims that this necessary prognosis of dangerousness is accepted in only 3 per cent of all the relevant cases related to Article 20 of the Penal Code, compared to more than half the penal decisions in cases of 'non-responsibility' (Article 21)[20].

The above discussion on the controversial, albeit powerful, position of psychiatric/psychological experts in court, has led to a wide debate on the legal role of the expert in court, and her/his actual power, which contradicts the law on criminal procedure. The debate also covers the possible conflicting roles of the expert because of her/his different professional functions (e.g. as a counselor or therapist). The expert is obliged to provide an objective opinion that is based on empirical scientific knowledge[21].

Scientific analyses of experts' opinions repeatedly point to the influence of common sense theories, personal norms and values, and prejudice[22]. In a study on 49 psychiatric and psychological experts, Heim found that their opinions reflected a formal and methodological point of view and were based on incomplete contents[23]. The results show, therefore, that the experts do not fulfill the theoretical scientific and judicial demands for a neutral and scientifically-based professional opinion when they carry out their role in providing expert opinions.

In another study, Kury analysed 197 cases where a written expert's opinion had been presented to the prosecution[24]. The study covered all the cases presented by the States of Lower Saxony and Hamburg between 1983 and 1984. Of these, 85 cases which had required a written expert's opinion in relation to responsibility had become legally effective. The study attempted to clarify the following points:

- the scientific and 'transparent' nature of the experts' arguments;

- to what degree the experts' opinions contained subjective and unscientifically proved appraisals;

- how many of the analysed expert opinions diagnosed the need to apply Articles 20 and 21, and in how many of the cases the court actually applied these Articles;

- the influence of the opinions on the type and duration of the sanctions applied.

With respect to the point relating to the scientific and 'transparent' character of the opinions, it can be said that 20 per cent of them did not mention the methods used in the examination. Only 1 per cent (N=2) of the analysed opinions made statements concerning the individual theoretical point of view, and 18 per cent (N=40) made statements on the professional sources on which the interpretation of the data was based.

Forty four per cent (N=96) of the analysed cases were scientific and 'transparent', a further 44 per cent (N=97) only partially met these criteria, and 12 per cent (N=26) did not fulfill them at all.

Only in 9.6 per cent (N=10) of the opinions expressing a diagnosis of a non-psychotic disturbance, did the experts ask for the application of Article 20 (non-responsibility), and 21.5 per cent (N=86) for Article 21 (diminished responsibility). On the other hand, where a psychotic disturbance had been diagnosed, the experts declared the patient non-responsible in 86.5 per cent (N=23) of the cases, and with diminished responsibility in 11.5 per cent (N=3) of the cases.

Table 2 presents the number of requests for the application of Articles 20 and 21 and the actual number of sentences applied by the judge.

Table 2:   **Requests for the application of Articles 20 and 21 and actual number of sentences applied***

	Neither Article 20 nor 21	Article 21	Article 20	Total
Court in agreement with the diagnosis	23 18.5% 40.4% 12.4%	73 58.9% 81.1% 39.5%	28 22.6% 73.7% 15.1%	124 67.0%
Court not in agreement with the diagnosis	34 55.7% 57.6% 18.4%	17 27.9% 18.9% 9.2%	10 16.4% 26.3% 5.4%	61 33%
Total	57 30.8%	90 48.7%	38 20.5%	185 100%

* The order of the values in the cells of Table 2 is as follows: number (N), row per cent; column per cent and total per cent.

In general, it can be said that the more qualified the opinions were, the greater was their influence on the decision of the courts.

SANCTIONS

Article 61 of the German Penal Code provides the following rehabilitation and security measures:

1) committal to a mental health institution;

2) committal to an institution for the treatment of chemical dependency;

3) committal to an institution of protective custody;

4) supervision of conduct;

5) withdrawal of driver's licence;

6) prohibition to practice a profession.

These measures are justified by the need to protect the community and by the obligation to resocialise and rehabilitate offenders who can be cured. If the offender is diagnosed as being non-responsible (Article 20) or with diminished responsibility (Article 21), and fits the criteria in Article 63f, s/he will not be punished, since punishment is associated with guilt, which is only possible when the offender is responsible. Depending on the cause of non-responsibility or diminished responsibility, the offender will be committed to a mental institution or to an institution for the treatment of chemical dependency. In the case of diminished responsibility, a security measure is also applied alongside the punishment, which does not necessarily mean that punishment has to be applied.

The German penal law is based on the principle of guilt (*Schuldstrafrecht*), so not all the needs to protect the public from dangerous offences and to provide treatment for mentally-ill offenders can be satisfied by the application of a sentence. This fact is the basis for the so-called 'double-track' (*Zweispurigkeit*) phenomenon, which means that punishment and preventive needs are kept separate; punishment does not involve any preventive element and nor are preventive needs considered as a form of punishment, but as special measures.

If the offender is found responsible, s/he may be subjected to one or more of the above-mentioned measures in addition to punishment. Except for the committal to an institution of protective custody, the measure is carried out prior to the application of the punishment.

According to sub-paragraph 2 of Article 67 of the German Penal Code:

... the court shall order, however, that all or part of the punishment shall be executed before the measure is applied, if the purpose of the measure would thereby be more easily achieved.

1. The court may subsequently make, modify or revoke an order under sub-paragraph 2, if this is so required by the conditions of the offender.

2. If all or part of the measure is carried out prior to the execution of the punishment, the time spent in applying the measure shall be credited towards the execution of the punishment, until two-thirds of the punishment has been completed...

With respect to the committal to an institution of protective custody, Article 66 of the German Penal Code states:

If someone is sentenced to at least two years' imprisonment for a crime of intent, the court shall order, in addition to punishment, committal to an institution of protective custody if:

1. the offender, before committing the latest crime, has already received two prison sentences for the duration of at least one year each, for intentional crimes;

2. prior to the latest crime, the offender has served at least two years' imprisonment for one or more of these offences, or on account of which s/he has been deprived of her/his liberty in an institution administering a measure of rehabilitation and security; and

3. the global evaluation of the offender and her/his crimes indicates that, because of her/his propensity to commit serious crimes, especially those inflicting serious physical or emotional injury on her/his victims or causing significant economic loss, s/he is a danger to society...

Role and function of the traditional criminal psychiatric hospitals in the German criminal justice system

The committal to a mental institution is one of the measures of rehabilitation and security. The definition of the measure as one of rehabilitation and security already describes the main function of the traditional criminal psychiatric hospital. In the best of cases, the offender has the possibility to be cured, and in the worse, s/he will not be healed but the public may feel safe since s/he is locked up in the 'security' of a psychiatric hospital.

Article 63 of the Penal Code states that the committal to a mental health institution is not limited to persons who require treatment or care in the proper medical-psychiatric sense. As the committal serves the dual purpose of healing and security, the requirement for treatment and care is not a precondition for the application of this kind of measure.

Alternatives to traditional criminal psychiatric hospitals in the German criminal justice system

When the committal to a socio-therapeutic institution (*sozialtherapeutische Anstalt*) envisaged by Article 65, was replaced by a solution within the punitive administration (under Article 2 of the Amendatory Act of Penal Administration - Strafvollzugsanderungsgesetz), no other alternatives to traditional criminal hospitals remained. The developments and discussions related to this topic are presented in Annex 1

REFORMS

No concrete plans for reform dealing with mentally-ill offenders in the criminal justice system are envisaged.

STATISTICS

Tables 3 and 4 show the number of offenders who, in 1989, were classified as mentally-ill according to Article 20 (non-responsibility), and according to Article 21 (diminished responsibility). It is possible to calculate the percentage of those offenders who were diagnosed as dangerous from the total number of offenders to whom some measure was applied.

Table 3:   Non-responsible offenders with and without committal to an institution

Offences	Sentenced according to Article 20 Total (m)*	Without committal to an institution Total (m)*	Committal to a mental institution Total (m)*	Committal to an institution for the treatment of chemical dependency Total (m)*
Total offences	554 (499)	264 (217)	252 (229)	56 (53)
Offences according to the Penal Code	539 (484)	237 (208)	249 (226)	53 (50)
Sexual offences	34 (33)	4 (4)	30 (29)	-
Offences against life**	74 (64)	5 (5)	61 (52)	8 (7)
Violent offences**	74 (69)	18 (16)	44 (41)	12 (12)
Theft and embezzlement	70 (58)	38 (27)	27 (26)	5 (5)
Robbery and blackmail, car vandalism	40 (37)	4 (4)	30 (27)	6 (-)
Fraud and patrimonial disloyalty	14 (12)	10 (9)	3 (3)	1 (-)
Offences against public security	109 (98)	62 (57)	34 (28)	13 (13)

*   (m) = number of male offenders.

**   Traffic offences excluded.

Table 4: Offenders with diminished responsibility, with and without committal to an institution

Offences	Sentenced according to Article 21 Total(m)*	Without committal to an institution Total(m)*	Committal to a mental health institution Total(m)*	Committal to an institution for the treatment of chemical dependency Total(m)*
Total offences	15 025 (13 584)	14 580 (13 162)	171 (167)	274 (255)
Offences according to the Penal Code	14 354 (13 041)	13 947 (12 650)	170 (166)	237 (225)
Sexual offences	589 (587)	507 (505)	58 (58)	24 (24)
Offences against life**	258 (235)	229 (206)	19 (19)	10 (10)
Violent offences**	2 559 (2 433)	2 528 (2 405)	12 (11)	19 (17)
Theft and embezzlement	4 612 (3 962)	4 538 (3 888)	16 (16)	58 (58)
Robbery and blackmail, car vandalism	744 (687)	666 (612)	15 (15)	63 (60)
Fraud and patrimonial disloyalty	404 (350)	392 (339)	3 (2)	9 (9)
Offences against public security	345 (318)	302 (277)	27 (25)	16 (16)

* (m) = number of male offenders.

** Traffic offences excluded.

AMENDATORY ACT OF PENAL ADMINISTRATION (STRAFVOLLZUGSÄNDERUNGSGESETZ) AND THE SOCIO-THERAPEUTIC INSTITUTIONS

INTRODUCTION

German penal law is based on the principle of guilt. As a consequence, no punishment can be applied in cases of innocence or non-responsibility, and in these cases the accused is discharged. If there is a definite probability that the offender will commit further serious offences, s/he is committed to a special institution in order to protect the public. This committal is not considered as a sanction or form of punishment, but as a security measure. Besides securing the offender, the measure aims at treating her/him and, according to the law, treatment should have priority over the security measure. In fact, the Second Penal Reform Act, which was implemented in the summer of 1969, changed the former order or priority in the Penal Code in that sense: the aim of curing the offender is now placed before that of securing her/him.

The concept of non-responsibility, as well as that of dangerousness and the need for improvement, is a matter of definition. It is easy to decide upon in extreme cases but becomes more difficult in the less clear-cut ones. Debate related to the grey area can be grouped around two opposing attitudes:

1) disapproval towards criminalising and punishing people who are ill and in need of help;

2) disapproval towards pathologising people who transgress social norms.

As Rasch mentions: 'It must be clearly understood that badly directed research and hypotheses analysis have played a determining role in justifying one type of reaction over the other: sanctioning or treatment'. Present criminal policy searches for and adopts those criminal theories that are most convenient for its purposes. Insufficient empirical investigation means, therefore, that this policy is not based on a secure foundation and thus makes it easy to exchange one attitude for another[25].

Article 65

During the 1940s and 1950s, in Denmark, The Netherlands and some of the United States, institutions were founded for the treatment of mentally-ill offenders. In Germany, this tendency took the form of counselling in accordance with the basic reform of German penal law.

The reform outline of 1962 established the creation of institutions for offenders with diminished responsibility. This requirement was dropped later on, although the recipients of the new measure were still offenders suffering from mental disturbances which required treatment[26].

Article 65 of the Penal Code, which refers to the committal to a socio-therapeutic institution as a measure of rehabilitation and security, was finally enacted in 1969 under the Second Penal Reform Act. This Article is considered as one of the most significant innovations of the Second Penal Reform Act and represents the main judicial basis of social therapy[27].

Criteria for selection of offenders

Article 65 of the Second Penal Reform Act considered four groups of offenders for inclusion in a socio-therapeutic institute:

- recidivists with a severe personality disturbance;
- offenders with a dangerous sexual drive;
- young adult offenders with a prognosis for criminal tendencies;
- non-responsible offenders, or offenders with diminished responsibility, if committal to a socio-therapeutic institution seems

to be more appropriate for their resocialisation than treatment in a psychiatric hospital.

The proclaimed aim of treatment in such institutes was to resocialise the offender and prevent recidivism.

Development of Article 65

Although the Second Penal Reform Act passed through the Lower House of Parliament without any resistance or discussion, it still appears to be a legislative gesture[28]. Since no practical or theoretical agreement was reached on both the committal into the institutions and treatment therein, and given the lack of personnel and material resources, the enactment of Article 65 of the Penal Code has been suspended several times. In the meantime, model institutions should take advantage of this period to gain experience in order to develop general concepts for the future[29].

The implementation of the Article concerning socio-therapeutic institutions was first postponed from 1 October 1973 until 1 January 1978, and then until 1 January 1985. It is doubtful that these regulations will ever become effective, for the following reasons:

1) the difficult financial situation of the Federal States has led to a cut-back in criminal therapy. Although it has been claimed that the treatment programmes carried out so far have been ineffective, this has not been backed by an analysis of their chances of working;

2) the implementation of the Penal Administration Act which mentions the term 'treatment' in several passages. By this, the ability of qualifying the offender to lead a life without offences is attributed to the penalty of imprisonment. 'Even the socio-therapeutic institution ranks here as an institution affected by law, which should not come into force as a special measure but as an integrated department in the penal administration'[30].

Given the lack of a judicial basis for commital by judicial order ('substantial judicial solution') during this period, committals to a socio-therapeutic institution were carried out according to the above-mentioned 'executive solution', which was regulated under Article 9 of the Prison Administration Act and which has been in effect since 1977.

After more than 15 years of debate on the formal principles, it is now certain that the 'executive solution' will continue to be applied in the future. The Amendatory Act of Penal of Penal Administration of 20 December 1984 substituted Article 65 of the old Penal Code with Article 9 of the Prison Administration Act. Only a few modifications have been made to the text, and the following version has finally been decreed:

Criteria for the transfer to a socio-therapeutic institute (Article 9)

Article 9 lists the following criteria for the transfer of a dangerous mentally-ill offender to a socio-therapeutic institute:

1. a prisoner can be transferred, upon her/his agreement, to a socio-therapeutic institution, if the particular therapeutic instruments and social assistance of this institution seem appropriate for her/his resocialisation. S/he may be transferred if these instruments and the assistance prove unsuccessful;

2. the transfer requires the approval of the director of the socio-therapeutic institution[31].

In fact, this institution was not established as a form of sanction under the penal administration.

Criteria for committal into the institution have not changed, the only requirement being that its programme should be appropriate for the resocialisation of the prisoner. No other requirements, including characteristics related to the prisoner, are necessary. Article 9 of the Prison Administration Act represents an optional provision.

The explicit obligation to institutionalisation socio-therapeutic institutions also included socio-therapeutic wards of regular imprisonment institutions in a few vaguely defined exceptional cases. Therefore, the old principle, whereby social therapy could only be applied in institutions that are separated from regular penal administrations, has been abandoned. This could lead to the danger of wards in regular penal institutions becoming labelled as 'socio-therapeutic', although there is no substantial difference between them and the ordinary institutions. Some enforcement of social therapy is envisaged by the revised version of Article 7 of the Prison Administration Act, which now requires, according to the executive plan, a review of the criteria for committing prisoners to a socio-therapeutic institution.

Penal administration reform

The Penal Administration Reform contains several paradoxes. The Penal Administration Act, which came into effect in 1977, did not amend any of the old errors and contains a few regulations which need another Federal Act in order to come into effect.

The fundamental belief of the right-wing rulers of the States, that penal administration should not only aim towards resocialisation but should also safeguard the public, has already become effective. They justified this belief by claiming that whatever serves resocialisation in an effective way, also serves security. The argument for including the redundant term 'safeguarding' was that some of the offenders do not need, or cannot be helped by, special resocialisation treatment. But, as with the principle of guilt, the sanction must not exceed the seriousness of the offence. Irrespective of the danger which the offenders present to the public, they may only be imprisoned for the period of time which is appropriate for the crime committed. 'In fact, the principle of revenge has been smuggled into the Penal Administration Act in the name of an appeal for security of the public'[32].

After much debate, the contradiction still remains, that after a sentence is passed that is proportionate to the offence, the offender is committed to an administration which should be defined as a resocialising agent. Therefore, the new law did not introduce any new impulses[33].

The present situation

It is obvious that, in its original version, Article 65 was rather difficult to apply, but even the implementation of the present regulations, both in theory and in practice, has not met expectations.

The most frequently proposed solution was probably the so-called 'enriched executive solution' (*angereicherte Vollzugslösung'*). Accordingly, Article 65 of the Penal Code was to be abolished and Article 9 of the Prison Administration Act was to be transformed from a permissive provision to a directive. The text therefore became: 'Prisoners whose behaviour indicates that, without social therapy, they would commit further serious crimes, should be accepted into a socio-therapeutic institute'. The selected criteria were not only 'criminal behaviour', but also a special psychic state of mind of the offender, which suggested the need for treatment[34].

At least at the beginning of the social therapy, according to Article 65, patients could include heavily compromised recidivists. However, their treatment was were strongly jeopardised by interruptions in the treatment and transfers to other institutions[35].

It was proposed to modify Article 65 by introducing, in particular, time limits, descriptions of the patients based on biographical records of the offence rather than a psychiatric categorisation of the offender, and the proposed form of treatment[36]. However, Article 65 contained several biographical characteristics of both the offender and the offence which could have provided a specific and concrete reference, and which Article 9 of the Prison Administration Act lacked.

As the prisoners were recruited exclusively according to Article 9 of the Prison Administration Act, it was not necessary to limit the selection of persons to those referred to in Article 65 of the Penal Code, or to provide precise diagnostic criteria for the selection. A wide gap exists between the theory behind the organisation of social therapy and its actual application. No homogeneous, or even homogeneously applied concept concerning the equipment, organisation and methods of treatment were used as a basis by the model institutions founded in the various States in Germany. The actual treatment varied according to the different socio-therapeutic attitudes, and material and personnel resources of each institution. As a result, considerable differences still exist between one socio-therapeutic institution and another. Social therapy is not considered as a specific therapeutic method, but as an intervention strategy which uses pedagogical, organisational and other means in order to cure personality disturbances, with the aim of aiding the offender's resocialisation into society[37].

Apart from the suspenssion and abolition of Article 65, the actual implementation of socio-therapy was far below expectations, even from a quantitative point of view. Originally, it was estimated that about 10 per cent of the prison population would be committed to socio-therapeutic institutions according to Article 65, and about 5 per cent according to Article 9 of the Prison Administration Act[38]. Instead, under the executive solution, 712 places are actually occupied, representing about 2 per cent of the prison population[39].

According to Jescheck, the abolition of Article 65 and the moderate quantitative consolidation of social therapy reflect the 'change of trend' in criminal policy which has been so extensively discussed at the international level. On the other hand, a gradual reorientation of criminal policy towards social therapy seems possible[40].

However, socio-therapeutic institutions have overcome the conceptual problems of the preliminary phase and have become relatively stable, which is essential for a systematic programme development and organisation[41].

Results of a meta evaluation study on recidivist rates of offenders committed to socio-therapeutic institutions

Lösel et al. carried out a meta evaluation study based on the most reliable and valid preliminary studies made by German scientists. For comparative reasons, different primary studies were included in the evaluation of the different variables, such as recidivist rates and personality characteristics[42].

The evaluation of recidivist rates was based on data related to the following socio-therapeutic institutions:

- The Socio-therapeutic Institution of Hamburg-Bergedorf[43];
- The Socio-therapeutic Institution of Ludwigsburg-Hohenasperg[44];
- The Socio-therapeutic Institution of Berlin-Tegel/House IV[45];
- The Socio-therapeutic Institution of Düren[46].

As expected, the results of the study confirmed that social therapy produced moderately positive effects. On the whole, although these results were not homogeneous, they were nevertheless remarkably consistent. For example, it is estimated that recidivism is 8-14 per cent lower in the population of social therapeutic institutions than in normal institutions.

REFERENCES

1　V Gessner & W Hassemer, *Gegenkultur und Recht Schriften der Vereinigung für Rechtssoziologie,* Nomos-Verlagsge-Jellschaft, Baden-Baden, no. 10, 1985.

2　O Kernberg, *Borderline Conditions and Pathological Narcissm,* Aronson, New York, 1967.

3　U Venzlaff, 'Die forensische Beurteilung der psychiatrischen Erkrankungen im Strafverfahren: Konfliktreaktionen, Neurosen und Persönlichkeitsstörungen im Erwachsenenalter', in U Venzlaff (ed), *Psychiatrische Begutachtung. Ein praktisches Handbuch für Ärzte und Juristen,* Gustav Fischer Verlag, Stuttgart-New York, 1986, pp. 327-359.

4　R Baer, *Psychiatrie für Juristen,* Beck, Münich-Stuttgart, 1988.

5　W Rasch, 'Die Zuordnung der psychiatrisch-psychologischen Diagnosen zu den vier psychischen Merkmalen der Paragraphen 20, 21 StGB', *Strafverteidiger,* 1984, no. 6, pp. 264-269.

6　E Kretschmer, *Medizinische Psychologie,* Thieme, Stuttgart, 1971, 13th edition.

7　E Dreher & H Tröndle, *Kommentar zum Strafgesetzbuch,* CH Beckische Verlagsbuch Handlung, Münich, 1985, 42nd edition.

8　H Schöch *et al.,* 'Rettet die sozialtherapeutische Anstalt als Massregel der Sicherung und Besserung', *Zeitschrift für Rechtspolitik,* 1982, no. 15, pp. 207-212; H Göppinger, *Kriminologie,* Beck, Münich, 1971.

9　G Kaiser, *Kriminologie,* Karlsruhe, Heidelberg, 1980.

10 *ibid.*

11 H Schöch, 1982, *op. cit.*

12 A Kaufmann, 'Das Problem der Abhängigkeit des Strafrichters vom medizinischen Sachverständigen', *Juristenzeitung*, 1985, no. 23, pp. 40 *et seq*; HL Schreiber, 'Zur Rolle des psychiatrisch-psychologischen Sachverständigen im Strafverfahren', *Festschrift für Rolf Wassermann*, Hermann Luchtehand Vlg, Neuwied, 1985, pp. 1007 *et seq.*

13 T Lenckner, 'Strafe Schuld und Schuldfähigkeit', in H Göppinger & H Witter (eds.), *Handbuch der forensischen Psychiatrie*, Springer, Berlin-Heidelberg-New York, 1972, vol. 1, pp. 3 *et seq.*

14 C Roxin, *Strafverfahrensrecht,* CW Beckische Verlagsbuch Handlung, Münich, 1983, no. 18.

15 R Baer, 1988, *op. cit.*

16 GA Lienert, *Testaufbau und Testanalyse,* Beltz, Weinheim, 1967.

17 WJ Schraml, *Abriss der klinischen Psychologie,* Kohlhammer, Stuttgart, 1969.

18 I Barbey, 'Die forensisch-psychiatrische Untersuchung', in U Venzlaff (ed.), *1986, op. cit.*, pp. 95-113.

19 H Göppinger, 'Das Gutachten', in H Göppinger & H Witter (eds.), *Handbuch der forensischen Psychiatrie*, Springer, Berlin-Heidelberg-New York, 1972, vol. II, pp. 1485-1502.

20 G Kaiser, *Kriminologie. Ein Lehrbuch*, CF Müller Juristischer Verlag, Heidelberg, 1988, 2nd edition; W Rasch, *Forensische Psychiatrie*, Kohlhammer, Stuttgart, 1986.

21 H Kury, 'Zur Begutachtung der Schuldfähigkeit: Ausgewählte Ergebnisse eines empirischen Forschungsprojektes', in R Egg (ed.), *Brennpunkte der Rechtspsychologie*, Forum Verlag Godesberg, Bonn, 1991, pp. 331-350.

22 HJ Plewig, *Funktion und Rolle des Sachverständigen aus der Sicht des Strafrichters*, Von Decker, Heidelberg-Hamburg, 1983.

23 N Heim, *Psychiatrisch-psychologische Begutachtung im Jugendstrafverfahren*, Heymanns, Cologne-Berlin-Bonn-Münich, 1986.

24 H Kury, 1991, *op. cit.*

25 W Rasch, 'Behandlungsvollzug oder Sozialtherapie', in A Gaertner (ed.), *Sozialtherapie. Konzepte zur Prävention und Behandlung des psychosozialen Elends*, Hermann Luchterhand Verlag, Darmstadt, 1982, pp. 129-144.

26 *ibid.*

27 F Lösel, P Köferl & F Weber, *Meta-Evaluation der Sozialterapie. Qualitative und quantitative Analysen zur Behandlungsforschung in sozialtherapeutischen Anstalten des Justizvollzugs*, Ferdinand Enke Verlag, Stuttgart, 1987.

28 W Rasch, 1982, *op. cit.*

29 F Lösel et al, 1987, *op.cit.*

30 W Rasch, 1982, *op. cit.*, p. 132.

31 F Lösel *et al.*, 1987, *op. cit.*

32 W Rasch, 1982. *op. cit.*, p. 134.

33 *ibid.*

34 W Rasch & KP Kühl, 'Psychologie Kriterien für die Unterbringung in einer sozialtherapeutischen Anstalt', in W Rasch (ed.), *Forensische Sozialtherapie*, CF Müller Juristischer Verlag, Heidelberg, 1977, pp. 203-259.

35 G Kaiser, F Dünkel & R Ortmann, 'Die sozialtherapeutische Anstalt - das Ende einer Reform?', *Zeitschrift für Rechtspolitik*, 1982, no. 15, pp. 198-207.

36 H Schöch *et al.*, 1982, *op. cit.*, pp. 207-212.

37 M Stemmer-Lüch & W Rasch, 'Diagnostik in der Sozialtherapie', in M Zielke (ed.), *Diagnostik in der Psychotherapie*, Kohlhammer, Stuttgart, 1982, pp. 179-202.

38 G Schmitt, "Synopse der Sozialtherapeutischen Anstalten und Abteilungen in der Bundesrepublik Deutschland und Westberlin", in Bundeszusammenschluss für Straffälligenhilfe (ed.), *Sozialtherapeutische Anstalten*, Selbstverlag, Bonn-Bad Godesberg, 1977, no. 19, pp. 182-219.

39 F Dünkel, R Nemec & A Rosner, *Organisationsentwicklung und Behandlungsmassnahmen in einer sozialtherapeutischen Anstalt. Unveröffentlichtes Manuskript*, Max-Planck-Institut für ausländisches und internationales Strafrecht, Freiburg i. Br., 1985; EW Hanack, 'Das Konzept der sozialtherapeutischen Anstalt im neuen deutschen Strafrecht', in HE Ehrhardt (ed.), *Perspektiven der heutigen Psychiatrie*, Gebhards, Frankfurt, 1972, pp. 229-237; R Egg, *Sträffalligkeit und Sozialtherapie*, C Heymanns, Cologne, 1984.

40 HH Jeschek, 'Die Krise der Kriminalpolitik', *Zeitschrift für die gesamte Strafrechtswissenschaft*, 1979, no. 91, pp. 1037-1064.

41 F Lösel *et al.*, 1987, *op. cit.*

42 *ibid.*

43 G Rehn, *Behandlung im Strafvollzug. Ergebnisse einer vergleichenden Untersuchung der Rückfallquote bei entlassenen Strafgefangenen*, Beltz, Weinheim, 1979.

44 G Dolde, 'Ein Vergleich der Rückfallquoten zwischen Probanden der sozialtherapeutischen Anstalt Ludwigsburg und Gefangenen der Vollzugsanstalt Mannheim', *Unveröffentlichtes Manuskript*, Stammheim-Stuttgart, 1980; G Dolde, 'Gefangenenstruktur und Wirksamkeit der Behandlung in der sozialtherapeutischen Anstalt Ludwigsburg, Sitz Hohenasperg', *Unveröffentlichtes Manuskript*, Stammheim-Stuttgart, 1980; G Dolde, 'Untersuchungen zur Sozialtherapie und Wirksamkeit der Behandlung in der sozialtherapeutischen Anstalt Ludwigsburg, Sitz Hohenasperg', in Bundeszusammenschluss für Straffälligenhilfe (ed.), *Sozialtherapie als kriminalpolitische Aufgabe*, Selbstverlag, Bonn-Bad Godesberg, 1981, no. 26, pp. 96-110; G Dolde, 'Effizienzkontrolle sozialtherapeutischer Behandlung im Vollzug', in H Göppinger & PH Bresser (eds.), *Sozialtherapie. Kriminologische Gegenwartsfragen*, Ferdinand Enke Verlag, Stuttgart, 1982, no. 15, pp. 47-64.

45 F Dünkel, *Sozialtherapeutische Behandlung und Rückfälligkeit in Berlin-Tegel. Eine empirische vergleichende Untersuchung anhand der Strafregisterauszüge von 1503 in den Jahren 1971 bis 1974 entlassenen Strafgefangenen in Berlin-Tegel*, Duncker und Humblot, Berlin, 1980.

46 W Rasch & KP Kühl, 1977, *op. cit*, pp. 203-259; W Rasch & KP Kühl, 'Psychologie Befunde und Rückfälligkeit nach Aufenthalt in der sozialtherapeutischen Modellanstalt Düren', *Bewährungshilfe*, 1978, no. 25, pp. 44-57.

BIBLIOGRAPHY

Cooke G., *The Role of the Forensic Psychologist*, Thomas Books, Springfield-Illinois, 1980.

Egg R., *Sozialtherapie und Strafvollzug. Eine empirische Vergleichsstudie zur Evaluation sozialtherapeutischer Massnahmen*, Haag & Herchen, Frankfurt, 1979.

Egg R., 'Wirkungen von sozialtherapeutischer Massnahmen' *Monatsschrift für Kriminologie und Strafrechsrteform*, no. 62, pp. 348-356, 1979.

Finzen A., 'Die forensische Beurteilung der psychiatrischen Erkrankungen im Strafverfahren: Die alkohol- und toximbedingten Störungen', in Venzlaff U. (ed.), *Psychiatrische Begutachtung. Ein praktisches Handbuch für Arzte und Juristen*, Gustav Fischer Verlag, Stuttgart-New York, pp. 267-278, 1986.

Foerster K., 'Der psychiatrische Sachverständige zwischen Norm und Empirie', *Neue juristische Wochenschrift*, no. 37, pp. 2049-2052, 1983.

Heim N., *Psychiatrisch-psychologische Begutachtung im Jugendstrafverfahren*, Heymanns, Cologne-Berlin, 1986.

Heinz G., 'Fehlerquellen und Irtümer in psychiatrischen Gutachten', in Venzlaff U. (ed.), *Psychiatrische Begutachung. Ein praktisches Handbuch für Arzte und Juristen*, Gustav Fischer Verlag, Stuttgart-New York, pp. 141-149, 1986.

Kaiser E., 'Methoden der Diagnostik zur Frage der Schuldfähigkeit', in Kerner H.J., Kury H. & Sessar K. (eds.), *Deutsche Forschungen zur Kriminalitätsentstehung und Kriminalitätskontrolle*, Carl Heymanns, Cologne, pp. 1264-1287, 1983.

Kaiser G. & Schöch H., 'Kriminologie, Jugendstrafrecht, Strafvollzug', in Beuthien V., Erischsen H.U. & Eser A. (eds.), *Juristischer Studienkurs*, CH Beck, Münich, 2nd edition, 1982.

Kaiser G., Dünkel F. & Ortmann R., 'Die sozialtherapeutische Anstalt - das Ende einer Reform?', *Zeitschrift für Rechtspolitik*, no. 15, pp. 198-207, 1982.

Kette G., *Rechtspsychologie*, Springer, Vienna-New York, 1987.

King M., *Psychology in and out of Court. A critical Examination of Legal Psychology*, Pergamon PR, Oxford, 1986.

Mende W., 'Die forensische Beurteilung der psychiatrischen Erkrankungen im Strafverfahren: Die affektiven Störungen', in Venzlaff U. (ed.), *Psychiatrische Begutachtung. Ein praktisches Handbuch für Arzte und Juristen*, Gustav Fischer Verlag, Stuttgart-New York, pp. 317-325, 1986.

Meyer J.E., 'Psychiatrische Diagnosen und ihre Bedeutung für die Schuldfähigkeit i.S. der Paragraphen 20 20, 21', *Zeitschrift für die gesamte Strafrechtswissenschaft*, no. 88, pp. 49-71, 1976.

Müller C., *Lexikon der Psychiatrie*, Springer, Berlin-Heidelberg, 2nd edition, 1986.

Opp K.D., *Strafvollzug und Resozialisierung*, Fink, Münich, 1979.

Ortmann R., 'Zur Persönlichkeitsstruktur der Insassen der sozialtherapeutischen Abteilung in der Justizvollzugsanstalt Berlin-Tegel', in Göppinger H. & Bresser P.H. (eds.), *Sozialtherapie. Kriminologische Gegenwartsfragen*, Enke, Stuttgart, 15th edition, pp. 101-118, 1982.

Ortmann R., 'Die Nettobilanz einer Resozialisierung im Strafvollzug: Negativ?', in Kury H. (ed.), *Gesellschaftliche Umwälzung, Kriminalitätserfahrung, Straffälligkeit und soziale Kontrolle*, Eigenverlag Max-Planck-Institut für ausländisches und internationales Strafrecht, Freiburg, 1992.

Ritter G., 'Die forensische Beurteilung der psychiatrischen Erkrankungen im Strafvenahren: Die himorganischen Störungen einschliesslich Anfallsleiden', in Venzlaff U. (ed.), *Psychiatrische Begutachtung. Ein praktisches Handbuch für Arzte und Jursten*, Gustav Fischer Verlag, Stuttgart-New York, pp. 201-229, 1986.

Ritter G., 'Die technischen Untersuchungen', in Venzlaff U. (ed.), *Psychiatrische Begutachtung. Ein praktisches Handbuch für Arzte und Juristen*, Gustav Fischer Verlag, Stuttgart-New York, pp. 115-125, 1986.

Schöch H., 'Die Beurteilung von Schweregraden schuldmindernder oder schuldausschliessender Persönlichkeitsstörungen aus juristischer Sicht.', *Monatsschrift für Kriminologie*, no. 6, pp. 333-334, 1983.

Schönke A. & Schröder H., *Strafgesetzbuch. Kommentar*, CH Beck, Münich, 1988.

Schorsch E., 'Die forensische Beurteilung der psychiatrischen Erkrankungen im Strafverfahren: Die sexuellen Deviationen und sexuell motivierte Straftaten', in Venzlaff U. (ed.), *Psychiatrische Begutachtung. Ein praktisches Handbuch für Arzte und Juristen*, Gustav Fischer Verlag, Stuttgart-New York, pp. 279-315, 1986.

Schraml W.J., *Abriss der klinischen Psychologie*, Kohlhammer, Stuttgart, 1969.

Schreiber H.L., 'Der Sachverständige im Verfahren und in der Verhandlung', in Venzlaff U. (ed.), *Psychiatrische Begutachtung. Ein praktisches Handbuch für Arzte und Juristen*, Gustav Fischer Verlag, Stuttgart-New York, pp. 151-165, 1986.

Schreiber H.L., 'Grundlagen der pscyhiatrischen Beurteilung im Strafverfahren: Juristische Grundlagen', in Venzlaff U. (ed.), *Psychiatrische Begutachtung. Ein praktisches Handbuch für Arzte und Juristen*, Gustav Fischer Verlag, Stuttgart-New York, pp. 3-77, 1986

Specht F., 'Die forensische Beurteilung der psychiatrischen Erkrankungen im Strafverfahren: Angeborene und früherworbene Beeinträchtigungen der geistigen Entwicklung', in Venzlaff U. (ed.), *Psychiatrische Begutachtung. Ein praktisches Handbuch für Arzte und Juristen,* Gustav Fischer Verlag, Stuttgart-New York, pp. 231-265, 1986.

Statistisches Bundesamt, ' Rechtspflege', *Reihe 4: Strafvollzug. Fachserie 10*, Metzler-Poeschel, Stuttgart, 1989.

Statistisches Bundesamt, *Strafverfolgung 1989*, Wiesbaden, 1991.

StGB, in Wasserman R. (ed.), *Kommentar zum Strafgesetzbuch,* Hermann Luchterhand Verlag, Neuwied, vol 1, 1990.

'The Penal Code of the Federal Republic of Germany', in *The American Series of Foreign Penal Codes,* Wayne State University, Rothman, South Hackensack (New York), no. 28, 1987.

Venzlaff U., 'Die Erstattung des Gutachtens', in Venzlaff U. (ed.), *Psychiatrische Begutachtung. Ein praktisches Hanbuch für Arzte und Juristen*, Gustav Fischer Verlag, Stuttgart-New York, pp. 127-139, 1986.

Venzlaff U., 'Die forensische Beurteilung der psychiatrischen Erkrankungen im Strafverfahren: Die zyklothymen Psychosen', in Venzlaff U. (ed.), *Psychiatrische Begutachtung. Ein praktisches Handbuch für Arzte und Juristen*, Gustav Fischer Verlag, Stuttgart-New York, pp. 189-200, 1986.

Venzlaff U., 'Methodische und praktische Probleme der forensisch-psychiatrischen Begutachtung', in Venzlaff U. (ed.), *Psychiatrische Begutachtung. Ein praktisches Handbuch für Ärzte und Juristen*, Gustav Fischer Verlag, Stuttgart-New York, pp. 79-94, 1986.

Waxweiler R., *Psychotherapie im Strafvollzug. Eine empirische Erfolgsuntersuchung am Beispiel der sozialtherapeutischen Abteilung einer JVA*, Beltz, Weinheim, 1980.

Witter H., 'Die Bedeutung des psychiatrischen Krankheitsbegriffs für das Strafrecht', in Warda G., Weider H., *et al.* (eds.), *Feschschrift für Richard Lange*, Walter de Gruyter, Berlin-New York, pp. 723-735, 1976.

Witter H., 'Zur gegenwärtigen Lage der forensischen Psychiatrie', in Witter H. (ed.), *Der psychiatrische Sachverständige im Strafrecht*, Springer Verlag, Berlin-Heidelberg, pp. 1-34, 1987.

ITALY
The Italian System from a Forensic Psychiatric Perspective

Francesco Bruno*, Paolo De Pasquali**, Iliana Bona**

INTRODUCTION

The perception of the pathology of the mind and its behaviour-altering effects is as old as man himself. Roman law (Modestino, Fourth Century AD) had already established formulations which excluded penal sanctions for offences committed by 'Furiosus', then likened to the 'Infans' for the purposes of criminal law. However, it was only after the long period of the Middle Ages, i.e. during the Eighteenth Century and the Age of Enlightenment, that we were to see the birth of scientific medicine on the one hand and, on the other, the affirmation of the universal values of man and the law as an imperative of utility, which allowed the progression from absolute power to legality. Man was considered to be 'responsible' for his behaviour, while the law undertook the task of defining the limits of 'criminal responsibility' according to the normative principle of the 'ethics of sovereign power' (*Nullum crimen, nulla poena sine lege*).

Subsequently, although the spread and affirmation of positivism, in both psychiatry and criminal law, brought about a temporary prevalence of rigidly mechanistic and deterministic conceptions, it also enabled further progress, which led to the formulation of concepts that remain fundamental today, such as diminished or complete lack of responsibility by reason of infirmity, social danger and social protection. The impact of such conceptions on the penal codes of most

*   Professor of Forensic Psychiatry and Criminological Medicine, University of Rome 'La Sapienza', Rome, Italy.

** Department of Psychiatric Sciences and Psychological Medicine, University of Rome 'La Sapienza', Rome, Italy. This report was prepared in November 1992.

countries was enormous, to the extent that, nowadays, not one of these codes is without special measures envisaging some form of social protection for those who have committed an offence and are at the same time suffering from a mental pathology which excludes or diminishes responsibility.

Naturally, the increasingly close relationship between psychiatry and law in the field of forensic psychiatry has generated numerous problems and stumbling blocks which must be overcome.

The first problem is of a structural nature: psychiatry is a biological, psychological and socially-based human science, whereas criminal law is a normative discipline based solely on social relations among men. It is clear, therefore, that psychiatry and criminal law can only partially keep pace with one another; more specifically, they can only do so as far as their social and political foundations are concerned. Furthermore, the concepts and theory of psychiatry are evolving very rapidly as a result of progress in the neurobiological and psychological sciences. Psychiatry cannot, therefore, guarantee the certainties which the law requires, but only theories which, once demonstrated, may soon be questioned by new and increasingly more reliable theories.

The second problem is a methodological one: psychiatry and criminal law have different parameters of reference and definitions. For the jurist, judgement is binary in nature, so that such a state as imputability can only be recognised or denied with, at the most, a normatively envisaged scale of intermediate steps. For the psychiatrist, on the contrary, a continuum of different situations and fluid gradations exists between normality and pathology, and does not just extend in one single direction, but rather encompasses a complex and three-dimensional space. By the same token, when moving from the judicial phase to that of prevention or treatment, it becomes evident that, for the psychiatrist, the world of 'man' is individual, relativistic, and probabilistic, whereas for the jurist the idea of 'man' is necessary, absolute, and based on the collective.

The third problem is political in nature: from a political point of view, the purpose of law is to regulate social relations among the individuals of a community, in accordance with the conventions that are accepted by all. These conventions generally reflect the power relations existing between the various members of society and are an expression of sovereignty.

Psychiatry is a medical science which has the purpose of eliminating or reducing psychopathological suffering. It assumes a prior knowledge of the normal and pathological functioning of the human mind, and the elements governing its behaviour, and hence is the science which studies precisely that border area between the individual and society. It is therefore impossible not to consider psychiatry *per se*, as a powerful instrument of social control. The broader that function of psychiatry appears to be, the more closely it will collaborate with the law, and this is precisely the case of forensic psychiatry.

The improper and harmful exploitation of individual rights becomes all the more possible for psychiatry when the democratic guarantees envisaged by the state order are few, and the separation of state powers is less radical. Conversely, the more guarantees there are that psychiatry is correctly used for forensic purposes, the more closely it is bound to a perception of justice as free, the expression of the people, separate from the executive and legislative power, and above the parties concerned.

Unfortunately, the above-mentioned problems are not always clearly defined. Furthermore, it is very difficult to discuss matters of political relevance in a scientific and objective way, and without projecting personal preferences and ideological beliefs into the discussion. For this reason, the terms of the problems sometimes become confused, and radical positions may even be assumed, advocating the general abolition of the concept of diminished or lack of responsibility because of mental illness.

RESPONSIBILITY

Italian legislation differentiates between the 'imputability' and 'non-imputability' of the offender. Before an offender can be punished, her/his capacity for cognition and volition (i.e. mental competence) must be ascertained; in other words, the legal and penal consequences of the offence committed can only be inflicted on a person if s/he is imputable. Article 85 of the Italian Penal Code sets forth the concept of imputability and establishes that:

No one can be punished for an act envisaged by the law as an offence if, at the time the offence was committed, s/he was not imputable. Anyone capable of cognition and volition is imputable.

'Cognition', in the legal-medical sense, is not simply the offender's ability to know what exists and happens around her/him, but also her/his ability to adequately discern the meaning and value, as well as the moral and legal consequences, of actions and events. Capacity for cognition denotes, therefore, the offender's ability to understand the social-juridical significance of her/his behaviour.

In the legal-medical sense, 'volition' denotes the offender's possession of self-determination in relation to the accomplishment of an objective, whether this involves carrying out, not carrying out, or preventing an action, without being coerced by others or affected by a pathological condition. This capacity thus implies both the possibility of choosing among alternatives and free self-determination.

Both concepts - capacity for cognition and capacity for volition - which were used by the legislator more than half a century ago, now seem open to extensive criticism from the scientific point of view. Capacity for cognition is, in fact, associated with the concept of intelligence; which has neither been defined nor is it definable, and is, in any case, a concept that can be interpreted in several ways, according to different perspectives. Intelligence can be thought of as a complex set of factors, the sum of different abilities, or more simply, as the most important factor (the capacity for logical reasoning) in maintaining that capacity for adaptation to the environment, which seems to be the most important purpose of intelligence.

The capacity for cognition envisaged by the legislator, is a mixed concept encompassing the ability for moral judgement on the one side and, on the other, the offender's state of awareness; only in this way can it be evaluated. With regard to the capacity for volition, it can be said that this is based on the concept of 'will', which modern psychology now does not recognise as one of the fundamental functions of the psyche.

Every intentional act is the result of a complex play of factors working in different directions; in particular, motivation is a force that drives a person to carry out a given deed while being opposed by other forces, which we identify as resistance and inhibitions. These counterforces may derive either from the subject or from the surrounding situation, if not from the object itself. For this reason, the 'will' described by the legislator should be regarded as being closer to the concept of self-determination, in other words, autonomous choice, than to the concept of moral obligation towards an end, which is more characteristic of will.

Articles 88 and 96 of the Penal Code have established the cases in which imputability is excluded or diminished. These cases are divided into the following: age-related conditions of a physiological nature, conditions of a pathological nature deriving from mental infirmity or from congenital anomalies and, lastly, conditions of a toxic nature due to the misuse of alcohol and drugs.

The causes of diminished or non-responsibility may be attributed to five factors:

a) the person is a minor;

b) mental infirmity;

c) deaf and dumbness;

d) drunkenness;

e) the effect of drugs.

With regard to mental infirmity (point b), Italian legislation considers the possible presence of psychopathological factors which may exclude (Article 88 of the Penal Code) or diminish (Article 89) the capacity for cognition or volition at the time of the act.

For imputability to be excluded or diminished, it is not sufficient for a mental anomaly to exist at the time of the act. In other words, for a chronological relationship to exist, a causal link must be traced between the act committed and the state of mind.

It is, in fact, possible to deny the judicial relevance of even severe psychopathological profiles if they did not interfere, either wholly or partially, with the criminal act committed by the offender. On the other hand, mental impairment can be recognised in a subject who has no persistent psychiatric disorders but who, at the time the offence was committed and in relation to that offence, was in a state of incapacity owing to an acute and transitory pathology.

Mental infirmity can manifest itself in varying degrees. It is 'total' when the state of mind is such, that it excludes the capacity for cognition or volition (Article 88). Mental impairment is 'partial' when this capacity is not excluded, but is greatly diminished: 'Anyone who, at the time s/he committed the act, was, by reason of infirmity, in such a state of mind that it greatly decreased, without excluding her/his capacity for cognition or volition, is accountable for the offence committed; nevertheless, the penalty is decreased' (Article 89).

With regard to treatment, total mental impairment results in the accused being absolved and, as a rule, being admitted to a prison psychiatric hospital (Article 222). Partial impairment, which does not exclude imputability, entails a reduction in sentence only; in addition to this, the person is normally placed under a hospital or custodial order as a safety precaution (Article 219).

The sentence is thus coupled with a safety measure: once the sentence restricting personal freedom has been served, the offender is admitted to a hospital or custodial centre following confirmation that the state of danger still exists (Article 31, Law 663, 10 October 1986).

It is clear, therefore, that there is a need to take into account mental infirmity when evaluating the degree of criminal responsibility of offenders, in order to meet three indispensable requisites of modern society.

The first of these requisites is simply that of justice: in the eyes of the law, all men must be regarded as being equal when conditions of criminal responsibility are equal.

The second is a humanitarian need: everyone has the right to physical and mental health, so any person suffering from a mental disorder, whether or not s/he has committed an offence, has the right to be treated in order to recover her/his maximum mental condition.

The third requisite is of a social nature: every organised social group has a duty to protect the safety and rights of its members; this is one of the reasons for the existence of the system of criminal justice.

Society must, therefore, adopt measures that will help to prevent or reduce the risk of criminal offenders relapsing into crime, whether they are mentally-ill or not. Clearly, none of these needs can disregard, or be in conflict with the protection of man's fundamental and inalienable rights.

PSYCHIATRIC EVALUATION

In those cases in which the judge deems it appropriate, either to establish or to rule out imputability, s/he appoints one or more psychiatrists to make a psychiatric assessment of the offender. In this context, in addition to the court experts, technical consultants representing the parties concerned may attend and take part in all the phases of the assessment.

The task of the psychiatric expert is to respond to the questions posed by the judge, which generally include at least the following: a) whether, at the time of the offence, the offender, due to infirmity, was in a state of mind that eliminated or greatly reduced her/his capacity for cognition and volition; and b) whether, at the present time, the offender should be considered a danger to society. To fulfill these tasks, the expert must examine the offender, possibly put her/him through specialised tests, observe her/his behaviour, consider the court proceedings, and then formulate a diagnosis.

What is of interest from the medical-legal point of view, however, is not so much the diagnosis of the offender's present mental infirmity, but rather the diagnosis of her/his prior state (at the time of the offence) and the prognosis of dangerousness, as well as the evaluation of the effects of the diagnosed illness on the offender's behaviour. The conclusion of the expert must include a detailed reasoning, as well as the responses to the questions posed.

It can be said that the expert's conclusions are generally related to different areas of information: the area of diagnosis, which is obviously medical-psychiatric in nature. The diagnosis is the first element which must necessarily underlie any other deduction of a prognostic, practical (with a view to treatment) or medical-legal nature.

In medicine, but even more so in psychiatry, the diagnosis has been recognised as a complex probabilistic procedure which has not escaped even well-founded criticism. This is inevitable, however, because the diagnostic process is that cognitive method or system which is able to discriminate between normality and illness, and because both normality and illness can only be defined in a relative way and not in a rigid, absolute fashion.

Nevertheless, on a material and operational level, as well as on the basis of common sense, illness or infirmity can be well defined by means of diagnoses which may be rendered more reliable, valid and sensitive through the use of appropriate tools (multiaxial diagnosis, multiple diagnosis, standardisation of testing and quantification methods, identification of signs and symptoms, etc.).

Of course, if a diagnosis is to be of any use, it needs a nosographic framework of reference; following an extensive conceptual crisis, psychiatric nosography is once again becoming ordered and is used internationally, through the adoption of modern diagnostic systems such as the DSM III-R or the tenth revision of the international classification of mental disorders compiled by the World Health Organization. These systems can be regarded as a working basis that can be used in the formulation of valid and internationally accepted diagnoses. The diagnosis is a necessary step which concludes the more strictly clinical part of the psychiatric report; once the diagnosis is established, the subsequent areas of information can then be considered.

One of these areas is that of criminal responsibility which, depending upon the penal system considered, can be defined in a binary manner as either present or absent, or with a series of intermediate phases of reduced responsibility. The judgement of responsibility is obviously not psychopathological, but rather judicial and philosophical in nature; however, to be formulated, it presupposes psychopathological knowledge of the facts and judicial knowledge of the terms of the law in the context of which the facts are being considered.

Not all authors agree that the psychiatric expert is the most suitable person for formulating such a judgement; indeed, many have categorically stated that it should be the judge who, on the basis of the technical knowledge made available by the expert, deduces whether the person is imputable or whether imputability should be reduced or even absent.

The question can be viewed from different angles. From a theoretical point of view, since the recognition or denial of responsibility can be regarded as a judgement, it would seem obvious that it should be pronounced by a judge, that is to say, without assigning the judging function to the psychiatric expert, since it is an essential part of the judge's own role. However, this could be opposed from a practical point of view, on the grounds that a judge has no specific preparation to take decisions in the psychopathological field, and that it is safer to entrust the psychiatric expert with a task that seems closer to her/his specific field of knowledge.

Several penal systems, including the Italian system, have tried to settle this long-standing issue by entrusting the judge with the task of *Peritus Peritorum*, namely of subjecting the experts to examination. On the basis of this power, the judge can, in theory, disregard the suggestions made by the experts and decide otherwise, obviously with a justification for the rejection of the results of the expert's report.

PSYCHIATRIC ILLNESS

Some psychiatric illnesses almost always give rise, or should give rise, to a state of non-imputability; this is the case of psychoses (schizophrenic and dysthymic), dementia, oligophrenia, exogenous and endogenous organic illnesses, and so forth.

Other infirmities, such as personality alterations and psycho neuroses, hardly ever lead experts and judges to the same decisions, either in terms of denying or affirming imputability. Psychiatric assessment is becoming increasingly concerned with people with personality abnormalities, rather than with real mentally-ill persons.

The grounds for non-responsibility can also be extended to include psychopathological profiles which cannot be classified as mental illnesses proper, provided it can be demonstrated that they influence the criminal conduct manifested by the offender.

On the whole, therefore, personality disorders can be neither admitted among the grounds for non-responsibility, nor excluded from them (as has occurred in the past for psychopathic personalities). Instead, it is of paramount importance to identify the criteria used in the evaluation and interpretation of the specific criminal conduct manifested by the subject with a personality disorder.

The nature and extent of the personality disorder must be so severe that it jeopardises the normal conduct of life and must also take the form of an illness. In other words, it must present a phase of onset and a clinical evolution, and must not be simply a quantitative alteration of the personality characteristics.

Psychopathic, neurotic and even borderline personalities, like all abnormal personality structures, are generally recognised as imputable. In fact, subjects with such personality disorders will not be considered as having a capacity for cognition and volition in the expert's report.

However, this assumption is not always correct, and it then becomes necessary to ascertain case-by-case, and on the basis of the specific offence committed as well as the *modus operandi*, whether or not the action or omission of the subject under assessment can be classified as being 'attributable to illness'.

The psychopathic personality is usually characterised by abnormal response patterns to environmental stimuli. These are, however, *ego* symptomatic responses, not accompanied by any feeling of guilt and generally made at the expense of others. This personality type appears to be well preserved and presents no signs of disintegration or deterioration.

Psychotic disturbances are also absent in the neurotic personality, and contact with reality and with others is preserved, although the personality is conditioned by problems of deficiency and inadequacy and by often unfounded feelings of guilt.

Often, the criminogenic behaviour of 'neurotic', 'psychopathic' and even 'borderline' individuals is represented by heterodestructive behaviour which occurs as a reaction to real, conflicting or pathological stimuli. When these reactions represent an 'habitual pattern of existence in the world', they have nothing to do with mental impairment. They can, instead, be classed as an illness when they are marked by the following elements:

a) a visible break in the offender's particular lifestyle;

b) a net, clear and significant disproportion between the causal event on the one side, and the intensity, type and duration of response on the other;

c) the possible presence of a condition which jeopardises the state of awareness, covered and followed by amnesia and dysmnesia;

d) the possible presence of disturbed perceptions or of preconceived, prevalent or delirious ideas, provided they are not induced by alcoholic and psychoactive substances (expressly excluded by Articles 92 and 93 of the Penal Code);

e) alterations that are not acted out and that do not derive from basic instincts;

f) strong emotional participation;

g) relatively short duration of the reaction, with reference to the criminal act.

If such indicators - variously combined with one other, although not necessarily co-existing - are apparent in the behaviour of the person under study, this may lead to the behaviour being classified as a psychiatrically significant illness.

The main trend with regard to borderline personality disorder is towards recognising a condition of diminished or lack of responsibility in cases in which the personality disorder shifts into the area of psychosis.

Because the defence and impulse mechanisms of a borderline case are fragile, a sense of heightened frustration and intense stress can cause a sudden upsurge of all the elements which represent normal psychosis, leading to severe disharmony of thought. In such cases, the *ego* takes over, and the patient loses all autonomy and ability to control her/his impulses as a result of the shift into the area of psychosis. This generates an unconscious behaviour that does not have a fixed objective, and is not equipped to prevent criminal conduct; and is followed by a rapid recovery of control. In this case we have something like a 'fixed-term psychosis', which will often be without any constant and evident delirium or hallucinatory phenomena, but in which any awareness is also suspended.

This profile gives shape to that type of crime which goes under the name of 'homicide lack of control', also known as 'blind rage', 'short-circuit reaction', 'explosive reaction', 'acting out'. These synonyms represent crimes of impulse and impetus which originate from an overreaction of the impulse. Although it is true that 'emotional distress' can help to trigger off an explosive reaction, it has no legal significance for the purposes of imputability. Indeed, Article 90 of the Penal Code states: 'Emotional or passionate states neither exclude nor diminish imputability'.

Hence, in a crime fired by an intense emotion, arising in response to emotiogenic existential situations, this state of the human mind is of no significance for the purposes of the application of Articles 88 and 89. In fact, considered separately, emotional and passionate states represent normal psychological conditions and not psychopathological states of the 'human being'.

These feelings, however, take on a psychiatric-forensic significance when they are integrated into a profile of mental pathology of which they are symptomatic (e.g. delusions of jealousy in intoxicated chronic alcoholics, emotional conduct of a mentally-deficient or demented person, acting out of schizophrenic behaviour, and so forth), or when they are re-absorbed into a profile of immaturity such that it excludes the capacity for cognition and volition in a minor between 14 and 18 years of age (Article 98).

Jurisprudence, therefore, is constant in its exclusion of the relevance of emotional distress, which is thus only able to affect responsibility when it represents the manifestation of an imbalance of the psyche integrating a clinically appreciable mental infirmity.

However, a more modern and extended interpretation of stress as a phenomenon which, in the long run, is capable of producing real infirmity, could produce several exceptions to the above rule, in the sense that certain psychopathological conditions induced by a form of chronic stress comparable to infirmity, could be regarded as influencing imputability.

SOCIAL DANGEROUSNESS

The area of social dangerousness can only be explored by the expert in certain systems and, generally, only in cases where the subject has been recognised as non-responsible. In other systems, the recognition of social dangerousness, even in the psychopathological field, remains entirely in the hands of the judge, or even the police authorities, in much the same way as for mentally sound offenders.

The judgement of social dangerousness, of course, encounters the same criticisms as that of responsibility, but it is also heavily criticised from the technical viewpoint. Formulating the prognosis of the possible danger represented by an offender suffering from mental disorders, is not exactly the same thing as forecasting the evolutive or involutive development of her/his illness.

Indeed, in the first case it is not a biological process, or even a psychological profile, to be judged, but a course of human conduct. The variables which may affect the determination of a course of human conduct are infinite and only partly depend upon the state of the offender. They depend to a much greater extent on the environmental and socio-cultural conditions preceding, during, or even after the manifestation of that conduct. In addition, nowadays, most scholars who have taken an interest in this particular sector, share the opinion that, in a functional and efficient system of out-patient controls and pharmacological or psychotherapeutic treatment, the social danger represented by mentally-ill offenders is clearly less than that of offenders who are not mentally-ill.

On the other hand, it can be intuitively acknowledged that in cases in which mental illness has been the foremost cause of a crime, treating the illness as effectively as possible becomes the best guarantee for the offender's social rehabilitation. If we consider that, nowadays, more than 90 per cent of the traditional psychiatric syndromes can be successfully treated, at least as far as the symptoms are concerned, it can be predicted that only by making progress in the area of therapy and treatment, will it be possible in future years to find a solution for the problem of criminal offenders suffering from mental disorders.

Danger is defined by the Italian Penal Code in Article 203, as follows: 'For the purposes of criminal law, a person who has

120

committed a crime is considered to be socially dangerous, whether punishable or not, when it is probable that s/he will commit further acts perceived by the law as crimes. The status of a socially dangerous person is deduced from the circumstances in Article 133 of the Penal Code.' The judgement of danger expressed in this way by the Penal Code is a predictive, or prognostic, judgement, based particularly on the assumption that it is highly probable that the person will commit further crimes.

In exercising her/his discretionary power in the application of the sentence, the judge considers the gravity of the criminal act, but (Article 133) must also take into account the culprit's capacity to commit a crime, which can be inferred from the following elements:

1) the motives for committing the crime and the character of the offender;

2) the offender's criminal and court record, and her/his general background and way of life before the commitment of the crime;

3) the offender's conduct before and after the crime;

4) the offender's individual, family and social living background.

This latter point involves a study, not only of the offender's personality, but also of her/his individual, family and social living conditions.

For the analysis of the danger represented by mentally-ill persons, the judge is assisted by the psychiatric expert who, from a motivational, dynamic and anthropological analysis, reaches conclusions on the psycho-sociological aspects of the individual case.

Many psychiatrists and forensic psychiatrists, on the basis of the results of different research studies conducted in the United States which have demonstrated lack of grounds for the prognosis of danger, believe they should not be called upon to make any prognosis that they do not feel equipped to make; these same specialists take the issue even further and also question the judgement of imputability, maintaining that it does not enter into their sphere of competence.

In reality, although every caution must be exercised in all predictive judgements, one cannot see who else might be better equipped than the forensic and criminal psychiatrist to undertake such a task, which is certainly more capable of producing results on the criminal level than on the sociological level.

The predictive appraisal of anomalous behaviour originating from, or linked to disease, (however difficult this may be, as in the case of a schizophrenic in a defective phase, or under 'neuroleptic protection', which enables her/him to become partially reintegrated into society), must be based, not only on the individual elements (clinical study), but also on the elements drawn from the subject's family and socio-cultural environment.

In practice, account is also taken of what are known as 'external indicators': the family and social environment to which the offender belongs, the existence and adequacy of the local psychiatric services, the possibility of the reintegration of the offender into the school or working world, the degree of acceptance of the offender's return by those with whom s/he lived before the crime.

These external indicators, however, should not be taken into consideration in the formulation of an opinion on the social danger of the patient (in that s/he cannot be responsible for resocialisation programmes), but only, possibly, to evaluate the level of risk to which the discharged patient who is not socially dangerous would be exposed.

In the evaluation of the psychiatric social danger, which is the task of the psychiatric expert in the case of confirmed mental impairment, internal indicators must be used, namely indicators of the individual type of pathology of the mind that is in progress. Thus, for example, in the case of schizophrenia:

a) the presence or persistence of strong psychotic symptoms at the emotional level, without the patient's awareness of the illness;

b) confirmed notable deterioration or a severe psychotic personality disintegration (irrespective of whether or not the offender has been treated on various occasions and/or suffered multiple relapses);

c) manifestation of one or more behavioural imbalances during a brief time span, of either a self- or heterodestructive nature, which can be directly linked to psychopathological imbalances;

d) progressively severe imbalance behaviour;

e) little or no response to therapeutic treatment;

f) refusal to follow the prescribed psychopharmacological therapies.

More than anything else, the above clinical indicators are important in deciding the type of social and health programmes to be put into effect. If the accused is regarded as being incapable of cognition and volition, but socially dangerous, s/he should be admitted to a prison psychiatric hospital, without receiving any alternative measures that are appropriate for her/his mental condition and therapeutic needs.

In practice, therefore, the mentally-ill offender who is discharged for total mental impairment is a 'different type' of mentally-ill person from those mentally-ill who have not infringed the rules of the Penal Code or who have done so but are not regarded as 'socially dangerous'.

There is a strong contrast between what is envisaged by the Penal Code and what is established by Law 180/78 on 'Voluntary and Compulsory Health Checks and Treatment'. This contrast highlights the 'cleavage' between clinical psychiatry (need for treatment) and forensic psychiatry (need for control), alongside the inequality between the mentally-ill person who has committed a crime and the mentally-ill person who is not an offender. Nevertheless, when the sick person's crime is related to one of the symptoms of the illness, it should not be interpreted other than in the context of that illness. The psychiatric report, therefore, is intended as a mere instrument at the service of psychiatric prognosis (concerning the existence or non-existence of social danger due to mental infirmity), rather than as a means to assist in the treatment of the mentally-ill person in need of social and health programmes.

In this way, preference is given to the aspects of 'control' and 'social protection' rather than to the therapeutic aspect. The expert's study has a static rather than dynamic form; it is a medium which takes no account of treatment at all, and yet the object of the tests is a dynamic, constantly evolving human entity.

Any custodial or care measures provided for the mentally-ill person undergoing a phase of acute psychotic imbalance, should merely precede the necessary therapeutic intervention, and this certainly cannot be ensured by the prison psychiatric hospital which, like all closed institutions, aggravates rather than resolves the problems of the mentally-ill.

TREATMENT

In many countries the field of treatment has not been sufficiently explored, or even indeed considered, by the psychiatric experts. In most countries, the response to the problems of mentally-ill offenders is simply to provide treatment under conditions of greater or lesser confinement in a psychiatric hospital, be it part of the health system or the penal system. It is obvious that the law, which by its very nature, is clearly established and definitive, has a greater interest in resolving the legal rather than therapeutic problem, in the name of the general safety of the population and the imperative of justice, rather than the rehabilitation of the individual subject.

Often, the penal system entrusts this rehabilitation to therapies that can be obtained under the health system without, however, forgoing the application of safety measures, if not indeed actual sanctions. In this respect, it could be useful to mention a number of problems concerning the administration of psychiatric treatment.

The effectiveness and safety of psychiatric therapies, and in fact of any medical therapy, depend upon two essential factors: the training and motivation of the health and welfare workers, and the availability of highly organised treatment resources and structures. The success of the therapies is not, therefore, guaranteed simply by the fact that it is possible to carry them out, but depends on where and how effectively they can be carried out, and, most importantly, by whom. In Italy, many programmes which in theory are possible, cannot in fact be carried out, because of the deterioration of the structures, the lack of specialised personnel and, above all, because the function of surveillance tends to prevail over that of treatment.

Lastly, as we have seen, in practice, any treatment will be carried out in a prison psychiatric hospital, which represents the most serious obstacle to the application of effective therapies.

Modern psychiatry has now ascertained that a long stay in the old, traditional psychiatric hospitals represents an evil to the patient that is probably even greater than the mental infirmity. Closed institutions produce an increasingly greater segregation and regression in the mentally-disturbed patient, bringing about a prematurely mental deterioration and uprooting her/him from her/his own environment. This often leads to a worsening of the psychiatric syndrome which becomes chronic, and prevents any possibility of rehabilitation.

With the exception of serious long-term cases, who suffer mainly from organic neurological conditions, and require assistance rather than therapy, nowadays, psychiatry envisages short stays in skilled psychiatric emergency departments, from which the patient is rapidly discharged and reintegrated into her/his natural environment, where s/he will then be placed under the constant care of the local psychiatric service and the social welfare service.

Both the pharmacological and psychotherapeutic therapies are conducted on a day-care basis. In order to be effective it is not sufficient for the offender to provide her/his consensus; s/he must also be motivated, and it is difficult to obtain both of these factors under conditions of therapy. Moreover, the psychiatric treatment of these patients follows no guaranteed method and does not conform to the norms of modern psychiatry. As already mentioned, effective therapy would also be the best form of prevention and social protection, and would enable the obstacles to the court orders to be removed, by allowing these subjects to circulate freely. At present these obstacles are still linked to the assumption that mentally-ill offenders are socially dangerous.

PRISON PSYCHIATRIC HOSPITALS

Law No. 180 (13 May 1978) 'Voluntary and Compulsory Health Checks and Treatment' completely modified the pre-existing situation by recognising the citizen's right to freedom with respect to health treatment, and by replacing the concept of 'danger' with that of 'protection of public health', with the aim of legitimating the compulsory nature of the treatment itself.

The aim of the above-mentioned law is to phase out psychiatric hospitals, which are accused of being 'places of exclusion and suffering'. What remains in operation, instead, in that no mention is made of them in the law and they are still subjected to the regulations in force, are the Prison Asylums, which are regulated by the new rules for enforcement introduced with Presidential Decree (DPR) No.431 of 29 April 1976.

Thus, what has come to be sanctioned is an inequality of treatment for those subjects who have become offenders and are judged as completely incapable of cognition and volition by reason of mental infirmity. If such a subject is regarded as socially dangerous, s/he will be required to undergo health treatment which is entirely in contrast with the spirit of the present health reform.

Admission into a prison psychiatric hospital is not regarded as a penalty, but as a security measure. By security measure is intended the means of social protection envisaged by criminal legislation against those who, by committing an act envisaged by the law as a crime, are found to be capable of committing further unlawful acts. Hence, security measures are envisaged and applied as a consequence of the state of danger in which the subject finds her/himself. Such measures, therefore, are a means of preventing crime. In other words, they aim towards readapting the criminal to a free social life, and thus to promote her/his education or treatment, depending on which of the

126

two might be required, making it impossible for her/him to cause harm in the meantime.

Security measures are not linked to the criminal law system but to the system of administrative law. They take the form of a series of provisions aimed at eliminating the physical, biological and social factors of crime, by releasing the subject from an illness that drags her/him into crime, by eliminating criminal tendencies and habits thus giving place to healthy and honest ways of life, and by making it materially impossible for a dangerous subject to cause harm. Therefore, sentences prevent crimes from being committed through an act of will, whereas security measures only indirectly avoid the infringement of criminal laws by acting on causes which, nevertheless, contribute to the occurrence of a crime.

Safety measures are applied where the sphere of action of the punitive system ends, to ensure that the state is protected against subjects who, because of mental immaturity or incapacity, must be subjected to special provisions to prevent the recurrence of further unlawful acts. The conditions required for the application of security measures are:

a) the carrying out of an act envisaged as a crime; and

b) the social danger of a subject.

The fundamental element for the application of a security measure in the case of a person discharged from a prison because of a mental infirmity, must consist in the persistence of that infirmity, and hence, of the danger at the time the judgment is made. In addition, once the security measure has been passed, it may be repealed by the judge whenever it is ascertained that the subject has recuperated her/his mental health and that the state of danger therefore ceases to exist.

The prison psychiatric hospitals operating in Italy are the following:

1) Aversa near Naples, housed in a sixteenth-century convent. In the early part of this century, the population of the Aversa Criminal

Asylum reached 350, but the figure had doubled by the beginning of the 1970s;

2) Naples, or Saint Efremio Nuovo, also housed in a sixteenth-century convent. Although it was designed to accommodate 50 patients, the number has now actually reached 300;

3) Reggio Emilia, located in an old convent which was converted in 1892;

4) Castiglione delle Stiviere in the Province of Verona. This is a private modern hospital which also runs a prison psychiatric section. A ward for 32 patients has been open since the early 1970s. Conditions here are more acceptable than those of the other institutions;

5) Barcellona Pozzo di Gotto, in the Province of Messina in Sicily;

6) Montelupo Fiorentino in the Province of Siena, which is installed in an old medieval fort.

Before Law No. 180 of 1978 came into force, there were two different institutions in Italy appointed to accommodate the mentally-ill: provincial psychiatric hospitals on the one hand, and prison psychiatric hospitals on the other.

The new law came into force as the result of the action of a strong and constructive cultural, political and social movement which, since the early sixties, had been increasingly radical in challenging not only the inhuman and uncivilised form of admitting patients to prison psychiatric hospitals, but also the therapeutic procedures that had been used until then. It even went as far as to totally reject psychiatry as a science of social control and the very concept of mental 'illness'.

The practical effects were dramatic, partly because the implementation of the law swiftly uprooted the former organisation without replacing it with a new and more functional one. A large number of patients were discharged from the provincial psychiatric hospitals, and it became practically impossible to deal with the acute critical situation, typical of certain mental pathologies.

Added to this was the great difficulty for the families and territorial institutions in assisting the chronically mentally-ill, in terms of therapy, prevention and rehabilitation. Admission to psychiatric hospitals has been replaced by other therapeutic programmes set up on a limited scale by the local health authorities, both on an out-patient basis and through the general hospitals. However, because these programmes are entirely voluntary in nature, they have been found to be inadequate precisely in their ability to control the behavioural disorders frequently manifested by the most serious patients. These sick people, therefore, often end up in a prison asylum. The prison psychiatric hospitals are now over-crowded and are unable to accept all mentally-ill prisoners, large numbers of whom therefore remain in prison.

Although, due to lack of relevant statistics, the actual number of mentally-ill people in prison is not known, it can be inferred from several indicators that it is now quite high. For example, the proportion of inmates in Italy's prisons who declare themselves to be drug addicts amounts to about 40 per cent, although virtually no prison has the facilities to treat drug addicts, despite the fact that this is expressly envisaged by the law.

To sum up, the present condition of the mentally-ill in Italy, whether or not they have committed a crime, can certainly be described as critical.

Table 1:   Data on prisoners and mentally-ill offenders in Italy from 1976 to 1989

Year	Prisoners	Patients in psychiatric hospitals or in public institutions	Mentally-ill offenders in forensic psychiatric hospitals	Percentage of prisoners held in psychiatric hospitals
1976	29 973	64 017	1 035	3.45
1977	32 337	59 663	1 116	3.45
1978	26 424	54 284	1 149	4.35
1979	28 606	46 826	1 280	4.47
1980	31 765	42 115	1 424	4.48
1981	29 506	38 358	1 570	5.32
1982	35 043	34 736	1 584	4.74
1983	40 031	32 214	1 508	3.77
1984	41 832	30 672	1 423	3.40
1985	41 536	29 188	1 344	3.21
1986	33 609	39 885	1 527	4.54
1987	31 377	38 043	1 741	5.47
1988	31 382	38 556	1 614	5.14
1989	30 680	37 512	1 152	4.95

BIBLIOGRAPHY

Adler F., *Jails as Repository for Former Mental Health Patients,* mimeographed edition, 1985.

Adler F., 'From Hospitals to Jail: New challenges to the Law-enforcement Process', *Criminal Law Bulletin,* vol. 17, no. 4, pp. 319-333, 1981.

American Bar Association, *First Tentative Draft Criminal Justice Mental Health Standards*, Washington D.C., 1983

Bayer R. *et al.*, 'The Insanity Defence in Retreat', *The Hastings Center Report,* vol. 13-16, 1983.

Bennet B. *et al.*, *Circular of the Association for the Advancement of Psychology, 1985.*

Canepa G., 'La Perizia sulla Personalità dell'imputato. Problemi Criminologici e Medico-legali', *Rassegna di Criminologia,* vol. 12, no. 1, pp. 23-37, 1981.

Canepa G. and Kerner N.J. (eds.), 'L'expertise Criminologique', *Annales Internationales de Criminologie*, vol. 19, no. 1-2, (special issue), 1981.

Cohen J., *Incapacitating Criminals: Recent Research Findings.* National Institute of Justice, United States Department of Justice, Washington D.C., 1983.

Council of Europe, *Legal Protection of Persons suffering from Mental Disorder placed as Involuntary Patients*, Legal Affairs, Strasbourg, no. R(83)2, 1983.

Fein R.A., 'How the Insanity Acquittal Retards Treatment', *Law and Human Behavior*, vol. 8, no. 3-4, pp. 283-292, 1984.

Greenwood P.W. and Abrahams A., *Selective Incapacitation,* Report to the National Institute of Justice, Rand Corporation, Santa Monica, 1982.

Dietz P.L., 'Why the Experts Disagree: Variations in the Psychiatric Evaluation of Criminal Insanity', *The Annals of the American Academy of Political and Social Science,* January, pp. 84-95, 1985.

Lugazzo A. and Beduschi G., 'Dal Manicomio Giudiziario all'ospedale Psichiatrico Giudiziario: un Problema Insoluto', *Rassegna di Criminologia,* vol. 15, no. 1, pp. 141-155, 1984.

Manacorda A., *Il Manicomio Giudiziario*, De Donato, Bari, 1982.

Moore H.S., *Law and Psychiatry: Re-thinking the Relationship,* Cambridge University Press, Cambridge, England, 1984.

Moran R. (ed.), 'The Insanity Defense', *The Annals of the American Academy of Political and Social Science*, (special issue), January 1985.

Morris N., *Madness and the Criminal Law,* The University of Chicago Press, Chicago, 1982.

Morse S.J., 'Undiminished Confusion in Diminished Capacity', *The Journal of Criminal Law and Criminology*, vol. 9, no. 2, pp. 209-219, 1984.

Mulvey E.P. and Lidz C.W., 'A Critical Analysis of Dangerousness Research in a New Legal Environment, *Law and Human Behavior,* vol 9, no. 2, pp. 209-219, 1985.

Potas I., *Just Deserts for the Mad,* Australian Institute of Criminology, Canberra, 1982.

Petrealla F., "Pensieri Sinistri ed Inquietanti", in 'Matti da Imprigionare', (supplement to no. 5 of *Difesa penale),* pp. 50-54, May-August 1984.

Pazzagli A. and Ballerini A., "La Botte Piena e la Moglie Ubriaca", in 'Matti da Imprigionare', (supplement to no. 5 of *Difesa penale),* pp. 43-49, May 1984.

Rogers R., Wasyliew O.E. and Cavanaugh J.L., 'Evaluating Insanity: A Study of Constructive Validity', *Law and Human Behavior*, vol. 8, no. 3-4, pp. 293-303, 1984.

Shah S.A., 'Dangerousness and Mental Illness: some Conceptual, Prediction and Policy Dilemmas', in Frederick C.J. (ed.), *Dangerous Behavior: A Problem in Law and Mental Health,* Department of Health and Welfare Publication No. (A.D.E.), 78-563, chap. 11, Washington D.C.,1978.

Shah S.A., 'Legal and Mental Health System Interactions: Major Developments and Research Needs', *International Journal of Law and Psychiatry,* vol. 4, pp. 219-270, 1981.

Shah S.A., 'Criminal Responsibility', in Curran W.J., McGarry A.L. and Shaw S.A. (eds.), *Contemporary Perspectives in Forensic Psychiatry and Psychology*, FA Davis, Philadelphia, forthcoming.

Smith J.S., *Forensic Psychiatry,* Potomac, Maryland, forthcoming

Steadman H.J., 'Empirical Research on the Insanity Defense', *The Annals of the American Academy of Political and Social Science,* pp. 58-71, January 1985.

Stengel R,, 'More Muscle for Crime Fighters', *Time Magazine,* p. 44, 29 October 1984.

Singer R,, 'The Aftermath of an Insanity Acquittal: The Supreme Court's Recent Decision in Jones v. The United States', *The Annals of the American Academy of Political and Social Science*, pp. 114-124, January 1985.

Slovenko R., 'The Past and Present of the Right to Treatment: A Slogan gone Astray', *The Journal of Psychiatry and Law,* vol. 9, no. 3, pp. 263-282, Autumn 1981.

Toplin L.A., 'Criminalising Mental Disorder: The Comparative Arrest Rate of the Mentally-ill', *The American Psychologist*, vol. 39, no. 7, pp. 794-903, July 1984.

Walker N., 'The Insanity Defence 1800', *The Annals of the American Academy of Political and Social Science*, pp. 25-42, January 1985.

ITALY
The correctional treatment of mentally-ill offenders and perspectives of reform
Adelmo Manna*

SANCTIONS

In order to understand how the Italian criminal justice system regulates sanctions concerning mentally-ill offenders, it is necessary to introduce the analysis with an historical overview of the system that existed under the 1889 Criminal Code, the so-called 'Zanardelli Code', named after the then Minister of Justice.

Although specific sanctions for mentally-ill offenders had not yet been introduced under the above-mentioned Code, the law demanded that this type of offender should be committed to the Authority of Public Security[1], which meant a temporary type of custody under observation in a psychiatric hospital[2]. This model was finally regulated by the 1904 law which also introduced the concept of 'dangerousness of the mentally-ill offender to her/himself and to others', and which was also applied to those people who had not committed any crime[3].

The reason why specific provisions regarding 'criminal mental hospitals' had not yet been introduced in the Zanardelli Code, despite the fact that the penal judge had been provided with this alternative by the 1887 Project, was that the 'conflict' between the 'classical school' and the 'positivist school' had, in this case, been won by the former[4].

In fact, prevention was still considered to be an administrative function, not concerning the penal judge, whose role was simply to

---

*   Professor, Faculty of Law, University of Bari, Italy, and UNICRI Scientific Consultant. This report was prepared in August 1992.

inflict sanctions on those people who were able to understand the meaning of their actions, since it was believed that penal sanctions should be of a retributive nature only. However, this did not mean that a preliminary system of measures, with an evidently preventive function - such as the 'house of custody' for those with diminished responsibility[5] - had already been introduced by the 1889 Code.

This system was a typical result of the influence of the positivist theories[6], according to which, on the contrary, the main objective of penal sanctions was to defend society, so that it was completely lawful, as well as useful, to use penal sanctions also against mentally-ill offenders[7].

Nevertheless, it was too early to introduce a proper system of so-called 'measures of security'[8] in the Penal Code, alongside the traditional penal sanctions *stricto sensu*, that also involved mentally-ill offenders (which, in fact, only appeared in the Penal Code of 1930). In any case, to better understand the Italian situation during the period 'of transition', one must take into account the wide differences that existed also in this field between the system adopted by the Penal Code of 1930, and its direct predecessor - the so-called 'Progetto Ferri' of 1921[9].

There was no place at all in this latter project for the traditional penal sanctions, due to the positivist school's fundamental concept which denied the existence of free will[10] and, consequently, of responsibility - the latter being a necessary precondition for the application of the traditional penal sanction, with an evidently retributive function[11]. On the contrary, according to the positivists, the main function of the penal sanction was social defence. As a result, the idea of prevention, which until then had remained outside the domain of the Penal Code and was only administered by public security, now become part of penal law.

This new concept produced two effects; not only was the concept of penal responsibility substituted by that of 'dangerousness'[12], but also the whole range of traditional penal sanctions was replaced by the so-called 'measures of security' - designed for different categories of offenders [13].

For the first time, these new measures also included the so-called 'criminal mental hospital' which, along the lines of the Ferri Project, involved the designation of special sections of the common mental hospitals for the treatment of totally or partially mentally-ill offenders[14]. A clear distinction was thus established between the 1930 Code and the Zanardelli Code. This consisted in the fact that the penal law now also provided for those people who, although mentally-ill, had committed a crime and therefore belonged to a category from which society also had to be protected. The problem, however, was that this kind of measure also had to be applied to those offenders who were only partially mentally-ill[15] and were therefore in control, although only to a limited extent, of their mental faculties. In these cases, partial penal responsibility also had to be taken into consideration.

This problem was solved in a different way by the 1930 Penal Code, which provided a cumulative system of penal sanctions and measures of security, such as the 'house of therapy and custody'[16] for partially mentally-ill offenders only, where 'custody' was related to diminished responsibility and security was related to cases of social dangerousness[17].

A measure of security only - the criminal mental hospital[18] - was provided for totally mentally-ill offenders who could not be judged as penally responsible, but who could be diagnosed as 'socially dangerous'[19].

Relationship between traditional criminal sanctions and measures of security

With the Penal Code of 1930, the Italian legislature adopted a system that is particularly clear as far as diminished responsibility is concerned; a measure of security was added to the traditional sanction that deprives people of their personal freedom.

The person is in fact responsible, although only partially, for her/his actions and thus a prison sentence is adopted; s/he is also considered to be dangerous by the law (Article 219 of the Italian Penal Code)[20], and hence a security measure is added - a centre of therapy and custody.

This formal definition of dangerousness and responsibility provides a judicial basis for both types of sanctions to be found in the cumulative system. This produces, however, an unreasonable dual form of repression[21], and it is therefore essential to identify both the origin and the real motives behind this system. Its origin is not to be found in Italy, but in the 'allg. Landrecht fuer die Preussischen Staaten', which dates back to the end of the eighteenth century, and particularly, in the Swiss 'avant-projet' of the Penal Code prepared by Stoos[22].

The main rationale behind this type of system was a belief that the traditional penal sanction and the 'new' measures of security had separate functions: whereas the former had a retributive function, the latter had a preventive one, both in terms of general and special prevention.

In the same way that diminished responsibility is dealt with under the present system, there was room for the application of both sanctions, given their different functions and the conditions for their application (responsibility/dangerousness). This system went through a major crisis with the introduction of the Constitution in 1948, and led to the recognition of a special preventive function of traditional penal sanctions[23].

In the author's opinion, by stating that penal sanctions should aim towards the re-education of the offender, the Constitution (Article 27, paragraph 3) clearly recognises the special preventive functions of these sanctions[24].

It must be remembered that an attempt to add the phrase 'in the field of execution' to Article 27 paragraph 3 only, with the obvious aim of confining prevention to that sector alone, was not accepted by the 'Assemblea Costituente'[25], and thus, the preventive idea was introduced 'in full sail'[26] into the judicial system.

It is also doubtful whether the penal sanction has retained a retributive nature, not only because retribution is not an independent function of the sanction, but merely an 'internal rule of regulation'[27], in that it assures a proportionality between the crime and the sanction[28], but also because it is not a convincing argument to trace the constitutional basis of retribution to the first paragraph of Article 27[29]. This paragraph, in fact, concerns another problem: the requirement that the imputation of a crime is 'personal', even in the more modern sense, of the requirement at least of 'negligence'[30], thus eliminating the possibility of strict liability[31], while not dealing at all with the sanctions aspect[32].

The recognition of a preventive function in the penal sanction in addition to the measure of security - which is not only constitutional (Article 27, paragraph 3), but also has an important basis in the evolution of the literature, especially since the beginning of the 1960s, when penal law was identified as only one of the systems for social control[33], so as to separate law and ethics and to deny the so-called absolute theories of the penal sanction, such as retribution[34] - has however plunged the cumulative system into a major crisis. In fact, at the basis of the cumulative system are the different functions of the two sanctions (retributive/preventive), so that the system loses its legitimacy if the functions are found to be the same[35]. Nor is it a convincing argument to base this legitimacy on the Constitution itself, since the latter provides for both types of sanction[36].

The inclusion of measures of security in the Constitution does not in fact imply an acceptance of the cumulative system, since the provision expressed in the last paragraph of Article 25 regards another aspect, i.e. the extension of the principle of strict legality to the measure of security[37]. Nevertheless, the crisis of the cumulative system has not yet brought about changes in the legislation. The only indication of a tendency towards a change in the present system in favour of a vicarial one, is the progressive development in case law of the sphere of the 'fungibility' between pre-trial and post-trial custody and the measure of security.

In fact, from an original position of rejection, according to which sanctions and measures of security have different functions despite the fact that they both produce a restriction of personal freedom[38], there is now a tendency towards a more open position. This is shown, for example, by a recent decision of the Supreme Court of Cassation to make it lawful to subtract the time spent under the measure of security (at first applied temporarily but not then confirmed) from the length of the sentence or pre-trial custody[39].

In the author's opinion, this represents a first important step towards a progressive acceptance of the idea of 'total' fungibility between penalty and measure of security, and thus of a more correct vicarial system.

The traditional forensic psychiatric hospital in the Italian penal system

In order to understand better the role of forensic psychiatric hospitals in the Italian legal system, it is necessary to look at the provisions of the Penal Code. From these, it is easy to identify the system adopted by the legislator, and in particular the people who will become the subjects of the sanction [40].

First, according to the first paragraph of Article 222, the forensic psychiatric hospital is foreseen for those people who are acquitted because of mental illness, chronic intoxication due to alcohol or drugs, or are deaf-mutes; this excludes those people who are acquitted for the same reasons, but have been brought before the court for petty offences, crimes of negligence, or other types of crime which are abstractly punishable with no more than two years' imprisonment, or by a fine.

Secondly, according to the last paragraph of the same Article, the psychiatric hospital is also foreseen for juvenile delinquents under 14 years of age[41], and those between 14 and 18 who are not guilty because of proved incapacity (lack of *mens rea*) and who have committed a crime under the conditions provided for by the first paragraph of Article 222.

Thirdly, the forensic psychiatric hospital is also foreseen for those people who have been placed under another measure of security[42], but are suffering from a mental illness for which they must be admitted to the hospital.

But in order to focus our analysis on the substantive penal law, it is important to consider: a) defendants to whom the criminal psychiatric hospital is temporarily applied during the trial as a measure of security; b) prison inmates who are affected by a mental illness and for whom, therefore, normal detention cannot be continued, (Article 148)[43]; and c) inmates placed under a different measure of security and who are also mentally ill (Article 212, second paragraph of the Penal Code).

Under these circumstances, it is evident that there has been an excessive increase in the traditional role of the forensic psychiatric hospitals. They have not only been used for the traditional categories of 'mentally-ill' offenders, but also as a 'psychiatric sanction'[44], or even as a temporary measure, for a variety of categories of people, despite the fact that ordinary psychiatric hospitals or (after Law 180/78) special sections of ordinary hospitals would better fit their needs[45].

In any case, the length of stay at the forensic psychiatric hospital depends essentially on an abstract view of the seriousness of the crime; i.e. ten years in cases of sentences of life imprisonment; five years for sanctions of not less than ten years; and two years in all other cases.

It is clear, therefore, that the forensic psychiatric hospital also assumes a retributive function, and therefore risks being used as a traditional penal sanction in a retributive sense. This could be seen as lacking constitutional legitimacy and was in fact raised before the Constitutional Court, which rejected the claim[46].

The Articles of the Constitution cited before the Court, concerning the principles of equality (Article 3) and strict legality (Article 25, paragraph 3), highlight the different roles of this kind of measure of security. This has only recently been mitigated by the fact that, following the so-called 'Gozzini Law', the dangerousness[47] of the mentally-ill offender cannot simply be assumed but must also be concretely proved before s/he can be judged as socially dangerous[48] and hence referred to the criminal psychiatric hospital. The different roles of the measure of security also have a very important influence in terms of its functions.

Originally, in 1930, the forensic psychiatric hospital was undoubtedly intended to perform two main functions: custody and therapy[49]. Custody clearly refers to the length of the sentence, decided upon in accordance with the abstract seriousness of the crime, while balancing in a curious way the need for retribution (which is evident from the proportional relationship between length of sentence and seriousness of crime)[50] with that of social defence, in the sense of general prevention. The therapeutic aspect was clear to the legislator in 1930, since at that time the psychiatric hospital was the only known type of system which took care of the mentally-ill, especially those suffering from psychosis. In any case, this system was also legitimate in terms of functions generally attributed to measures of security - general and special prevention - with an emphasis on the latter[51].

Although the custodial function has remained unmodified, the therapeutic function is, without doubt, undergoing a major 'crisis'. This is a result of the movement in the seventies which lead to Law 180/78 - the 'Basaglia Law' - which abolished psychiatric hospitals in Italy[52].

The main characteristics of this Law are that treatment became essentially voluntary[53], thus in conformity with Article 32 of the Constitution, and was compulsory in exceptional cases, with recovery in special sections to be set up in the hospitals[54]. The rationale behind this Law is the idea that the mentally-ill have various 'levels of responsibility'[55]. It is therefore no longer necessary to provide permanent custody within a closed institution, and indeed, a more open kind of treatment is more effective.

Although this idea has been criticised, mainly because the above-mentioned special sections in the normal hospitals have not yet been fully set up in Italy[56], with the result that many mentally-ill individuals are now 'treated' within the family, carrying obvious risks for the personal safety of other people, it does, however, reveal that even the legislator believes that the traditional psychiatric hospital is no longer the most suitable model of therapy. If this is the case, then the forensic psychiatric hospital, which is the only traditional type of institution still in existence, can be judged as contrary to some of the provisions of the Italian Constitution.

The first objection concerns the principle of equality, in the sense of the need for equal treatment in similar situations[57], and this could also be the case for the mentally-ill, since there is no longer a case for retaining forensic psychiatric institutions when 'similar' normal psychiatric hospitals have already been abolished. A reply to this criticism, however, could be that a difference exists between the mentally-ill and mentally-ill offenders since only the latter have committed a crime; therefore, the institution foreseen for them must also have a greater custodial function. In the author's opinion, this is not a very persuasive argument if one agrees that the criminality of a mentally-ill offender is often a symptom of the illness itself. Hence, the difference between mentally-ill and mentally-ill offenders is not sufficient to contemplate such different types of treatment, even in the criminal justice system[58].

The second argument concerns Article 32 of the Constitution, which not only states that the right of health is a fundamental right of the person, and only 'afterwards' does it become an interest of the community, but also that compulsory treatment is legal only if prescribed by the law, and must in all cases guarantee the respect of the human being[59].

In this respect, as is demonstrated by Padovani[60], the forensic psychiatric institution can be considered as going against this provision, for two main reasons. The first concerns the disciplinary measures that can be adopted against mentally-ill offenders[61], at least some of which could be judged as being contrary to the dignity of the person. The second concerns the contents of the treatment that is provided in the forensic psychiatric institutions, which is in fact too similar to that prescribed for ordinary offenders in prison[62], and therefore makes it difficult to speak of actual 'therapeutic' treatment, given the greater role of the custodial aspect. It is therefore questionable whether the treatment provided in traditional forensic-psychiatric institutions conforms to the provisions laid out in Article 32 of the Constitution.

In the author's opinion, however, this aspect must be viewed in relation to another fundamental provision of the Constitution (i.e. Article 27, paragraph 3) which states that 'the penal sanctions must aim towards the re-education of the sentenced person'. It must, in fact, be considered that measures of security can also be classified as penal sanctions, not only because it is the penal judge who applies them, but also because this takes place within penal proceedings, so that they cannot be classified as administrative[63]. It must also be added that the dominant opinion is that the freedom of a person can only be removed by penal sanctions[64]. Having established this, it is also necessary to verify whether the measures of security, and thus also those which were once known as 'criminal asylums' and which are now known as forensic psychiatric hospitals, fall within the provisions of Article 27, paragraph 3 of the Constitution.

Unfortunately, in this respect, the Italian Constitutional Court has always denied that Article 27, paragraph 3 could also be applied to measures of security, by stating that this provision only regards penalties *stricto sensu*, because measures of security have *per se* this tendency, which must be expressly recognised in penalties on the basis of a clear constitutional provision[65]; just as it would appear superfluous to extend the provision to measures of security.

This idea, which is frankly difficult to understand[66], has permitted the Constitutional Court to accept the exceptions to the constitutional legitimacy of the measures of security, but only on the basis of provisions other than those contained in Article 27, paragraph 3[67].

The idea itself seems unfounded, in any case, since it cannot be said that all measures of security are structurally directed toward special prevention, although this may have been the original objective of the legislator, as in the case of the criminal asylums. According to the Constitutional Court's interpretation, on the contrary, measures of security cannot be constitutionally controlled according to Article 27, paragraph 3, although these can no doubt be included in the category of penal sanctions. This does not appear correct, especially since the same Court, in a famous sentence on 'plea bargaining'[68], formally recognised that re-education is a primary function of the penalty, and is not only valid in the field of execution, as stated earlier[69], but also in the fields of judicial application and legislative provision[70].

Once it has been established, that even according to the Constitutional Court, the ordinary legislator is bound to introduce penal sanctions which are evidently preventive in nature, this also has to apply to the measures of security, particularly with respect to the required control for constitutional conformity of those that are already found in the criminal justice system.

Alternatives to traditional criminal psychiatric hospitals in the Italian criminal justice system

The main reason why forensic psychiatric institutions, notwithstanding the above-mentioned doubts on their constitutional illegitimacy, have not yet been declared illegal by the Constitutional Court, seems to be the risk of a legislative 'vacuum', especially since real 'alternatives' have not yet unfortunately been experimented on a large scale in Italy.

In many European countries, so-called 'socio-therapeutic institutions'[71] have been in use for a long time. These facilities were built for a variety of categories of offenders; not only for those who were mentally-ill in the 'classical' sense, but also sexual offenders and those who committed particularly serious crimes, such as murder, and are generally subject to mental disorder[72]. These types of institutions are not really alternatives to the traditional criminal asylums, which in fact continue to exist in these countries[73], but present an intermediary solution between providing penalties and measures of security. This can be seen, for instance, in the development of German legislation[74].

This kind of institution could provide a useful example of an alternative, more effective way to 'punish' very dangerous criminals, whether or not they are mentally-ill to all intents and purposes, under a new perspective which foresees both measures of security and the concept of penalty[75]. Unfortunately, as already stated, socio-therapeutic institutions have not yet been introduced in Italy, either through legislation or in practice, with the important exceptions of Lonate Pozzolo (near Milan) and Civitavecchia (near Rome)[76], as mentioned by Kaufmann[77]. However, the situation with respect to these two institutions has changed somewhat; Lonate Pozzolo's 'Work Centre' was closed around 1989-1990, in order to make way for 'Malpensa 2000'. All the furniture and equipment were removed and the building will be demolished.

As for Civitavecchia, an institute for the re-education of young offenders existed until 1970, after which it was transformed into an ordinary prison which still operates today. This 'involution' should perhaps be seen in relation to the crisis in the idea of re-education itself[78] but, in any case, it led to the failure of new perspectives in this area, so that the situation has now returned to its point of origin, which is based upon the traditional distinction between punishment (imprisonment or fine) and measure of security (forensic psychiatric hospital or - for those offenders with diminished responsibility - therapeutic centres, limited obviously to the present area of investigation)[79].

Under these circumstances, it is very difficult for the Constitutional Court to declare the constitutional illegitimacy of the, by now, outdated 'criminal asylums' since no other concrete alternatives exist.

REFORMS

In order to understand the aims of the reform in the field of mentally-ill offenders, it is necessary to relate these to the wider reform of the psychiatric law of 1904 (Law No. 180/1978), introduced

144

by the so-called 'Basaglia Law', named after the leader of sociological psychiatry at that time[80].

As is well known, this Law abolished the traditional asylums and substituted, or rather, attempted to substitute[81] them by special sections in normal hospitals, for use in cases of emergencies and as non-custodial therapy in normal cases, subject to individual consent[82].

It is clear that this Law was inspired by a concept of mental illness in which social factors are more important than individual ones, i.e. biological and psychological factors[83]. This explains the abolition of the old asylums, which received popular support but which was not accompanied by the introduction of a new, more modern type of institution for mentally-ill offenders, such as socio-therapeutic institutions. This is also the reason why it is still necessary to reform Law No. 180, since the mentally-ill are often cared for by their families with the evident risks[84].

It was under this same cultural inspiration, that Draft Law No. 177, which was presented to the Senate on 29 September 1983 and later withdrawn[85,] attempted to regulate the problem of mentally-ill offenders. This draft proposed the abolition of traditional criminal asylums, but pointed to the resulting problem of an important change in the field of criminal responsibility[86]. The idea was to cancel the distinction between responsibility and non-responsibility so that all offenders would be considered responsible for their actions; later, at the stage of execution, different forms of treatment would be decided upon within the penitentiary structures themselves.

This draft, which is not really new since the aim of the old Italian positivist school[87] in this area was to abolish the concept of criminal responsibility and substitute it with that of dangerousness[88], found interesting models in the criminal justice systems of Sweden and Belgium[89]. In these countries, however, this type of system does not seem to have produced positive results since, although the distinction has been abolished in the field of criminal responsibility, it reappears in the field of execution (of the sanction). This is due to the need, in this latter area, to distinguish between mentally - and non-mentally-ill offenders in order to provide the most appropriate sanction for each individual[90]. One must also consider that the draft is based upon a so-called *fictio juris*, since it does not represent the real picture for which all mentally-ill offenders are responsible for their actions[91]. On the contrary, most modern penal systems are based on the concept of 'criminal responsibility' as a sort of guideline and orientation for the behaviour of members of society[92], as well as being accepted[93] as a 'social convention'[94].

The problem is, however, completely different and consists in the extension of the cases of non-criminal responsibility (as in other legal systems[95]) to neurosis, psycho-pathologies, and all forms of mental disturbances in general which do not have a clear medical basis[96]. It is clear from this new concept that the traditional distinction between prison and criminal asylum is no longer adequate, particularly for the above-mentioned syndromes, since those suffering from them require other new types of institutions, such as the socio-therapeutic centres[97].

In those countries where socio-therapeutic institutions have been introduced, although very expensive, they have produced positive results in that the recidivism rate seems to be much lower (about 16 per cent) than in the case of normal treatment within the prison[98]. As a result, they could be considered favourably by the legislator during the preparation of a new series of penal sanctions.

Status of the reform

As already mentioned, the draft was withdrawn, so that the only present solution to the problem of the judicial treatment of mentally-ill offenders would be to reform the penal code. As a matter of fact, an *ad hoc* Commission was set up, but consisted only of criminal law professors nominated by the former Minister of Justice, Giuliano Vassalli.

The Commission has completed its work, consisting of an outline of 'legge-delega', which aims to reform the Penal Code of 1930 and which is now being discussed by the Legislative Commission of the Ministry of Justice.

This draft has been published[99], so it can be discussed briefly to the extent that it relates to the matter under discussion. At first, a definition of the concept of imputability could not be found. This was left to the 'delegated legislator', although it would have been better if some indications had been given in this respect since, like other concepts such as 'malice' and 'negligence', the differences in the literature and court decisions are many[100]. 'Other abnormalities' was added to the concept of mental illness, evidently following the German Penal Code[101], but with a more vague definition. In any case, this new formulation is very important, especially since it is clear that, in this way, neuroses and psychopathics are included in the concept of mental illness[102].

Unfortunately, the concept of dangerousness has remained notwithstanding its evident lack of definition, accentuated by the fact that today, compared with the original version of the 'Rocco' Penal Code, the dangerousness is never 'presumed'[103], but is always 'decided upon by the judge'.

Finally, as far as the measures of security are concerned, the vicarial system has finally been adopted so, nowadays, the old irrational 'double system' no longer exists[104].

It must be added, however, from a more specific point of view, that the single measures for mentally-ill offenders have not, unfortunately, been specified since in the outline reference is only made to a vague 'psychiatric structure', in addition to outpatient treatment[105]. It would have been better not to leave this fundamental problem with the 'delegated legislator', but to take a stance as to whether to abolish or maintain the traditional forensic institutions and eventually, to integrate them with other specific institutions, such as socio-therapeutic institutes. In this way, the draft would have been seen to be 'in step' with the most important experiences in the field of sanctions, focusing on resocialisation and, thus, in accordance with the Article 27, paragraph 3 of the Italian Constitution[106].

It is hoped, however, as debates continue on the draft, that it might be possible to modify, in the name of clarification, some of the sections that, in the author's opinion, require reforming.

NOTES AND REFERENCES

1   Article 46 of the 1889 Italian Penal Code; E Dezza, 'Imputabilità e infermità mentale: la genesi dell'articolo 46 del Codice Zanardelli', in G Tarello (ed.), *Materiali per una storia della cultura giuridica*, Il Mulino, Bologna, 1991, vol. XXI, pp. 131 *et seq.*

2   L Majno, *Commento al Codice Penale Italiano,* D Tedeschi e figlio Editore, Verona, 1902, 2, p. 122; Articles 13 and 14 of Decree No. 6509 of 1 December 1889.

3   A Manna, 'Trattamento medico-chirurgico', in *Enciclopedia del Diritto, 1992,* XLIV, pp. 1301 *et seq.*

4   Article 47 of the 1887 Project; E Majno, 1902, *op. cit.*

5   Article 47 of the 1889 Italian Penal Code; E Majno, 1902, *op. cit.*, p. 121.

6   S Moccia, 'Ideologie e diritto nel sistema sanzionatorio del Codice Zanardelli', in S Vinciguerra *et al.* (eds.), *I codici preunitari e il Codice Zanardelli*, Cedam, Padova, 1993, pp. 562 *et seq.*; compare this with E Musco, *La misura di sicurezza detentiva, profili storici e costituzionali*, Giuffrè., Milan, 1978, pp. 7 *et seq.*

7   C Lombroso, *L'uomo delinquente in rapporto all'antropologia, alla giurisprudenza ed alla psichiatria*, Fratelli Bocca Editore, Turin, 1898, III, pp. 54s *et seq.*

8   For the history of the introduction of the system of the so-called 'measures of security' in Switzerland, in the project of LOOS, at the end of the XIX Century, see E Musco, 1978, *op. cit.*, pp. 43 *et seq.*

9   E Ferri, *Principi di diritto criminale*, UTET, Turin, 1928, pp. 756 *et seq.*

10 E Ferri, *Teorica dell'imputabilità e negazione del libero arbitrio*, Florence, 1878; E Ferri, in Soto & Hernandez (eds.), *Sociologia criminale*, (Spanish edition), Gongora, Madrid, 1907, vol. III, pp. 3 *et seq.*

11 E Dreher, *Die Willensfreiheit - Ein zentrales Problem mit vielen Seiten*, Beck, München, 1987, pp. 379 *et seq.*

12 E Ferri, 1928, *op. cit.*, pp. 652 *et seq.*

13 On the concept of 'free will', see E Dreher, 1987, *op. cit.*, pp. 379 *et seq.*

14 Article 32 of the Draft, in E Ferri, 1928, *op. cit.*, p. 764.

15 Another problem is whether 'partial mental illness', foreseen in legislation, also exists in nature. On the fact that the relative provision was generally introduced for practical purposes, see A Crespi, 'Imputabilità (diritto penale)', in *Enciclopedia del Diritto,* 1970, vol. XXI, p. 775.

16 Articles 219 and 220 of the Italian Penal Code of 1930.

17 On the definition of social dangerousness, see Article 303 of the Italian Penal Code.

18 Article 222 of the Italian Penal Code.

19 After Article 31 of the Law of 10 October 1986, N. 663, this term is no longer a *'praesumption iuris de jure',* deriving from the mental illness, but must be proved in the concrete case, even if the offender is mentally-ill.

20 See the important change introduced by Article 31 of Law No. 663 of 1986.

21 E Musco, *1978, op. cit.,* pp. 128 *et seq.*

22 *ibid,* pp. 43 *et seq.*

23 *ibid,* pp. 165 *et seq.* E Musco is in favour of this recognition. Compare this with I Caraccioli, *I problemi generali delle misure di sicurezza,* Giuffrè, Milan, 1970, p. 43, who states that the system of the so-called 'doppio binario' is also recognised by the Constitution.

24 Article 27, line 3 of the Constitution; G Fiandaca, 'Il III comma dell'art. 27' in G Branca & A Pizzorusso (eds.), *Commentario della Costituzione. Rapporti Civili, Articoli 27-28,* Zanichelli, Bologna-Rome, 1991, pp. 222 *et seq.*

25 For the history of this attempt by Leone and Bettiol, see A Manna, 'Sull'illegitimità delle pene accessorie fisse. L'Art. 2641 della pena', in *Giurisprudenza costituzionale,* 1980, pp. 910 *et seq.*

26 G Vassalli, 'Funzioni e insufficienze della pena', in *Rivista italiana di diritto e procedura penale,* 1961, pp. 296 *et seq.*

27 F Bricola, 'Tecniche di tutela penale e tecniche alternative di tutela', in F Bricola *et al., Funzioni e limiti del diritto penale,* CEDAM, Padova, 1984, pp. 3 *et seq.* and pp. 43 *et seq.*

28 The reassessment is highlighted as a form of guarantee of the retributive function; M Gallo., 'Conclusione', in M Gallo *et al. Orientamenti per una riforma del diritto penale,* Jovene, Naples, 1976, pp. 93 *et seq.*

29 G Turnaturi, 'Aspetti problematici della costituzionalità delle pene pecuniarie fisse e proporzionali', in *Rivista italiana di diritto e procedura penale,* 1977, pp. 1412 *et seq.*

30 For a description of the famous decision No. 364/88 of the Italian Constitutional Court, see D Pulitanò, 'Una sentenza storica che restaura il principio di

colpevolezza', in *Rivista italiana di diritto e procedura penale*, 1988, no. 2, pp. 686 *et seq*. On Article 27, paragraph 1 of the Constitution, see A Alessandri, 'Il I comma dell'art. 27', in G Branca (ed.), 1991, *op. cit.*, pp. 1 *et seq*.

31   See also the above-mentioned sentence No. 364/88 of the Constitutional Court. On the other hand, for a view that tends only to modify strict liability in sense that is concordant with the Constitution, see A Pagliaro, 'Colpevolezza e responsabilità obiettiva: aspetti di politica criminale e di elaborazione dogmatica', in A Pagliaro *et al.*, *Responsabilità oggettiva e giudizio di colpevolezza*, Jovene, Naples, 1989, pp. 3 *et seq.*; V Militello, *Rischio e responsabilità penale*, Giuffrè, Milan, 1988.

32   A Manna, 1980, *op. cit.*

33   C Roxin, 'Sinn und Grenzen staatlicher Strafe', in *JuS*, 1966, pp. 377 *et seq*.

34   L Eusebi, 'La "nuova" retribuzione', in G Marinucci & E Dolcini (eds.), *Diritto penale in trasformazione*, Giuffrè, Milan, 1985, pp. 93 *et seq*.

35   E Musco, 1978, *op. cit.*, p. 257.

36   I Caraccioli, 1970, *op. cit.*

37   F Bricola, 'Art. 25, II e III comma', in G Branca, 1981, *op. cit.*, pp. 227 *et seq*.

38   I Caraccioli, 1970, *op. cit.*, p. 375.

39   Cass. pen., S.U. 29 aprile 1978 (unpublished); E Musco, 'Misure di sicurezza', in *Enciclopedia giuridica*, 1990, vol. XX, p. 8; G Fiandaca & E Musco, *Diritto penale, parte generale*, Zanichelli, Bologna, 1989, 2nd edition, p. 645.

40   E Musco, 1990, *op. cit.*, pp 4-5. It should also be mentioned that, according to Article 62 L, 26 July 1975, N. 354, related to the penitential order and Article 98, D.P.R. of 29 April 1976, N. 432, i.e. the related law or enforcement, the original term 'judicial lunatic asylum' adopted in the Italian Penal Code of 1930 was replaced by the more modern, although only in form, term of 'judicial psychiatric hospitals'.

41   It would have been better for them, given their youth, to be placed in the so-called 'judicial reformatory'.

42   T Padovani, 'L'ospedale psichiatrico giudiziario e la tutela costituzionale della salute', in *Il Tommaso Natale*, 1978, pp. 853 *et seq.* and p. 881.

43   On this provision, see the decision of parial illegitimity, of the Constitutional Court, 19 June 1975, N. 146, in *Giurisprudenza costituzionale*, 1975, pp. 1372 *et seq.*; see also G Vassalli, 'Fine poco gloriosa di una norma poco civile: l'art 148 codice penale', in the same publication, pp. 2021 *et seq*.

44   T Padovani, 1978, *op. cit.*, p. 881.

45   On Law 180/78, see A Baratta *et al.*, 'Libertà e salute: la nuova legislazione psichiatrica', in La *Questione criminale*, 1979, pp. 347 *et seq.*

46   G.I. Trib. Rome, 4 August 1971, in *Giurisprudenza costituzionale*, 1971, II, p. 2561; G.I. Trib. Nuoro, 9 September 1971, in same publication, 1972, I, p. 630. The decision of the Constitutional Court is N. 106 - see E Musco, 1978, *op. cit.*, p. 5.

47   See the previous note.

48   Article 31 of the 'Gozzini Law'.

49   I Cappelli, 'Manicomio giudiziario', in *Enciclopedia del diritto*, 1975, vol. XXV, pp. 427 *et seq.*

50   M Gallo, 1976, *op. cit.*, pp. *94-95.*

51   I Caraccioli, 1970, *op. cit.*

52   A Manna, 1992, *op. cit.*, p. 1301.

53   Articles 1 and 2 of Law N. 180/187.

54   Article 6 of Law N. 180. On this point, see MG Gianichedda, 'Salute, diritti, controllo sociale: modelli di psichiatria dopo la riforma', in *Dei delitti e delle pene*, 1986, no. 1, pp. 5 *et seq.*

55   A Manacorda, 'Lineamenti per una riflessione sulla responsabilità penale dell'operatore di salute mentale', in A Manacorda *et al.*, *Tutela della salute mentale e responsabilità penale degli operatori*, GESTIS, Perugia, 1989, pp. 7 *et seq.*; F Bricola, 'La responsabilità penale dell-operatore di salute mentale: profili penalistici generali', in the same publication, pp. 137 *et seq.* and pp. 140 *et seq.*

56   On the criticisms and the related new draft reforms of the 'Basaglia Law', see AG Renzulli *et al.*, Oltre la 180: 'Le proposte dei socialisti', in *Argomenti socialisti*, 1991, no. 1 (supplement), pp. 5 et seq. See also Bill No. 790 proposed by Senator Zuffi *et al.*, transmitted to the Premiership on 19 November 1992; Bill No. 216 prepared by Senator Zito *et al.*, transmitted on 20 May 1992; Bill No. 71 prepared by the Right Honourable Tassi and transmitted on 23 April 1992; Bill No. 1528 proposed by the Honourable Garavaglia *et al.* and transmitted on 2 September 1992. Finally, on 10 February 1993, the Cabinet approved the Government Reform Project (substituting Law No. 180), presented by the then Minister of Health, Mr. De Lorenzo. Among other things, this envisaged a series of gradual *ad hoc* measures such as the Centre of Mental Health (a kind of decisional filter), the Semi-residential Resocializing and Therapeutic Service (in other words, a day hospital), the Relief Health Residence, where patients are recovered for treatment 'that cannot be effected at home' or if 'the patient is in need of protracted and continuous assistance', and finally - something that is obviously quite worrying, given the risk of substantial

revirement - the Protected Community (i.e. a 'closed number structure' for ex-asylum patients). Furthermore, 'obligatory health treatment' can be imposed on the patient following a simple medical opinion and without the prior provision of the Mayor. Although, in the author's opinion, this represents a step backwards, it is, neverthless, too early to express a final judgement on the matter (see *La Repubblica*, 11 February 1993, p. 24 and *La Repubblica*, 12 February 1993, p. 22).

57   A Manna, 1980, *op. cit.*, pp. 910 *et seq.*

58   To the extent that some people, *de jure contendo,* have proposed to refer mentally-ill offenders to the normal psychiatric institutions; for example: HJ Hirsch, in G Küpper (ed.), 'Diskussionsbericht über die Arbeitssitzung der Fachgruppe Strafrechtsvergleichung der Tagung der Gesellschaft für Rechtsvergleichung am 14.9.1989 in Würzburg', *ZStW*, 1990, pp. 448 *et seq.*

59   Article 32 of the Constitution. In particular, see: V Amato, 'Art. 32, 2° comma' in G Branca (ed.), *Commentario della Costituzione. Rapporti Civili, articoli 27-28,* 1974, Zanichelli, Bologna-Rome, pp. 167 *et seq.*

60   T Padovani, 1978, *op. cit.*, pp. 874 *et seq.*

61   Such as the so-called 'fasce di contenzione ai polsi' (wrist restraining straps) and others.

62   T Padovani, 1978, *op. cit.*, p. 884.

63   G Vassalli, *La potestà punitiva*, UTET, Turin, 1942, pp. 325 *et seq.*

64   For a significant exception, in the Pre-colloquium of Stockholm of the IAPL (14-17 June 1987) on the problem of depenalisation, see: E Viano, 'The legal and practical problems posed by the difference between criminal law and administrative penal law: questions relating to the legal structure of the two systems', in *Revue Internationale de Droit Penal*, 1988, vol 59, no. 1-2, pp. 95 *et seq*. The acts of the colloquium are published in the same publication.

65   For example, see Decision No. 68 of 1967, in *Giurisprudenza Costituzionale.*, 1967, p. 742; Decision No. 1 of 1971 with an observation by G Vassalli in 'Le presunzioni di pericolosità sociale di fronte alla Constituzionale', in *Giurisprudenza Costituzionale*, 1971, no. 1, p. 3; Decision No. 168 of 1962 in F Dassano, C Maccagno & M Ronco (eds.), *Sentenze della Corte Constituzionale sugli art. 25 c. 2 e 3 e 27 c. 1 e 3 (1956-1975)*, Giappichelli, Turin, 1976, p. 644; Decision No. 19 of 1974 in the last-mentioned publication, p. 442.

66   G Vassalli, 'L'abolizione della pericolosità presunta degli infermi di mente attraverso la cruna dell'ago', in *Giurisprudenza Costituzionale*, 1982, I, p. 1229; and, more recently, G Fiandaca, 'Art. 27, 3°comma' (just cited), p. 319.

67   Decision No. 1 of 1971; *ibid*; and Decision No. 146 of 1975, with an observation by A Alessandri in 'Pena ed infermità mentale', in *Rivista italiana di diritto e procedura penale*, 1976, p. 277

68   See the sentence No. 313 of 2 July 1990 of the Constitutional Court, with an observation by G Fiandaca in 'Pena "patteggiata" e principio rieducativo: un arduo compromesso tra logica di parte e controllo giudiziale', in *Foro italiano*, 1990, no. I, pp. 2385 *et seq*.

69   See the decisions mentioned in notes 65 and 67.

70   G Vassalli, 1961, *op.cit.*

71   H Kaufmann, 'Kriminologie', *Strafvollzug und Sozialtherapie*, Kohlhammer, Stuttgart, 1977, no. III, pp. 1152 *et seq*.

72   The legislative evolution of these institutions in Germany is particularly significant, and for which see further on.

73   For example, in Germany.

74   In the reform of 1975, the 'socio-therapeutic institutions' were, in fact, classified as measures of security, but in the 1985 law of penal execution they were no longer classified as such, but as 'alternatives to longer punishment' and were no longer compulsory but subject to 'voluntary' admission. For a different point of view see: G Kaiser, F Dünkel & R Ortmann, 'Die sozialtherapeutische Anstalt - das Ende einer Reform?', in *ZPR*, 1982, pp. 198 *et seq.*; HH Schüler-Springorum, 'Die sozialtherapeutischen Anstalten ein Kriminalpolitisches Lehrstück?', in *Gedächtnisschrift für Hilde Kaufmann*, 1986, p. 167.

75   Especially in the sense of a better development of the special preventive function.

76   One could add the Center of Observation of Rome - Rebibbia, although it is not actually a 'socio-therapeutic institution'.

77   H Kaufmann, 1977, *op. cit.*

78   G Fiandaca, 1991, *op. cit.*, pp. 258 *et seq*.

79   With the additional application of the so-called 'doppio binario', i.e. a cumulative system, between punishment and measure of security.

80   A Baratta *et al.*, 1979, *op.cit.*

81   Particularly as a result of the difficulties encountered in the practical implementation of the law.

82   A Manna, 1992, *op. cit.*

83   G Balbi, 'Infermità di mente ed imputabilità', in *Rivista italiana di diritto e di procedura penale*, 1991, pp. 844 *et seq*.

84 A Manna, 1992, *op. cit.*

85 On this subject, see: A Gatti *et al.*, 'Matti da imprigionare. A proposito del progetto di legge N. 177 del Senato', in *Difesa penale*, May-August 1984, supplement to no. 5; E Musco, 'Massreglen der Besserung und Sicherung im strafrechtlichen Rechtsfolgensystem Italiens', in *ZStW*, 1990, pp. 415 *et seq.*; O De Leonardis, G Gallio, D Mauri & T Pitch (eds.), *Curare e punire. Problemi e innovazioni nei rapporti tra psichiatria e giustizia penale*, UNICOPLI, Milan, 1988.

86 G Balbi, 1991, *op. cit.*

87 E Ferri, 1878, *op. cit.*

88 See the Ferri Draft of 1921.

89 For Sweden, see: D Victor, 'Massreglen der Besserung und Sicherung im strafrechtlichen Rechtsfolgensystem. Eine swedische Perspktive', in *ZStW*, 1990, pp. 435 *et seq.* For Belgium, see the *Loi d'execution penale* of 1930.

90 D Pulitanò 'L'imputabilità come problema giuridico', in D Pulitanò *et al,* 1988, *op. cit.*, pp.127 *et seq.* and p. 137.

91 E Musco, *op. cit.*, 1988, p. 434.

92 Also on the basis of general prevention which includes the function of orientation.

93 On the related question of 'free will', see: E Dreher, 1987, *op. cit.*

94 C Roxin, 'Schuldunfähigkeit Erwachsener im Urteil des Strafrechts', in *Festschrift für Spann*, 1986, pp. 457 *et seq.*

95 See in particular the reform of 1975 of the general part of the Penal Code of Germany (paragraphs 20 and 21 StGB); A Schönker, H Schröder & T Lenckner, *StGB Kommentar*, München, 1988, no. 23, sub paragraphs 20 and 21.

96 As above.

97 H Kaufmann, 1977, *op. cit.*

98 H Schüler-Springorum, 1986, *op. cit.*

99 In *Documenti Giustizia*, 1992, no. 3, pp. 305 *et seq.*

100 For a discussion on malice and negligence, but with an emphasis on the method, see: D Pulitanò, 'Appunti sulla disciplina dell'imputazione soggettiva nello schema di proposta di legge delega', in *Prospettive di una nuova Codice Penale - La Parte Generale*, report presented at a seminar organised by the International Institute of Higher Studies in Criminal Sciences, Siracusa, 15-18 October 1992.

101   Paragraphs 20 and 21 StGB in the revised version, drawing from the reform of 1975, which introduced the concept of 'other serious abnormality'. See HH Jescheck, 'La Riforma del diritto penale in Germania - Parte Generale', in *Indice Penale*, 1976, pp. 393 *et seq.*

102   Article 34, sub-articles b) and d) of the draft of the new Italian Penal Code, p. 347. On the regulation of imputability in the draft, see: F Tagliarini, 'Considerazioni sullo schema di delega per il nuovo codice penale in tema di imputabilità (art. 34, punti b) e d)', in *Prospettive di un nuovo Codice Penale - La parte generale*, report presented at a seminar organised by the International Institute of Higher Studies of Criminal Sciences (ISISCS), 15-18 October 1992, Siracusa.

103   This was partly abolished by the Constitutional Court, and definitely by the so-called 'Gozzini Law' of 1986 which constitutes a 'mini reform' of the penitentiary execution.

104   Article 48 of the draft in the new Italian Penal Code, p. 354, also because the measures of security in the outline are only applied to those judged non-responsible. On the 'vicarial system', see: E Musco, 1978, *op. cit.*

105   See Article 48 (a) mentioned in note 104.

106   G Fiandaca, 1991, *op. cit.*

JAPAN

*Ryosuke Kurosawa**

INTRODUCTION

In Japan, there is only one criminal justice system and, therefore, all judiciary policy decisions are made and carried out at a national level (see Figure 1).

Article 3 of the Mental Health Law defines a mentally-ill person as follows: a) a psychotic person, even if this is due to intoxication; b) a mentally-retarded person or, c) a psychopath. Article 39 of the Japanese Penal Code prescribes that:

a) a person who has committed an illegal act and lacks mental capacity (i.e. is not responsible for her/his actions) cannot be punished; and

b) a person who has committed an illegal act and has insufficient mental capacity (i.e. diminished responsibility) must receive a mitigated sentence.

In addition to this, on 3 December 1931, the Supreme Court defined a person who is lacking in mental capacity as someone who does not understand the nature and quality of her/his action, or who cannot control the act.

As indicated in Table 1, of all the offenders dealt with in Japan in 1989 (excluding traffic and professional negligence offenders), those who were either mentally-disturbed or suspected of being mentally-disturbed amounted to 1833 (1 750 adults and 83 juveniles). The percentage of mentally-disturbed offenders included in the total number of offenders was only 0.6 per cent (of which 1.2 per cent were

---

*   Chief Specialist, Naniwa Juvenile Training School, Osaka, Japan, and former UNICRI Associate Research Officer. This report was prepared in March 1992.

adults and 0.1 per cent juveniles); whereas the percentage was remarkably high for certain classes of offences, for example, 19.5 per cent for arson and 9.4 per cent for homicide.

DANGEROUSNESS

There is no provision in the Japanese criminal justice system for the category of dangerousness. Nor is there a specific provision in the Japanese Penal Code for the relationship between mental disorder and responsibility. Since this is principally a psychiatric issue and therefore a a matter of controversy, it is difficult to provide a conclusive description. Nevertheless, the following description by Fukushima[1] can be provided as an example:

Developmental disorder or response disorder

1) personality disorders: psychopaths and people suffering from a personality disorder are considered responsible for their criminal action;

2) response disorder: persons suffering from a neurosis, psychosomatic or adjustment disorder are, in principle, responsible for their actions;

3) as far as mental retardation is concerned, borderline cases with an IQ above 70 are considered to be responsible; persons with mild retardation and an IQ of between 70 and 50 are considered to be suffering from diminished responsibility; and, finally, people suffering from moderate and severe mental retardation with an IQ below 50 are not considered responsible for their actions.

Intrinsic mental disorder

1) schizophrenics are not responsible for their actions;

2) manic-depressives only manifest the intrinsic mental disorder symptom periodically. Therefore, they are not considered responsible for their actions during the manifestation of these symptoms, and responsible when the symptoms are not present.

Organic mental disorder

1) organic mental disorder (to a limited degree) exhibits the following symptoms: a) intelligence disorder; b) personality change, and c) psychotic disorder. When a person appears to be suffering from the third disorder (psychotic symptoms), s/he is not deemed to be responsible for her/his actions;

2) people suffering from epilepsy are not considered responsible for their action if this occurs during an epileptic fit.

PSYCHIATRIC EXAMINATION

Psychiatric examinations to evaluate the mental condition of the patient are carried out by designated physicians. The role of the designated physician (*Shitei'i*) is more important under the new law than that of the previous evaluative physician (*Kantei'i*) under the 1950 Law. Under the old law, the Ministry of Health and Welfare's only requirement to become a *Kantei'i* was at least three years' experience in the diagnosis and treatment of people with mental disorders (although in practice the usual actual requirement was 5 years). By contrast, the 1988 Law introduced a rigorous and comprehensive set of educational, training and clinical requirements for obtaining S*hitei'i* status, as well as continued updating of knowledge in the field in order to maintain the required level of competence.

The K*antei'i* was only required to examine persons following a governor's hospitalisation order. The duties of the S*hitei'i* extend to determining the need for continued hospitalisation of both voluntary patients and patients who have been hospitalised under a governor's order. The S*hitei'i* must also determine the need for, and type of physical and other restrictions[2].

TREATMENT OF MENTALLY-ILL OFFENDERS

The medical health system envisages three types of hospitalisation in the case of mentally-ill offenders:

a) voluntary admission;

b) hospitalisation for medical protection;

c) compulsory hospitalisation.

In the case of voluntary admission, for the first time, the 1988 Law provides for the voluntary admission of patients into a mental hospital. In fact, it imposes a firm obligation on the head of a mental hospital to admit mentally-disordered persons upon the latters' written consent.

Hospitalisation for medical protection involves the patient being hospitalised with the consent of the person responsible for the patient's protection and welfare. For example, a relative or member of the family can decide to hospitalise a patient even without the latter's consent. However, in order to reduce the possibility of abuse, collusion or subterfuge in this category of hospitalisation, the new law has added the following procedural safeguards: a) an initial examination, to determine whether the person concerned is 'mentally disordered' and in need of hospitalisation, must be conducted by a designated and certified physician; and b) the need for hospitalisation is subject to review by a panel of the Prefecture Psychiatric Review Board, which was established under the 1988 Law.

The governor of the Prefecture can decide to hospitalise a patient following the request of any member of the general public for the examination and necessary protection of a person who is, or is suspected of being, mentally-disordered. It can also be applied when the governor receives a report from the head of a mental hospital, a police officer, public prosecutor, head of a probation office or of any correctional institution. Upon receipt of such a request or report, or on her/his own initiative, the governor must order the person concerned to be examined by a physician who has been certified by the Ministry of Health and Welfare to carry out certain medical tasks as stipulated by the new law. If, during the examination, the person is deemed mentally-unfit and therefore likely to cause harm to her/himself without hospitalisation, the governor may commit the person to a hospital of the Prefecture or other designated hospital. Once hospitalised, the patient must be examined by at least two certified physicians who must confirm this diagnosis.

Although the procedures for this type of involuntary hospitalisation are essentially the same under both the old and new laws, it was only with the 1988 Law that certain criteria to determine the likelihood of a person injuring her/himself or others by reason of mental disorder unless hospitalised were established. Physicians are now instructed to decide that hospitalisation is necessary when, due to symptoms that are set forth and described in the regulations, the person is deemed likely to commit such acts as attempted suicide or 'actions posing a threat to the life, body, chastity, reputation or property, etc. of others or to the protected legal interests of society, such as murder, injury, assault, problematic sexual behaviour, slander, vandalism, robbery, intimidation, theft, fraud, arson and playing with fire, etc.'

Treatment of mentally-ill offenders in the criminal justice system

As prescribed in Article 39 of the Penal Code, at the stage of prosecution, those accused who are deemed not responsible are not prosecuted, and are acquitted at the subsequent trial, whereas those who are judged to have diminished responsibility are given mitigated sentences.

Table 2 presents the number of persons who, due to diminished or lack of responsibility, received an acquittal or mitigated sentence instead of being prosecuted. In 1989, 397 persons were not prosecuted by reason of insanity at the prosecution stage and, during the preliminary court hearing, 9 were acquitted for the same reason, while 63 were given mitigated sentences on the grounds of insufficient mental capacity.

In Figure 1, Fukushima[3] illustrates the flow in the decision-making process of mentally-ill offenders based on the 185 cases on which he carried out a preliminary psychiatric examination. According to his research, out of the 185 cases who underwent a preliminary psychiatric examination before the prosecution, 84 persons (45 per cent) were diagnosed as being not-responsible, 47 persons (25 per cent) were judged to have diminished responsibility and 48 persons (26 per cent) were considered responsible for their actions.

Between 1985 and 1989, as shown in Table 3, out of a total of 3 995 persons, 3 601 were not prosecuted on the grounds either of lack of, or insufficient mental capacity, while 394 went under trial. The large majority of the latter were acquitted on the grounds of lack of mental capacity.

As shown in Table 4, which refers to the same total, 2 393 (59.9 per cent) were suffering from schizophrenia, 421 (10.5 per cent) were suffering from alcoholism and 290 (7.3 per cent) were suffering from manic-depressive psychosis. Finally, out of the 3 995 persons, the large majority of offenders accused of all crimes fell into the category of schizophrenia, 13.2 per cent of the offenders accused of homicide suffered from manic-depressive psychosis, 17.1 per cent of the cases for arson were accounted for by alcoholism, and mental deficiency accounted for 13 per cent of the cases of rape and indecent assault.

Correctional institutions

In the Japanese correctional system, all inmates are incarcerated according to a classification system which includes special categories for mentally- or physically-disabled inmates; i.e. Class Mx: mentally retarded; My: psychopaths and cases with considerable psychopathic tendencies; Mz: psychosis and those with psychotic tendencies; Px: physically disabled; Py: physically handicapped; and Pz: inmates aged 60 years or more.

Japan has five medical prisons in which serious cases are hospitalised and given intensive care. Two of these prisons are specialised in Class M, one in Class P and two in both Class M and P. In addition, there are five other medical centres attached to large prisons, where sick prisoners are hospitalised. Those prisoners who need special medical treatment may be transferred to medical centres or medical prisons, depending upon their condition.

As indicated in Table 5, in 1989, 3 088 (7.6 per cent) of the prisoners were diagnosed as being mentally disturbed.

In the same year, 202 (5.4 per cent) mentally disturbed juveniles were in juvenile training schools.

Measures of security

There is no provision for so-called security measures or, in fact, for criminal psychiatric hospitals in the Japanese criminal justice system.

REFORMS

The new Mental Health Law was promulgated on 26 September 1987 and came into effect on 1 July 1988. The main features of this new law are that it clarifies hospitalisation procedures and categories, the qualification requirements and role of the physicians designated to carry out physchiatric examinations, post-admission safeguards and intermediate community-based social rehabilitation facilities

With regard to the new hospitalisation measures, the law has placed greater emphasis on the patient's human rights and has given voluntary hospitalisation priority over the three above-mentioned hospitalisation measures.

In order to protect the human rights of the patients, the 1988 Law introduced a system of safeguards which involved the submission of regular reports and reviews on the patient's condition and status. It introduced a formal method for presenting a request for discharge or improved treatment, as well as a statement of the patient's rights under the new system, which must be explained to the patient upon admission into the hospital. The most important institutional reform of the new law was the establishment of a Psychiatric Review Board in each Prefecture. This Board was to act as a special body to receive and review requests and reports that have been authorised and mandated respectively, under the new system of safeguards.

The Ministry of Health and Welfare recognised the need for intermediate community-based social rehabilitation facilities and outlined a fully-integrated rehabilitation system, complete with day- and night-care facilities, group residential facilities, etc. The new law authorised the establishment of a variety of rehabilitation facilities, i.e. 'Social Reintegration Activities' and 'Training Facilities' (*seikatu kunren shisetsu*) and 'Sheltered Workshops' (*jusan shisetsu*).

STATISTICS

Statistics related to the treatment of mentally-ill offenders in Japan are presented in the following tables and charts.

Table 1:   Number of mentally-ill offenders cleared by the police (1989)

Offence	No. of cleared offenders		No. of mentally-ill offenders		No. of offenders suspected to be mentally-ill	
	Adults	Juveniles	Adults	Juveniles	Adults	Juveniles
Total	147 939	165 053	411	28	1 339	55
Homicide	1 207	116	46	-	77	1
Robbery	870	574	1	1	12	2
Bodily injury	15 706	9 360	47	-	122	3
Assault	5 896	3 097	16	-	43	-
Threat	861	78	8	1	5	-
Extortion	4 315	5 152	2	-	8	-
Larceny	74 186	121 194	184	22	783	37
Fraud	8 543	626	13	1	67	-
Embezzlem.	15 870	19 769	1	-	5	2
Rape	891	438	3	1	9	-
Indecent assault etc.	2 407	454	15	-	22	-
Arson	543	97	42	1	76	6
Others	16 644	4 098	33	1	110	3

*   a) 'mentally disturbed' means psychotic persons, mentally deficient persons and psychopaths who were diagnosed by psychiatrists as needing medical care or protection.

    b) 'suspected to be mentally disturbed' means those who are subject to the notification to the governor stipulated in Article 24 of the Mental Health Law, excluding the mentally-disturbed.

** Indecent assault, etc. includes public indecency and distribution of obscene literature.

Source: National Police Agency.

Table 2: Number of persons found lacking and insufficient in mental capacity (1985-1989)

Year	No. of persons not prosecuted on grounds of lack of mental capacity	No. of persons acquitted on the grounds of lack of mental capacity	No. of persons given mitigated sentences on the grounds of insufficient mental capacity
1985	399	10	86
1986	417	3	78
1987	392	5	72
1988	414	6	62
1989	397	9	63

* Non-prosecution does not include traffic professional negligence and road traffic violations, and mitigated sentence excludes Special Law offences.

Source: Criminal Affairs Bureau, Ministry of Justice.

Table 3: Dispositions for offences committed by mentally-disturbed persons by offences and category of mental disturbance (total from 1985 to 1989)

Category	Total	Non-prosecution			Trial		
		Sub-total	Lack of mental capacity	Suspended prosecution (insufficient mental capacity)	Sub-total	Convicted (insufficient mental capacity)	Acquitted (lack of mental capacity)
Total	3 995 (100.0)	3 601 (90.1)	2 019 (50.5)	1 582 (39.6)	394 (9.9)	33 (0.8)	361 (9.0)
Offence							
Homicide	835 (100.0)	704 (84.3)	674 (80.7)	30 (3.6)	131 (15.7)	17 (2.0)	114 (13.7)
Robbery	141 (100.0)	125 (88.7)	96 (68.1)	29 (20.6)	16 (11.3)	1 (0.7)	15 (10.6)
Bodily injury	608 (100.0)	561 (92.3)	262 (43.1)	299 (49.2)	47 (7.7)	3 (0.5)	44 (7.2)
Bodily injury resulting in death	77 (100.0)	63 (81.8)	61 (79.2)	2 (2.6)	14 (18.2)	-	14 (18.2)
Rape, indecent assault	77 (100.0)	59 (76.6)	37 (48.1)	22 (28.6)	18 (23.4)	3 (3.9)	15 (19.5)
Arson	521 (100.0)	453 (86.9)	400 (76.8)	53 (10.2)	68 (13.1)	1 (0.2)	67 (12.9)
Others	1 736 (100.0)	1 636 (94.2)	489 (28.2)	1 147 (66.1)	100 (5.8)	8 (0.5)	92 (5.3)
Mental disturbance							
Schizophrenia	2 393 (100.0)	2 293 (95.8)	1 419 (59.3)	874 (36.5)	100 (4.2)	23 (1.0)	77 (3.2)
Manic-depressive psychosis	290 (100.0)	255 (87.9)	136 (46.9)	119 (41.0)	35 (12.1)	4 (1.4)	31 (10.7)
Epilepsy	68 (100.0)	60 (88.2)	27 (39.7)	33 (48.5)	8 (11.8)	1 (1.5)	7 (10.3)
Alcoholism	421 (100.0)	346 (82.2)	162 (38.5)	184 (43.7)	75 (17.8)	-	75 (17.8)
Stimulant drug toxicosis	161 (100.0)	126 (78.3)	62 (38.5)	64 (39.8)	35 (21.7)	-	35 (21.7)
Mental deficiency	137 (100.0)	88 (64.2)	26 (19.0)	62 (45.3)	49 (35.8)	-	49 (35.8)
Psychopathic disorder	48 (100.0)	39 (81.3)	8 (16.7)	31 (64.6)	9 (18.8)	-	9 (18.8)
Other mental disturbances	477 (100.0)	394 (82.6)	179 (37.5)	215 (45.1)	83 (17.4)	5 (1.0)	78 (16.4)

Source: Criminal Affairs Bureau, Ministry of Justice

Table 4: **Offences committed by mentally-ill offenders by category of mental disorder (total from 1985 to 1989)**

Offence	Total	Schizo phrenia	Manic depres- sive psychosis	Epilepsy	Alcohol- ism	Stimulant drug toxicosis	Mental deficie- ncy	Psycho- pathic disorder	Other mental disturb- ances
Total	3 995	2 393	290	68	421	161	137	48	477
	(100.0)	(59.9)	(7.3)	(1.7)	(10.5)	(4.0)	(3.4)	(1.2)	(11.9)
Homicide	835	494	110	9	48	29	11	5	129
	(100.0)	(59.2)	(13.2)	(1.1)	(5.7)	(3.5)	(1.3)	(0.6)	(15.4)
Robbery	141	101	2	3	15	4	3	1	12
	(100.0)	(71.6)	(1.4)	(2.1)	(10.6)	(2.8)	(2.1)	(0.7)	(8.5)
Bodily injury	608	394	26	11	66	25	5	14	67
	(100.0)	(64.8)	(4.3)	(1.8)	(10.9)	(4.1)	(0.8)	(2.3)	(11.0)
Fatal bodily injury	77	53	2	1	9	1	4	2	5
	(100.0)	(68.8)	(2.6)	(1.3)	(11.7)	(1.3)	(5.2)	(2.6)	(6.5)
Rape, indecent assault	77	48	6	3	4	-	10	1	5
	(100.0)	(62.3)	(7.8)	(3.9)	(5.2)		(13.0)	(1.3)	(6.5)
Arson	521	272	37	9	89	19	28	3	64
	(100.0)	(52.2)	(7.1)	(1.7)	(17.1)	(3.6)	(5.4)	(0.6)	(12.3)
Others	1 736	1 031	107	32	190	83	76	22	195
	(100.0)	(59.4)	(6.2)	(1.8)	(10.9)	(1.8)	(4.4)	(1.3)	(11.2)

* Figures in parentheses show percentages.

** Alcoholism and stimulant drug toxicosis include toxic psychosis; other mental disturbances include toxicosis by substances other than alcohol and stimulant drugs.

Source: Criminal Affairs Bureau, Ministry of Justice.

Table 5: Mentally-disturbed inmates in correctional institutions (as of 20 December 1988 and 1989)*

Category	No. of inmates	Mentally-ill inmates				
		Sub-total	Mental deficiency	Psychopathic disorder	Neurosis	Other mental disturbances
1. Prison						
1988	44 663 (100.0)	3 181 (7.1)	1 188 (2.7)	613 (1.4)	137 (0.3)	1 243 (2.8)
1989	40 796 (100.)	3 088 (7.6)	1 074 (2.6)	597 (1.5)	120 (0.3)	1 297 (3.2)
2. Juvenile training school						
1988	3 851 (100.0)	209 (5.4)	117 (3.0)	4 (0.1)	5 (0.1)	83 (2.2)
1989	3 742 (100.0)	202 (5.4)	102 (2.7)	1 (0.0)	2 (0.1)	97 (2.6)

* Figures in parentheses show percentages.
** Number of inmates does not include inmates whose mental diagnosis was not conducted or was too difficult to be conducted.
Source: Correction Bureau, Ministry of Justice.

Figure 1:   The treatment of mentally-ill offenders in the criminal justice system

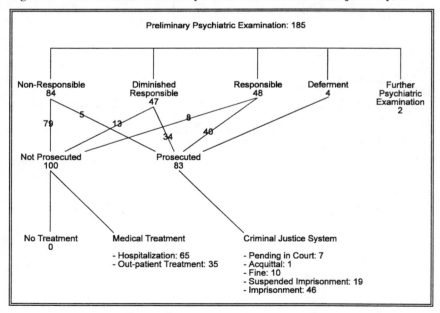

Source: A Fukushima, 'Mentally-ill and crime in Miyazawa', in Miyazawa & Fujimoto (eds.), *Criminology*, 1978.

REFERENCES

1   A Fukushima, *Psychiatric Examination*, 1985.

2   The sections on psychiatric examinations, treatment of mentally-ill offenders and reform are taken mostly from: SM Salzberg, 'Japan's New Mental Health Law: More Light Shed on Dark Places?', in *International Journal of Psychiatry*, 1991, no. 14.

3   A Fukushima, 'Mentally-ill and Crime', in Miyazawa & Fujimoto (eds.), *Criminology*, 1978.

NIGERIA
Tolani Asuni *

INTRODUCTION

There are two different sets of statutes which are relevant to the administration of criminal justice in Nigeria. The first is the Criminal Code and the Criminal Procedure Act which is applicable to federal offences and to the federal jurisdiction of Abuja and all the southern states of the Federation. The second is the Penal Code and the Criminal Procedure Code which is applicable to all the northern states of the Federation. Although the language used in the statutes may differ, the provisions are substantially the same as far as this report is concerned.

RESPONSIBILITY

Both the Criminal Code and the Penal Code reflect the so-called classical (neo-classical) school in their notions of responsibility. According to the theory of this school, all human actions originate from *free will* after the application of *reason*, since both of these endowments have been given more or less equally to all human beings. Neo-classical theory concedes however, that both endowments may be impaired or impinged upon by, for example, mental illness, and in such a case there would be no responsibility. However, Section 28 of the Nigerian Criminal Code provides in particular for two major mind afflictions which are relevant to non-responsibility:

a) mental disease;

b) natural mental infirmity.

---

* Professor of Psychiatry, University of Lagos College of Medicine and Chairman of the Psychiatric Hospitals Management Board, Lagos, Nigeria; former Director of UNICRI. This report was prepared in May 1992.

Therefore, the Nigerian criminal justice system distinguishes between responsibility and non-responsibility, and provides criteria for the distinction in Section 28 of the Nigerian Criminal Code, according to which responsibility is:

a) the capacity of the individual to understand what s/he is doing;

b) the capacity of the individual to control her/his actions;

c) the capacity of the individual to realise that s/he should not commit a wrongful act.

The concept of 'diminished responsibility' is not envisaged in the Nigerian Criminal Code; nor do provisions exist for the treatment of borderline cases in the Nigerian judicial system.

With respect to the treatment of offenders who are determined 'not responsible', the Criminal Code states that they should not receive criminal sanctions of a punitive nature for their illegal actions. Although, according to the criminal legislation, the first step in the administrative stage of criminal procedure is a court order to confine the offender in an 'asylum', this is not regarded as a criminal sanction. According to the Criminal Procedure Act, the asylum 'includes a lunatic asylum, a mental or other hospital, a prison and any other suitable place of safe custody for medical observation'. In this respect, 'security' is the essential element.

Offenders who are determined as being 'not responsible' are either sent to a psychiatric hospital for treatment, or kept in a prison clinic where they are placed under the treatment of a visiting psychiatrist or the prison medical officer. The duration of the offender's stay in hospital or prison, which might even be a life term, is always decided upon by the state governor. If the inmate responds positively to intense therapeutic treatment after a reasonable period of time, s/he may be recommended for discharge and placed in the care of relatives who will be responsible for her/his continued care.

Psychiatric/psychological examinations to diagnose mentally-ill offenders

Mentally-ill offenders have to undergo a series of examinations, to be carried out by a qualified psychiatrist, who has to prepare a comprehensive psychiatric assessment of the mental condition of the patient. In particular, the following aspects should be taken into consideration:

a) the detailed personal history of the offender, supplied by the offender her/himself and supplemented by relatives or a relevant third person;

b) circumstances of the offences as provided by the police and other witnesses;

c) in the absence of a qualified psychiatrist, a general physician carries out the examination to the best of her/his ability.

DANGEROUSNESS

Although there is no legal concept of dangerousness in Nigerian criminal law, in practice it is implied. For example, a frequent question posed by judges in cases of serious offences such as homicide, is whether the offender will commit the crime again. In fact, the term 'danger' only appears once in the Criminal Procedure Act, i.e. in Chapter 233 which deals with the 'procedure where a person of unsound mind is reported fit for discharge'. The relevant statement reads 'If the medical officer ... certifies that such a person, in her/his judgement, may be discharged without the danger of doing harm to her/himself or to others, the Governor may order that s/he be discharged or detained in custody...'.

No written criteria exist that determine the concept of dangerousness in relationship to the principle of strict legality and legal precision. This is because it is considered impossible to provide a legal definition of the determination of human behaviour - including the concept of dangerousness - in which so many factors come into play in a complex manner.

The usual approach of the psychiatrist with respect to the dangerousness of the patient is that, if the patient remains under the psychiatrist's supervision and, with the co-operation of relatives, takes the required medication regularly and responds positively to treatment - as is compulsory for most psychotic patients - the chances of the offender repeating a criminal action will be reduced.

Since the concept of 'dangerousness' is not legally recognised, all mentally-ill offenders are treated as non-offenders who have been certified and committed for treatment by the court, and are placed in appropriately secure facilities to prevent them from escaping. The emphasis is on the mental illness of the offender, and not on the legal status with respect to the crime. The treatment of dangerous mentally-ill offenders is also the same as that for all mentally-ill offenders, as described above.

PSYCHIATRIC EXAMINATION

The function of the psychiatric examination in the criminal justice procedure is to:

a) determine the fitness of the offender to plead to the charge or otherwise;

b) determine the criminal responsibility of the offender at the time of the commission of the offence;

c) recommend disposal options, the objective being to assist the court at reaching a just decision.

In the absence of a qualified psychiatrist, which is the normal praxis in Nigeria, a medical officer (who is usually a general practitioner), attached to a prison or an asylum, is called upon to give a report on the state of the mind of the accused.

Although no criminological examination is foreseen in the evaluation of mentally-ill offenders, a chemical test - i.e. a drug-induced abreaction - may be used if necessary. At present, there is no specific psychological test in use. However, an electroencephalogram (EEG) is used when indicated.

In Nigeria, expert psychiatric opinion is usually taken into consideration when a decision has to be made on the state of mental health of the offender. The opinion of a single expert is usually sufficient and the report of more than one expert on the part of both the defence and the prosecutor is rare.

SANCTIONS

Since the verdict regarding mentally-ill offenders can be 'unfit to plead or stand trial', 'not guilty by reason of insanity', or 'guilty but insane', the sanction provided in these cases is committal to a prison or confinement in a psychiatric hospital. In practice, however, the offenders are given psychiatric treatment, where available, just as they would receive treatment for any physical illness if this proved necessary.

If the accused show signs of improvement after treatment, one of the following measures may be applied: they may be sent back for trial if this had previously been postponed; they may be acquitted on the grounds of insanity and hence released; or they may be discharged by the governor under whose order they were detained, if the governor considers the report of the medical officer(s) satisfactory with respect to the state of mind of the accused. There is also provision that allows relatives and/or friends to request that the patient be placed in their care, on condition that the governor is completely satisfied about the security of the offender, and that the offender will be taken care of properly and prevented from doing injury to her/himself or to others. Furthermore, the relatives and/or friends must guarantee that the accused will appear for trial and inspection upon the requirement and order of the governor.

Role and function of the traditional criminal psychiatric hospitals in the Nigerian criminal justice system

There are no traditional criminal psychiatric hospitals as such in the Nigerian criminal justice system. The few psychiatric hospitals that do exist may have a more secure unit for the mentally-ill offender and other certified cases that may attempt to escape. If no psychiatric hospital is available, mentally-ill offenders are kept in prison where they are attended to by a visiting psychiatrist or the prison medical officer.

REFORMS

Plans for reforms related to the treatment of mentally-ill offenders in the criminal justice system do exist in Nigeria. In fact, the reform recommended by the Association of Psychiatrists in Nigeria deals with the Mental Health Act, and contains some measures dealing with the mentally-ill. The present law is old and obsolete, as can be seen from the description of the sanctions above, and the reform aims at bringing it up-to-date by taking into account modern treatment methods and the rehabilitation of the mentally-ill. It also aims to increase the recognition of the art and practice of psychiatry in the new law.

The status of the reform is still at the level of debate, with proposals being put forward by the various organisations concerned, such as psychiatrists, criminologists, prison officers, and so on. Reports from panels set up by the government to look into the question of prison conditions and mentally-ill offenders are also being prepared and made available for consideration.

LEGISLATIVE BIBLIOGRAPHY

Criminal Code, Chapter 77 of the 1990 Laws of Nigeria.

Criminal Procedure Act, Chapter 80 of the 1990 Laws of Nigeria.

Penal Code, Chapter 89 of the 1963 Laws of Northern Nigeria.

Criminal Procedure Code, Chapter 30 of the 1960 Laws of Northern Nigeria.

PERU
Victor Prado Saldarriaga*

INTRODUCTION

The following is a description of the main characteristics of the treatment that is applied to mentally-ill offenders by the Peruvian system of penal control. The empirical and statistical information in this national report was elaborated from archives of the Judicial Ward at the National Institute of Mental Health 'Victor Larco Herrera', which is the only centre in Peru dealing with the treatment of non-responsible offenders.

The new Penal Code and Penal Procedure of 1991 has brought about important changes in the law on the application of security measures for non-responsible individuals or individuals with diminished responsibility who show signs of dangerousness. The main problem with the treatment of the mentally-ill in Peru can be directly linked to the financial constraints of both the health and judicial sectors which, unfortunately, no government has bothered to improve for the last fifteen years. The result is that mentally-ill offenders have constantly been neglected by the Peruvian penal system, and have suffered most from the violation of human rights.

RESPONSIBILITY

Although national legislation has not provided any legal definition of responsibility, it has always indicated in which cases the author of a prosecutable act cannot be responsible for her/his act. In this respect, the Codes have simply stated that penal responsibility cannot be imposed upon any person who is incapable of understanding the

---

*   Professor of Penal Law and Criminal Policy, Major National University of San Marcos, Catholic Pontifical University of Peru, Lima, Peru. This report was prepared in March 1992.

criminal nature of an act, as well as being able to determine her/his conduct according to this comprehension. Moreover, the legal literature has been explicit about which types of psychological or psychopathological abnormalities can weaken an individual's capacity for comprehension and determination. Peruvian penal law has often considered mental psychosis, oligophrenia, and a deep alteration of the consciousness[1] as causes of non-responsibility.

The Penal Code of 1991 states in Article 20, paragraph 1 that: 'The following are exempt from penal responsibility: s/he who, due to psychological abnormality, deep alteration of the consciousness or perceptions and distortions that greatly alter her/his concept of reality, is incapable of understanding the criminal nature of her/his act or to intend according to this understanding'.

The formula that was implemented by the 1991 Code was a combination of the revoked Penal Code of 1924 (Article 85, paragraph 1), and the Draft Project of the Spanish Penal Code of 1983 (Article 22, paragraph 4).

Peruvian law is classified by the Doctrine as descriptive-normative. According to Hurtado, this implies that 'the decision (or judgement) as to whether the subject is responsible or not depends on the judge, on the basis of a concrete condition (resulting from scientific examinations)'[2]. It is to be pointed out, however, that the legal concept of responsibility is applied in every penal trial as a presumption *juris tantum* and can only be questioned on the basis of a psychiatric diagnosis. In this sense, the proposal made by the Supreme Court, in its judgement of 10 August 1981, appears to be coherent: 'Penal exemption cannot be based upon a mere possibility, but requires a certain, precise and evident causal factor. If this factor is not clearly indicated by either a medical certificate or by a previous scientific debate, a precise expert opinion must be expressed before the sentence can be passed'[3].

178

Diminished responsibility

The Codes of 1924 and 1991 do not specify in which cases the concept of diminished responsibility can be applied. Nevertheless, both codes refer to it as a condition of the offender which qualifies her/him for a mitigated sanction, as well as for the application of security measures in place of, or alongside the sanction[4]. The Code that is presently in force deals with the effects of diminished responsibility in the following articles:

(Article 21) In the cases mentioned in Article 20, whenever no requirements are necessary to completely remove responsibility, the judge can carefully reduce the sanction to a limit below the legal minimum.

(Article 76) Out-patient treatment will be diminished and applied to the defendant alongside the sanction whenever this is required for therapeutic or rehabilitative purposes.

The national Doctrine and Jurisprudence consider diminished responsibility to be applicable in the following cases: partial inebriation, pharmacodependency, preliminary symptoms of mental weakness and some manifestations of psychopathic personality such as acts of necrophilia[5].

As far as judicial rulings that qualify the defendant for diminished responsibility are concerned, the following can be cited[6]:

1) It is a mitigating circumstance to find the accused under the effect of alcohol when committing the offence (Supreme Court, 3 April 1951);

2) The sanction should be prudently reduced if, at the moment of a single act of homicide, the offender was suffering from an abnormal, pathological state of intoxication, with conscience worries and psychomotorial excitability, or was suffering from a slight mental weakness or a slight mental deficiency (Supreme Court, 4 April 1974).

3) A mitigated sanction must be applied to the perpetrator of an act of infanticide on a six-year old daughter if, following a psychiatric examination, the accused is defined as having an abnormal schizophrenic personality without being disturbed by any mental illness (Supreme Court, 18 July 1974).

The treatment of non-responsible offenders

Those individuals who have gone through trial and have been declared by the court as non-responsible are exempt from any sanction. If, however, they manifest any signs of dangerousness, the current penal law authorises the judge to apply a security measure, such as committal to a hospital or to specialised out-patient treatment. According to the medical personnel at the Larco Herrera Hospital, the criteria provided for by the 'IX Clasificaciòn Psiquiatrica de la OMS' (WHO IX InternationalPsychiatric Classification) must be adhered to when diagnosing the mental illness of the non-responsible offender.

Thus, the security measures are based upon the principles of necessity and proportionality, and cannot exceed the length of the sentence corresponding to the crime committed by the non-responsible offender. In fact, the following articles of the Penal Code of 1991 can be cited:

(Article 72) Security measures will be applied in the following circumstances:

1) when a person has committed an act which is considered an offence; and

2) when, considering both the character of the person and the offence committed, it is possible to predict a high likelihood of her/his committing other offences.

(Article 73) The security measures must be proportionate to the level of dangerousness of the offender, the seriousness of the crime committed and the likelihood of another offence being committed if no further treatment is received.

(Article 75) The duration of the medical treatment must not exceed the length of the corresponding custodial sentence that would have been applied for the offence. Every six months, and upon the request of the judge, the specialists of the in-patient treatment centre must submit the results of the medical examination related to the offenders so as to enable the judge to decide whether the factors leading to the application of the measure have disappeared. If this is the case, the judge will withdraw the imposed hospitalisation measure.

Yet, despite the significant and rational character of the above-mentioned norms, the non-responsible offender faces a very uncertain reality under the Peruvian penal justice system. First of all, given the lack of space in the only psychiatric hospital that treats 'judicial patients', those individuals that have been declared non-responsible remain in correctional institutions, where they are exposed to all kinds of risks without receiving any psychiatric treatment whatsoever.

Secondly, no judicial control is effected on those prisoners who are subjected to security measures. This results either in an indefinite extension of their stay in the hospital or in a lack of authorisation for those patients who have reached adequate levels of cure to receive out-patient treatment.

Thirdly, psychiatric reports related to those sentenced offenders showing symptoms that qualify them as being penally non-responsible, take a long time to be prepared and submitted to the court. This is the cause of the sad 'exhibition' of tried mentally-ill individuals waiting in the audience-chambers in deplorable conditions.

In conclusion, the facts show that the non-responsible offender is abused, and not cured, under the Peruvian penal system. What is even more serious is that the situation has become chronic, and no concrete measures of improvement have been proposed by the organisms of the penal system[7].

Penal treatment for particularly abnormal cases

This section describes the treatment which is applied, under the Peruvian penal system, to particular types of abnormal personality traits, neurotic disorders, borderline cases and cases of epilepsy. It should be pointed out that, in general, there is common agreement in both the legal and psychiatric-forensic doctrines of the country, that all the above-mentioned disorders, despite their origins or clinical manifestations, do not determine a loss of the sense of reality; as a result, the individual is penally responsible. In this case, it has been suggested by forensic psychiatrists that a thorough and detailed examination be carried out on those sentenced individuals who show psychopathic or neurotic traits or borderline cases associated with mental weakness or psychosis. Forensic science has also detected cases of neurosis with dissociative crises or consciousness disturbances. Offenders suffering from these disorders should receive the appropriate penal treatment, as is the case of dangerous offenders with diminished responsibility[8].

Peruvian jurisprudence is also quite explicit with regards to those abnormal personality traits which qualify an offender as being responsible for her/his actions. An example of a resolution of the Supreme Court[9] in this sense is:

> The murderer who has an antisocial, psychopathic personality and who therefore cannot be defined by forensic psychiatry as either mentally-sane or mentally-ill, does not fall into the sphere of non-responsibility, since s/he is responsible for her/his actions (Supreme Court, 5 May 1975).

As for 'borderline' cases, no previous data are available in the national judicial-psychiatric files, since this kind of patient is not included in the statistics of the Larco Herrera Hospital. However, according to the staff of the judicial sector of this hospital, borderline cases refer to those individuals who are responsible for their actions and must therefore be penally sanctioned for the crime committed. According to the staff: 'The criteria of the medical staff is that they should be confined, due mainly to the difficulty in controlling the

182

instability and aggressiveness of this type of patient, as well as a lack of sufficient staff and equipment'[10].

With respect to cerebral syndromes, including disturbances of conscious perception or epilepsy, Peruvian forensic psychiatry and jurisprudence have paid particular attention to cases of personality disorders that are characterised by impulsiveness. In these cases, as Gutierrez Ferreira aptly stresses, 'patients are driven by powerful forces which cause them to behave abnormally, commit crimes with the precision of a bright individual and with the unconsciousness of a sleepwalker'. This is called a 'crepuscular state of consciousness', whereby the mentally-ill individual remains in a state of total or almost total amnesia with respect to what has happened. This particular mental state is oriented and coherent, but there are also other forms of mental disorder whereby the patient might suffer from hallucinations, strong disorientation or perplexity, act as a typical psychotic or remain mentally absent for a few hours or for several days'[11]. Although this kind of epileptic criminality has normally qualified the offender for diminished responsibility, nevertheless, in some decisions these cases can be considered as reasons for penal non-responsibility: 'The length of the sentence for perpetrators of crimes such as infanticide or homicide must be reduced if a psychiatric report or a psychological and electroencephalographic examination show that previous cases of epilepsy have existed in the family, that the offender has also suffered from such attacks, that s/he is only partially oriented, exhibits a negative relationship between her/his natural impulses and intellect, presents certain paranoid traits, has a very low intellectual level, and has such a weak *ego* as to make her/him irresponsible for her/his actions, since all these factors qualify the person as having diminished responsibility' (Supreme Court, 21 August 1974). 'The accused mentally-ill offender who suffers from epileptic psychosis which prevents her/him from recognising the criminal nature of her/his acts, and thus from making decisions according to this understanding, is not responsible; nevertheless, since s/he shows signs of dangerousness, s/he must be confined in a hospital in the name of public safety' (Supreme Court, 5 May 1975)[12].

DANGEROUSNESS

Both the Penal Codes of 1924 and 1991 have related non-responsibility to a post-crime diagnosis of dangerousness. Furthermore, as many penal codes in Latin America have been profoundly influenced by 'Italian Positivism', that of 1924 indicated 'social dangerousness' as a criterion which justified a sanction proportionate to the level of guilt.

For example, the meaning and function of Article 83 in the repealed Code clearly stated that: 'The perpetrator of an unintentional or unpunishable offence will nevertheless be remanded if s/he is expressly judged according to the law as being socially dangerous, although the penal sanction will be substituted by the most appropriate security measure determined by law'. With reference to this provision, Hurtado Pozo declared that 'it does not include, however, the principle of social responsibility provided for by Article 18 of the Italian Project of 1921. In fact, it is a kind of guiltless responsibility on the part of non-responsible dangerous individuals'. As is expressly demonstrated by the application of the sanction related to responsibility and guilt in Articles 51, 81, 82 and 85, Annex 1, the legislator has simply pointed out in Article 83 that the state of dangerousness provides a basis for the application of some kind of security and preventive measure[13].

The Penal Code of 1991 ratified dangerousness as a determining factor for the judicial application of security measures to non-responsible perpetrators of crime. In particular, Article 72, paragraph 2 refers to the prognosis of dangerousness in the following terms: 'That from the personality of the perpetrator and the act committed, it is possible to prognose a high likelihood that s/he will commit other offences'. On the other hand, Article 73 states that the criminal dangerousness of the perpetrator also constitutes an indicator for the proportional application of security measures. In any case, the law does not provide a precise definition of the indicators of dangerousness and, consequently, an ambiguous normative notion is created that has an effect upon the principle of legality.

It must be pointed out that the new legal concept of dangerousness has been taken from the Preliminary Project of the Spanish Penal Code of 1983[14]. Therefore, given the short period of enforcement of the 1991 Penal Code, it has not been possible for the national Doctrine and Jurisprudence to provide concrete suggestions regarding the interpretation of both the legal concept of dangerousness and the acts and circumstances that must be considered when making a prognosis and reaching a decision. However, the following criteria for interpretation can be deduced from the normative text:

1) The concept of dangerousness must be prognosed on the basis of the type of crime committed, the conditions under which it was committed and a psychological evaluation of the perpetrator of the crime;

2) the declaration of dangerousness acts as a prognosis that the author will commit other offences;

3) the prognosis of dangerousness is a judicial decision, but must be based upon the results of the tests carried out on the offender by the experts.

The legislation (Article 116 of the 1924 Penal Code) and jurisprudence have traditionally considered the recidivist and chronic character of the offence as indicators of dangerousness, although such criteria have only been applied to responsible offenders and cannot therefore be incorporated by the norms on dangerousness included in the new Peruvian Penal Code[15].

Medical-legal aspects

The psychological and/or psychiatric evaluations that lead to an indication of dangerousness of the offender are based upon the crime committed by the offender, her/his background, past psychological or psychiatric records, level of integration in her/his social environment, etc. What mainly concerns the scientific experts are the results related to the individual's affectivity. The affective disorders of the examined person are normally used to associate her/his condition with the prognosis of future criminal dangerousness. As an example, the medical-legal conclusions of a psychiatric examination conducted on the perpetrator of an assault can be used, which showed the presence of a chronic cerebral syndrome, dysthymia and paranoia[16].

From the precedents of, and examinations carried out on the offender, it can be concluded that:

a) The patient suffers from a chronic cerebral syndrome that seriously compromises his affectivity - aggressiveness and violent dysthymia - and produces an antisocial, disordered effect on his mental capacity, paranoid ideas that cause him to temporarily lose his sense of reality and a marked lack of intelligence and learning ability;

b) if the assault was committed under the mental condition outlined in the above paragraph, in our opinion, this mitigates his responsibility since we have to accept the fact that his dysthymia cannot be controlled, and the attacks of paranoia temporarily cause him to lose his sense of reality, despite the fact that he may not be psychotic or alienated according to the real sense of the word;

c) on the other hand, the disorders that affect him are of a cerebral etiopathogenic origin for which no scientific cure seems to exist at present; the drugs that can be administered to him can only partially control his dysthymic disorders and convulsive crises, and must be taken throughout the whole of his life and under the control of specialised doctors;

d) we suggest that the investigating judge should, for security reasons, order the patient's confinement in a mental hospital in order to prevent him from committing other more serious offences.

According to the clinical praxis of the Judicial Psychiatric Service of the Larco Herrera Hospital, the evaluation procedure is as follows: 'The psychological and psychiatric evaluations, which lead to the conclusion that a psychiatric patient is dangerous, are always based on both the diagnosis and the crime committed, as well as on the description provided by the patient or the patient's family and other institutions. The tests themselves only help to orientate auxiliary examinations, as the interviews and the medical examinations might be more precise'[17].

The treatment of dangerous mentally-ill offenders

The material limitations of the Judicial Psychiatric Service greatly restrict the therapeutic effects of the treatment received by the dangerous non-responsible offenders, and operates more as a disciplinary measure, or to maintain order within the prisoners' ward. The staff mentioned that 'In the experience of the Service, the hospitalised offenders who are considered to be dangerous are treated by means of group psychotherapy, where they are informed of the kind of relationship existing between each member and the limitations of the Service, after which they are left to create their own rules which must, however, be adhered to. The dangerous inmates have then always created small power groups. It should also be pointed out that those patients who are "dangerous" and suffer from cerebral organic syndromes are administered pharmacological medication, which usually produces positive results'[18].

PSYCHIATRIC EXAMINATION

Legal framework

Although the psychiatric evaluation generally takes place during the preliminary stage of the trial, it can be requested by the judge, prosecutor general or defence attorney during any phase of the penal process. With respect to the cases for, and results of the psychiatric tests, Article 93 of the Penal Code of 1924 stated that:

The judge or the court dealing with the case can request an expert examination to be carried out on the non-responsible offender with an unstable mental condition, and in all cases related to epileptic or deaf-mute individuals. The experts will report on the mental condition of the offender and express their opinion as to whether s/he should be confined in a hospital or institution, and/or whether s/he represents a danger to the public and to public order.

Article 189 of the 1940 Code of Penal Procedure stated that:

> Whenever there is a suspicion that the responsible offender suffers from a mental illness or other pathological disorder that might affect her/his responsibility, the investigating judge, an official, the defendant or prosecuting agent, will request this to be confirmed by means of a psychiatric examination to be carried out by two psychiatric experts. The defendant or the prosecuting agent can also nominate the expert. The judge will then order that the responsible offender undergoes the examination.

The Penal Procedural Code promulgated in 1991 has included similar norms on psychiatric evaluation in Articles 71 and 72. This has resulted in the identification of a distinct set of regulations on both the psychiatric evaluations and on the experts who carry them out. The most important of these are the 'Regulation of Psychiatric Experts' of 11 August 1939 and the 'Regulation of Law No. 11272 on Mental Hygiene' of 14 October 1952. According to the latter, in order to become a Medical Assistant of the Psychiatric Service, the candidate must possess the following requisites:

a) Peruvian citizenship;

b) valid qualifications to carry out this type of professional activity within the country;

c) a vocation for this specialisation.

The criminological examination

The psychiatric evaluation requested by the judicial authority takes a long time to be applied to the mentally-ill offender. The results of these evaluations are also usually presented to the judge and the court with considerable delay. These dysfunctions, that condition the effectiveness and utility of the psychiatric reports in a penal trial, are justified by the responsible agencies (i.e. the Institute of Forensic

Medicine or the Larco Herrera Hospital) as being caused by the lack of medical and psychiatric personnel.

In Peru, it usually takes 45 days for the psychiatric report to be completed and delivered to the judicial body. During this time, the mentally-ill offender under examination is temporarily moved from prison on two or three occasions, in order to be sent to the psychiatric hospital.

As Gutierrez Ferreira states, in Peru, the psychiatric report is presented in the form of a 'psychiatric-clinical history' of the patient[19]. In addition, the psychological examination is completed by a report, a psychopathological examination and, depending on the case, one or more auxiliary examinations (such as the electroencephalogram, mental tests, etc.). It is essential for the report to provide a clear prognostic and categorical forensic conclusion and it is at this point that the function of the psychiatric report meets its main drawback in the Peruvian penal trial. According to Articles 190 and 191 of the 1940 Penal Code, only if the judge is convinced of the existence of a mental illness, based on the conclusions provided by the medical report, can the custody of the mentally-ill offender in a psychiatric hospital be decided upon[20]. However, many judicial resolutions accuse the psychiatric reports of being ambiguous, incomplete and unhelpful in determining the judicial decision. Examples of these resolutions include[21]:

1) If the examinations provide very general prognoses and are not in conformity with Article 189 of the Code of Penal Procedures, which establishes that an examination of the accused person by two psychiatric experts must be requested if there is a suspicion that the individual is mentally deranged, both the sentence and all decisions taken during the oral session are annulled (Supreme Court, 10 February 1984).

2) If the forensic reports provide an inadequate description of the mental condition of the accused, the latter must undergo another examination since it is impossible to define whether

s/he is responsible or not for her/his actions (Supreme Court, 3 January 1961).

3) If the mental state of the accused is not sufficiently determined, s/he can be neither sentenced nor obliged to pay civil damages once her/his custody in the Larco Herrera mental asylum has been requested (Supreme Court, 16 April 1936).

4) The exemption of a sanction cannot be based upon a mere possibility, but requires a certain, precise and clear cause. If this is not evident from either the medical certificate or the medical examination, a precise declaration on the part of the expert is necessary (Supreme Court, 10 August 1961).

Thus, according to the doctors in charge of the judicial psychiatric ward of the Larco Herrera Hospital, the conclusions and recommendations contained in the psychiatric reports are not taken into consideration by the judicial authorities. According to them: 'The psychiatric evaluations include both the psychiatric reports and the examinations related to the progress of the patients who are already hospitalised'.

The aims of these evaluations are to provide a medical classification for those people who have committed an offence and show signs of mental disorder, and also to inform the judicial authority of the progress of out-patients. It should be mentioned that the role of the psychiatric evaluations does not match their function, since the judicial authority does not generally take their suggestions into consideration[22].

In Peru, psychiatric reports usually have the following structure and content:

- *Personal description and circumstances of the examination*

This identifies the individual under examination and refers to the reasons, conditions and place of the examination as well as to aspects related to the evaluation.

- *Precedents and interviews*

  Both the precedents and the psychopathological data (past and present illnesses) of the examined person, as well as interviews with her/him, are registered by indicating her/his precise responses and attitudes to the questions posed.

- *Actual clinical examinations*

  The results of the general clinical, somatic, neurological, psychological and psychiatric examinations are presented under this item.

- *Diagnostic and auxiliary examinations*

  These examinations provide a summary of the remarks and diagnoses of the examined patient's mental condition. Reference is also made to the results obtained from the auxiliary tests when these are relevant to the suggested diagnosis.

- *Legal-medical conclusions*

  These refer to the relationship between the psychiatric diagnosis and the penal responsibility of the patient; in other words, whether the patient was able to understand the criminal character of the act and make decisions on the basis of this understanding. A prediction of the individual's likelihood of committing another offence is also provided.

Then, as claimed by the doctors at the Judicial-Psychiatric Service of the Larco Herrera Hospital: 'No special criminal evaluations are included in the psychiatric evaluations conducted on judicial patients, although these are affected by the clinical history and the psychological evaluation'[23].

SANCTIONS

As already mentioned, security measures are only applied to non-responsible offenders or to offenders with diminished responsibility, when there is a risk of their committing other offences. The 1991 Penal Code provides for two types of security measures: recovery and out-patient treatment. Articles 74 to 76 define the characteristics of each of these measures as follows:

(Article 74) Recovery consists in the irresponsible offender being recovered and treated, for therapeutic or custodial reasons, in a medical institution or other appropriate establishment. Recovery can only be imposed when there is a risk of the offender committing other offences.

(Article 75) The duration of the measure of security cannot exceed the length of the equivalent custodial sentence that is foreseen for the act committed.

Every six months, and subject to the judge's request, the specialists of the centre must provide the judge with a medical report which will enable her/him to establish whether the causes for applying the medical measures no longer persist. Should this be the case, the judge will order the suspension of the hospitalisation.

(Article 76) Out-patient treatment will be established and applied alongside the sentence whenever this is requested by the offender for therapeutic or rehabilitative reasons.

Therefore, the new Penal Code adopts a vicarial court model in its application of both penal and medical measures. In practice, whenever the law establishes that measures of recovery have to be applied to either a non-responsible offender or to an offender with diminished responsibility, this must be carried out before the penal sanction, and the length of the recovery must be deduced from the total length of the custodial sentence. However, Article 77 established that the judge may reduce or drop the sanction if the security measures produce positive results.

It should be pointed out that the rules related to security measures contained in the current Penal Code have been elaborated along the guidelines of the 1984 Brazilian Penal Code (Articles 96 to 98) and the Spanish Draft Outline (Articles 87 to 89). Nevertheless, the Peruvian Code does not include norms that deal specifically with the application of security measures. It should be understood, however, that all matters related to the application of these measures are influenced by the decisions of the psychiatric division to whom the mentally-ill individual has been assigned by the judicial authority. In this sense, the norms under Chapter III of the Regulations of Law No. 11272 on Mental Hygiene must be taken into consideration, particularly Articles 33 and 38 which deal with 'mentally-ill individuals who are subordinate to judicial power'. According to Article 37 of the above regulation: 'The medical director of the establishment or the chief medical officer of the specific sector must keep the judicial authority regularly informed about the treatment being administered to the patient'.

Problems of application

The lack of norms related to the application of the security measure, as well as the serious infrastructural weaknesses of the state's health and penal system, have almost always resulted in the mental patients not being treated in specialised hospitals or centres, as ordered by the judicial authorities. Instead, they often find themselves under a sporadic and disorderly form of medical control in the correctional facilities. According to the latest official penitential census, in Peruvian prisons, mentally-ill offenders rank second among the total prison population: 'According to available data, gastroenteritis and tuberculosis represent the major form of illness, i.e. 7 per cent of the nation's prison population. These are followed by mentally-ill individuals (suffering from nervous illnesses, schizophrenia, mental retardation, etc.) which accounts for 3 per cent. Patients suffering from skin and infectious diseases come third with 2 per cent of the prison population and, lastly, patients with venereal diseases which represent 1 per cent of the entire prison population'[24]. The above-mentioned census stated that of a total penal population of 14 891 prisoners, 426 were mentally-ill[25].

During discussions with the staff of the prisoners' ward in the Larco Herrera Hospital, it was explained that the presence of mentally-ill, non-responsible offenders in prisons was mainly due to poor estimates and a lack of co-ordination between the Ministry of Health and the National Penitentiary. In this respect, it was mentioned that neither the Ministry of Health nor the Ministry of Justice, and least of all the National Penitentiary, had attempted to improve the state of neglect in the prisoners' ward at this hospital. As a result, it was possible to recover only a very limited number of mentally-ill offenders in the ward, and this led to the creation of a long waiting list of some 150 incarcerated patients, who were waiting for a bed and some attention in the psychiatric prisoners' ward.

The neglect of the mentally-ill in the prison centres led to the Supreme Court's Resolution No. 155-81-JUS of 15 December 1981. The Resolution authorised the mentally-ill inmates of the Lurigancho Prison to be put under the care of their closest relatives, who then became responsible for their treatment. Article 2 of the above-mentioned Resolution stated that: 'Before such an assignment can be approved, a psychiatric examination is necessary which confirms the non-aggressiveness of the non-responsible offender, as well as an analysis which determines the ability of the family to take care of the individual'. In fact, it should be pointed out that 32 inmates were immediately assigned to their families following this Resolution. Similar measures are no longer applied, although the condition of the mentally-ill in Peruvian prisons remains critical.

Treatment of mentally-ill offenders[26]

The following description of the treatment of mentally-ill offenders in Peru is based on a report on the treatment afforded to completely non-responsible offenders at the Larco Herrera Hospital.

The Larco Herrera Hospital came into operation in 1918 under the direction of Hermilio Valdizan. New wards have since been added to the hospital, according to the financial funds and types of illnesses to be treated. Ward No. 16 was built in the 1930s, under the auspices of the Ladies' Patronage, which provided all the necessary support to ensure that the mentally-ill offenders were placed in an environment that was compatible with their treatment and also guaranteed the necessary custody and security.

During the last decades, the above-mentioned ward has received numerous mentally-ill offenders from all parts of the Republic. This is still the case today, and is one of the factors that have made it impossible for the inmates to receive adequate treatment. It has also led to many responsible criminals using the excuse of a mental illness to apply for penal exemptions, and has created chaos and threatened the safety of the real patients in the hospital. In addition, it has worsened the negative social reputation of this class of patients and their treatment.

The current situation

At the moment, out of a total of 600 patients, 31 have been recovered in the hospital by judicial order. Although the hospital can host up to 1 200 patients, only a small number of patients are actually recovered due to lack of funds and staff. Of these, 30 patients are recovered in the above-mentioned Ward 16, the only female patient being recovered in another ward.

The 31 patients were evaluated according to their mental condition and were divided into 9 large categories of illnesses. However, such groups should not be considered as representing clear-cut conditions but, on the contrary, are more precisely defined by nuances and within the clinical field. These patients are all recovered for crimes classified under the Penal Code of 1924 and upon the authorisation of the courts of justice and courts. It should be pointed out that the hospital is only equipped to accept 31 patients at a time and that, at present, there is a waiting list of approximately 120 people waiting for treatment in the different penal centres of the country (Figures 1 and 2).

Once the non-responsible individual is recovered in the ward, a diagnostic evaluation is made to confirm and define her/his mental illness. To avoid the recurrence of past cases of erroneous evaluations, the classification recommended by the WHO (IX International Psychiatric Classification) is used. Upon the completion of the provisional diagnostic examination, the patient is placed under observation and provided with provisional treatment for a certain length of time. At the end of this period, a final diagnosis is made to confirm the illness, as well as a prognosis of the likely evolution and temporary improvements resulting from the recovery. The aim of the treatment is to rehabilitate the patient or at least to prevent the illness from becoming worse.

The staff in charge of the treatment of the non-responsible patients is classified as follows: 1 psychiatrist, 1 psychologist, 1 case worker, 2 nurses, 7 assistant nurses, 1 nutritional assistant. It should be pointed out that a permanent psychiatrist has recently been assigned to the judicial ward, whereas previously the patients were treated by the doctors of other wards on a shift basis.

The treatment is divided into 2 stages: a) recovery; and b) successive out-patient treatment that is not legally framed. The first stage consists of 3 phases:

a) pharmacological treatment;

b) internal rehabilitation by taking part in special activities;

c) family therapy for social reintegration.

The second stage, on the other hand, provides for socialisation by:

a) role adaptation;

b) progressive rehabilitation through participation in everyday activities; and

c) pharmacological treatment.

In both stages, most of the therapy, apart from the pharmacological treatment, is directed towards the reaffirmation or creation of those values that characterise the environment to which the patient will return upon leaving hospital. Therefore, the treatment should be essential and subject to the prescription, and should teach the patient's family how to recognise symptoms of behavioural modifications (for example, in cases of alterations of relatively aggressive impulses).

It should be noted that legal norms have produced a negative effect in this area. This is witnessed by the compulsory recovery of non-responsible offenders when it would have been preferable for them to be treated by a psychiatrist, since recovery might have worsened the illness and, in any case, does not improve the condition of the patient.

This negative influence is even stronger in the operative field, where, according to present legislation, irresponsible offenders:

a) must first go through the penal system with the risk of their pathological character becoming even more acute;

b) must receive permission from the competent judicial region before being admitted or discharged from the hospital. This often causes administrative delays, leading to greater confusion for both the patient and the hospital, considering the above-mentioned waiting list.

In fact, most of the criticism related to the distorted legal system implemented by the 1924 Penal Code comes from the medical personnel.

Administrative laws

The Larco Herrera Hospital belongs to the health sector and is not part of the 'special facilities' referred to by the Code of Penal Execution. It depends on funds from the National Penitentiary (a decentralised organ of the Ministry of Justice), which, however, only provides financial assistance for the treatment of 5 psychiatric patients. Although recent attempts have been made to improve the co-ordination between the hospital and the National Penitiantial Institute, as well as the level of funding, they have not proved very successful.

STATISTICS

Figures 1 and 2 and Table 1 provide statistics on the types of illness and offence committed by the patients recovered by judicial order in the Larco Herrera Hospital.

Figure 1: Classification of patients recovered by judicial order in the Larco Herrera Hospital, according to mental illness

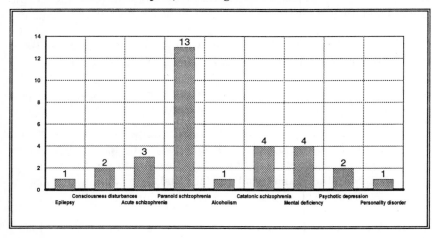

Figure 2: Classification of patients recovered by judicial order in the Larco Herrera Hospital, according to offence committed

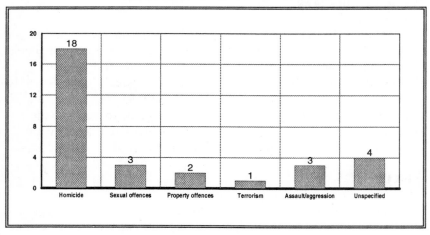

Table 1: Classification of patients recovered by judicial order in the Larco Herrera Hospital, according to offence committed and type of mental illness

Type of offence committed	Mental illness of the patient
Rape	Consciousness disturbance
Assault	Acute schizophrenia
Assault	Residual schizophrenia
Rape	Slight mental deficiency
Homicide	Paranoid schizophrenia
Unspecified	Residual schizophrenia
Assault	Alcoholism
Theft	Acute schizophrenia
Theft	Catatonic schizophrenia
Homicide	Personality disorder
Homicide	Serious mental deficiency
Unspecified	Simple schizophrenia
Homicide	Paranoid shizophrenia
Theft	Personality disorder
Homicide	Paranoid schizophrenia
Homicide	Catatonic schizophrenia
Parricide	Paranoid schizophrenia
Assault	'Hebefuridic' schizophrenia
Parricide/Assault	Paranoid schizophrenia
Rape	Psychosis associated with mental deficiency
Homicide	Paranoid schizophrenia
Assault	Personality disorder
Homicide	Mental deficiency
Homicide	Paranoid schizophrenia
Homicide	Psychotic depression
Rape	Paranoid schizophrenia
Homicide	Paranoid schizophrenia
Terrorism	Depression
Homicide	Paranoid schizophrenia

REFERENCES

1   Article 13 of the 1836 Penal Code of Peru, paragraph 2; Article 8 of the 1863 Penal Code, paragraph 1; Article 85 of the 1924 Penal Code, paragraph 1.

2   J Hurtado Pozo, *Manual of Penal Law - General Part*, Sasator, Lima, 1978, p. 265.

3   J Espino Pérez, *Penal Code*, Cultural Cuzco, Lima, 1988, fifth edition, p. 103.

4   Articles 90, 91 and 94 of the Peruvian Penal Code.

5   J Hurtado Pozo, 1978, *op. cit.*, pp. 273 and 274.

6   J Espino Pérez, 1988, *op.cit.*, pp. 110 and 111.

7   M Macedo describes the critical situation of mentally-ill offenders in her realistic report 'El Mundo de la sin razón: setenta y dos horas en el Larco Herrera', published in the supplement 'Domingo' of the *Diario La República*, 18 November 1990, pp. 13-16.

8   C Gutierrez Ferreira, *Forensic Psychiatry*, EDDILI, Lima, 1986, p. 69.

9   J Espino Pérez, 1988, *op.cit.*, p.102.

10 Interview made to the medical staff of the Judicial Psychiatric Service of the National Victor Larco Herrera Hospital, in October 1991.

11 C Gutierrez Ferreira, 1986, *op.cit.*, p. 56.

12 J Espino Pérez, 1988, *op.cit.*, pp. 102 and 111.

13 J Hurtado Pozo, 1978, *op.cit.*, p. 55.

14 See Article 87.2 of the draft version of the 1983 Spanish Penal Code.

15 J Espino Pérez, 1988, *op.cit.*, p. 139.

16 C Gutierrez Ferreira, 1986, *op.cit.*, p. 145.

17 Cited interview.

18 *ibid.*

19 C Gutierrez Ferreira, 1986, *op.cit.*, p. 113.

20 Article 190 states that: 'If the investigating judge, following the conclusions of the mental expert, is convinced that the accused person does not have a mental disorder,......'; Article 191: 'If, on the contrary, the investigating judge is persuaded that the accused person is suffering from a mental disorder, prior to the opinion of the revenue officer, s/he will order her/his recovery in a mental home, and will transfer the case to the court of justice which will then take a final decision on the case.

21 Extract from Julio Espino Pérez, 1988, *op.cit.*, pp. 103, 112 and 113.

22 Cited interview.

23 *ibid.*

24 National Penitential Institute, *The National Penitential Census of 7 April 1986 - Final Results*, INE, Lima, 1986, p. 112.

25 *ibid*, Note No. 22, p. 92.

26 Based on a report of treatment of mentally-ill offenders at the Victor Larco Herrera Hospital, which was elaborated in November 1991 with the valid contribution of Moises Martinez (student) and thanks to the support and assistance of the medical personnel of the Victor Larco Herrera Hospital.

SWEDEN

Anita Werner*

INTRODUCTION

Swedish legislation on mentally-ill offenders was recently reformed by the new rules which came into force at the beginning of 1992. The main purpose of the reform was to modernise psychiatric terminology. The former definition in the Swedish Penal Code was 'mental disease, feeblemindedness or other mental abnormality of so profound a nature, that it must be considered equivalent to mental disease'. This definition has now been replaced by the term 'grave mental disorder', in accordance with the new Compulsory Mental Care Act. This Act now allows for greater differentiation in initiating new restrictions for discharge and to moderate psychiatric examinations.

RESPONSIBILITY

In principle, there is no distinction in the Swedish criminal justice system between responsibility and non-responsibility. This distinction was abandoned when the present Penal Code came into force in 1965. However, the difference between the legislation before and after 1965 is of greater significance from a theoretical, rather than a practical point of view. For example, without using the concept of non-responsibility, the law states that an offender who is found guilty of committing a crime while suffering from a grave mental disorder cannot be sentenced to imprisonment. If no other sanction is adequate, s/he will not be punished.

The criminal justice system does, however, adopt the concept of 'diminished responsibility' in that the law states that if the offenders'

---

*   The Supreme Social Insurance Court, Stockholm, Sweden. This report was prepared in April 1992.

ability to control their behaviour has diminished, due to a mental disorder or similar reason, this should be regarded as extenuating circumstances.

Offenders who are deemed non-responsible and cannot, therefore, be sentenced to imprisonment can, however, be sentenced to any other sanction in the Penal Law. There is a special sanction for mentally-disordered offenders, which is committal to forensic psychiatric care. This sanction is applicable if, at the time of the trial, the offender is suffering from a grave mental disorder and, taking into consideration her/his mental and physical condition, it is required that s/he be admitted to a psychiatric institution, where s/he will be treated but will also be deprived of liberty and be subjected to other constraining measures.

Up to the present date, borderline personalities have been regarded as psychotic and, as such, no special consideration has been given to this type of personality. Nor are any specific methods of psychiatric and psychological examinations used to diagnose this kind of patient, since, generally speaking, forensic psychiatrists regard the diagnosis of borderline cases as doubtful.

The Swedish criminal justice system deals with various types of mental illness in different ways. For example, victims who have been suffering, for a long period of time, from a grave neurosis are classified as suffering from a grave mental disorder and are not usually imprisoned. Acute depression, especially if it might lead to suicide, is also regarded as a grave mental disorder, as is the so-called irresistible impulse of a psychotic nature. Psychopathic disorder, on the other hand, is seldom used as a diagnosis, the usual conception of personality disorder being a disturbed character or likewise. If there is no other diagnosis, the offender should not receive any special treatment according to the law.

DANGEROUSNESS

Although, in principle, the concept of dangerousness is not envisaged by the Swedish criminal justice system, it does in fact exist with respect to parole. Offenders who are sentenced to imprisonment are normally parolled after having served half of their prison term. However, if the term of imprisonment is fixed at more than two years, the offenders are not released on discretionary parole until they have served two-thirds of the prison term. If, on the other hand, the crime is serious and directed against, or involves a threat to life or health of a person, and if there is a clear risk of the offender repeating the crime after release, the question of release is investigated by a special correctional board. This rule normally applies to people convicted of violent or drug-related crimes.

For mentally-ill offenders who are committed into psychiatric care, when passing sentence, the court may prescribe that the question of discharge from the institute be investigated by the county administrative court, provided that the crime was committed under the influence of a grave mental disorder, and that there is a risk that, given her/his mental condition, the offender may relapse into serious criminality.

Although dangerousness is not normally used as a diagnosis, according to the rules, it must be given careful consideration in relation to the discharge of an offender. If the offender has repeatedly committed acts of violence, s/he will normally be characterised as 'dangerous' during the mental examination.

PSYCHIATRIC EXAMINATIONS

Two types of mental examinations exist in the Swedish criminal justice procedure. One comparatively short mental examination, called 'the paragraph 7 examination' (which receives its name from paragraph 7 of the Law on Personality Investigation in Criminal Cases, in which it appears), comprises a complete mental examination in accordance with the Law on Forensic Psychiatric Examinations. A 'paragraph 7 examination' can be ordered by the court in any criminal case; it is sufficient to commit an offender into forensic psychiatric care without any special restrictions for her/his discharge.

A complete mental examination can be ordered for the purpose of discovering: a) if there are any medical reasons for committing the offender into forensic psychiatric care; or b) if the offender was under the influence of a grave mental disturbance at the moment of the commission of the offence.

In the first case, the court order should also reveal whether the examination should include the prerequisites for special restrictions for discharge. In this case, a complete mental examination is compulsory. If, however, at the time of the trial, the offender is already being treated in an institution for forensic psychiatric care and with special restrictions on discharge, a report prepared by the chief psychiatrist of that institution will suffice. This also applies if the offender, without such a prescription, is treated in accordance with the Law on Forensic Psychiatric Treatment or the administrative Compulsory Mental Care Act.

The length of the mental examination thus depends on the court order. It should be carried out as rapidly as possible, and should not exceed four weeks if the offender is in custody, and six weeks in other cases. A complete mental examination can only be ordered if the offender has confessed to the crime or if it has been proved beyond doubt that s/he has committed it.

A criminological examination is also envisaged by the criminal justice procedure and consists of an investigation into the social life and background of the offender, including her/his criminal record and an analysis by the social worker. As a general rule, psychological tests are also used to determine the mental state of the offender and are carried out by a psychologist. They include an IQ test, a test for detecting a possible lesion of the brain, and a personality test (for example the Rorschach Test). The mental examination report is always signed by the psychiatrist, but the complete examination always involves a team which includes a psychiatrist, a psychologist, a social worker, the offender's personal contacts, and the nursing staff.

The final decision on the responsibility and dangerousness of the offender rests with the court, irrespective of the conclusions or recommendations made by the psychiatrists. Nevertheless, it is extremely difficult for the court to go against the results of an examination as far as the mental condition of the offender is concerned. If the court has any doubts on the results of the examination or on the report from an institution, it can refer to the National Board of Health and Welfare for advice. However, this has only occurred on rare occasions.

SANCTIONS

As mentioned at the beginning of this report, an offender who has committed a crime while under the influence of a grave mental disorder cannot be sentenced to imprisonment, although s/he can be considered for any other sanction. If the offender is in need of psychiatric care, the medical authorities will decide into which institution s/he should be committed. This procedure also applies in other cases; for example, if there is no clear causal connection between the crime committed and the mental disorder, and yet it appears obvious that the offender is suffering from a grave mental disorder and is in need of psychiatric care, then committal to a psychiatric hospital is considered to be an adequate sanction. As was also already mentioned earlier in the report, special measures are prescribed by the court with regard to the release of the offender.

Apart from committal to forensic psychiatric care, no other special sanctions are designed for mentally-disordered offenders. Nevertheless, it is taken for granted that offenders who are sentenced to traditional criminal sanctions will be provided with the necessary physical or psychiatric treatment, either on a temporary basis while within the prison, or for shorter or longer periods in a psychiatric hospital.

It should be mentioned, that in cases when it is obvious that the offender is mentally-ill and is committed to an appropriate institution and there is no public or private interest in taking the case to court, the prosecutor can decide not to prosecute.

Some prisons have special psychiatric departments for the temporary care of prisoners. Apart from this, Sweden has no so-called 'criminal hospitals' in that all hospitals are administered by the general health service system. In effect, however, some hospitals - or rather, hospital departments - are reserved for criminal patients who are in need of special treatment or special security measures.

Criminal patients who do not have special restrictions are discharged when the chief psychiatrist considers that the patient no longer suffers from a grave mental disorder or when the patient's mental and physical condition no longer requires her/him to be kept in an institution. If the treatment continues for more than 4 months, the doctors must apply to the administrative court to detain the patient for a further period of time, which can be prolonged for a period of 6 months at a time. If the patient has special restrictions for discharge, then the administrative court should decide when there is no longer a risk that the patient, because of her/his mental illness, will relapse into criminality and that it is no longer helpful to keep the the offender in an institution.

REFORMS

Plans for reform in the Swedish criminal justice system refer to changing the general rules concerning parole. The reform envisages the entitlement of the offender to parole after serving half of the sentence. No new reforms are planned, however, as far as mentally-ill offenders are concerned.

STATISTICS

Since the new legislation has only recently come into force, the statistics are not really relevant. It is expected that the number of offenders committed to psychiatric care will be reduced; in 1990, 322 offenders were committed into psychiatric care and 15 527 were sentenced to imprisonment; a total of 37 164 persons were sentenced to sanctions other than fines.

THAILAND
*Thamrong Dasananjali**

RESPONSIBILITY

The Criminal Code of Thailand (BE 2500) clearly distinguishes between the concepts of responsibility and non-responsibility. Hence, according to Section 65:

Whenever a person commits an offence, and at the time of committing the offence is unable to appreciate the nature or illegality of the act, or is unable to control her/himself on account of a deficient mind, mental disease or mental infirmity, such an individual shall not be punished for the offence committed. If, on the other hand, the offender is partially able to appreciate the nature of her/his act and to partially control her/himself, s/he will be punished, but the court may inflict a lesser punishment than that provided by the law for such an offence.

In order to apply the above criteria, however, it must first be ascertained whether the offender is suffering from a mental illness or not. Unfortunately, no precise definition of the terms cited in Section 65 exist and, despite the attempts of many psychiatrists to provide a complete definition of these terms, no consensus has yet been reached on the matter.

For example, in previous works, the author of this report has described *Chit Brokprong* (Thai for incomplete state of mind) as a mental deficiency or mental retardation and *Rok Chit* (psychosis - a disease of the mind) as mental illness. He therefore suggested that *Chit*

* Director, Division for the Co-ordination of Drug Abuse Treatment, Department of Medical Service, Ministry of Health, Bangkok, Thailand. This report was prepared in February 1992.

Funfuen (alteration of the mind) should not be used in that it fits into the category of *Rok Chit.* However, others have described *Rok Chit* as psychosis, *Chit Brokprong* as mental retardation and *Chit Funfuen* as an alteration of the conscious level of the mind (organic in origin).

The law dealing with responsibility and non-responsibility was drawn up on the basis of the criteria used in McNaughten's principle.

Section 65 of the Criminal Code of Thailand also deals with the concept of diminished responsibility but, as in the case of responsibility and non-responsibility, divergences exist on its interpretation.

Treatment of non-responsible offenders

If the offender is determined non-responsible for the act committed, then the following provision is made in Section 48 of the Criminal Code:

> If the court is of the opinion that the liberation of any person with a deficient mind, mental disease or mental infirmity, who is not punishable or whose punishment is reduced according to Section 65, would be a threat to public safety, the court may give an order for her/him to be detained in a hospital. This order may, however, be revoked by the court at any time.

If the court does not decide to revoke the order, the decision on the state of dangerousness of the offender is left with the hospital personnel, who might decide to release the offender or allow her/him the possibility of being treated in the hospital on a voluntary basis.

Although no clear guidelines exist on the treatment of borderline cases, in practice, this depends on the court's decision which, in turn, relies upon the evaluation of the psychiatrist.

The first phase of the psychiatric and psychological examinations to diagnose the responsibility of the offender involves the compilation of forms related to her/his personal history, criminal record and other relative information. The social worker will then investigate the offender's social and family environment. The mental state of the offender is diagnosed and recorded by the psychiatrist and nurse in charge of the case, while the psychological tests are conducted by a psychologist. Laboratory tests are also carried out, as well as a special examination.

When the information is ready a meeting is held to discuss the results of the report and make a final diagnosis on the mental health of the offender. This meeting is chaired either by the director of the hospital or by the head of the team dealing with the case. A report is then prepared and sent to the authorities concerned.

DANGEROUSNESS

Reference is made to the concept of dangerousness in Section 48 of the Criminal Code, although the term 'danger to the public' is not clarified. In practice, it is the court that examines the criminal act and the state of illness of the offender.

Offenders who are determined dangerous are usually detained in a restricted area of a mental hospital, although this sometimes depends on medical technicalities. For example, a psychopath is not included in this category and therefore the behavioural treatment and sexual regime would not apply in this case.

PSYCHIATRIC EXAMINATIONS

As mentioned in Section 14 of the Criminal Procedure Act, if the court, police or public prosecutor suspect that the accused is suffering from a mental illness, the latter will be sent to a doctor for an evaluation of her/his condition. The doctor in question is usually a medical practitioner or a psychiatrist. The offender might then be admitted into a mental hospital for an indefinite period, or become an out-patient and visit the hospital periodically.

The criminological examination is not used here but, instead, a psychiatric examination is carried out so as to prepare a report or psychiatric evidence for the court.

In most cases, the psychological tests used to evaluate the mental state of the offender are the MMPI, the IQ test, the Rorschach Test and the Bender Gestalt Test. Every mental institution has a clinical psychologist, whose role is to carry out tests and provide counselling and psychotherapy to the patient.

Although the relationship between the judicial decision and the psychiatric examination is not very clear, studies show that most of the medical evidence concerning the offender is accepted by the court. Nevertheless, the court makes a final decision irrespective of the medical evidence presented. Thus, ultimately, the decision regarding the dangerousness of the offender rests upon the court.

SANCTIONS

If the offender is considered a danger to the general public, according to Section 48 of the Criminal Act, s/he must be placed in a mental hospital upon the order of the court, and can only be released after the submission of a satisfactory medical report.

At present, only one hospital has been constructed to deal with forensic psychiatric cases and this is the Nitichitawej Hospital. Although most forensic psychiatric cases are sent to this medical institution for evaluation, nevertheless, any person who is labelled dangerous (according to the law) can be detained there. However, some cases, especially from the provinces, can be sent to a normal mental hospital for treatment.

REFORMS

Although discussion on reform commenced several years ago, it is still in a preliminary phase. During a Workshop on Forensic Psychiatry held in Bangkok in 1985, the conclusion was reached that a better understanding was needed among doctors, lawyers, judges and the agencies dealing with mentally-ill offenders, as well as a clearer definition of the law. At another seminar held in Songkha in 1991, it was recommended that greater knowledge of forensic psychiatry must be made available. In the author's opinion, although the system in

Thailand is satisfactory and is working in the right direction, greater comprehension and clarification is needed.

Status of the reform

Despite the fact that the implementation of the reform is slow and gradual, some results can already be seen. For example, law faculties in universities now accept the idea that law students in Thailand should have a sound knowledge of forensic psychiatry. At present, however, this subject is not an obligatory part of the university curriculum.

STATISTICS

Table 1 presents statistics issued by the Forensic Psychiatric Services for the years 1989 to 1992.

Table 1: **Number of cases treated by the Forensic Psychiatric Services (1989-1982)**

	1989	1990	1991	28 February 1992
Total No. of in-patients	3 293	3 148	3 203	563
Diagnosed with psychoses	3 248	3 065	3 057	551
Compulsory detention	7	6	2	-
New admissions	315	439	512	104
Discharges	326	478	543	114

SUMMARY OF THE NATIONAL REPORTS

RESPONSIBILITY

The distinction between responsibility and non-responsibility is envisaged in all the criminal justice systems presented in this volume, with the exception of Sweden, where it was abandoned in 1965 when the new Penal Law came into force. The criteria to determine the distinction between these two concepts varies, however, from country to country.

Canada: The Canadian Criminal Code states that persons who, at the time they committed a criminal act or omission, were suffering from a mental disorder that rendered them incapable of appreciating the nature and quality of the act or omission or of knowing that it was wrong, are not held responsible by the criminal law.

Egypt: The Egyptian Penal Code prescribes that no person shall be liable to punishment for any act committed at a time when s/he had lost consciousness and freedom of choice, for reasons of insanity, mental infirmity or intoxication.

England & Wales: In England and Wales, the criterion used to distinguish between responsibility and non-responsibility, is that mentally disordered persons are not convicted if the act was committed when the defendant was in such a state of mental disorder that s/he could not be held to be criminally responsible. In such cases, the offenders are not guilty by reason of insanity.

Germany: According to the German Penal Code, a person is not criminally responsible if, at the time of the act, due to a psychotic or similar serious mental disorder, or profound interruption of consciousness or feeblemindedness, or any other type of serious mental abnormality, s/he is incapable of understanding the illegality of the conduct and to act in accordance with this understanding.

Italy: The Italian Penal Code decrees that no one can be punished for an act envisaged by the law as an offence, if, at the time the offence was committed, s/he did not have the capacity of 'recognition' and/or 'volition'. 'Recognition' in the medical-legal sense is not simply the offender's ability to know what exists and happens around her/him, but also the ability to adequately discern the meaning, value and moral and legal consequences; i.e. the ability to understand the social-judicial significance of the behaviour. 'Volition' denotes the offender's ability for self-determination in relation to the accomplishment of an objective. The cases which exclude diminished responsibility are divided into 3 categories: they may be of a physiological nature (age), pathological nature and toxic nature. Therefore, non-responsibility or diminished responsibility may be attributed to 4 causes: a) the offender is a minor; b) mental infirmity; c) the offender is handicapped; and d) intoxication.

Japan: The Japanese Mental Health Law defines a mentally-ill person as follows:

a) a psychotic person, including someone who is psychotic due to intoxication;

b) a mentally-retarded person;

c) a psychopathic person.

The Japanese Penal Code states that an act committed by someone who lacks the mental capacity to distinguish between right and wrong (i.e. is not responsible) and is unable to understand the nature or quality of her/his act, is not punishable: this was verified by the Japanese Supreme Court on 3 December 1931.

Nigeria: The Nigerian Penal Code specifies responsibility as being the capacity of an individual to understand what s/he is doing, control her/his actions, and know that s/he should not commit the act.

Peru: Although the Peruvian legislation does not provide a legal definition of the term 'responsibility', the Peruvian Penal Code considers it sufficient to mention that no legal responsibility can be

216

imposed upon a person who is unable to comprehend or determine the delictual character of her/his act.

Sweden: Swedish legislation states that an offender who commits a crime under the influence of a grave mental disorder cannot be sentenced to imprisonment.

Thailand: The Thai Criminal Code indicates that whenever a person commits an offence at a time when s/he is not able to appreciate the nature or legality of the act, or unable to control her/himself on account of a deficient mind, mental disease or mental infirmity, that person shall not be punished for such an offence. However, it does not provide a definition or explanation of mental illness.

Diminished responsibility

Canada: In Canada, there is no concept of 'diminished responsibility' in the sense of a specific defence. However, evidence of the type of abnormality of mind required to establish the defence of diminished responsibility would, in certain circumstances, be sufficient to reduce the charge of murder to manslaughter and would be taken into consideration by the judge in sentencing for offences where there is no mandatory sentence.

Egypt: There is no provision for diminished responsibility in Egyptian criminal law. Nevertheless, the court, can apply the system of 'mitigating circumstances' which is the only way to instigate the legal method of establishing the balance between the capacity to accept responsibility and the penalty.

England & Wales: In England and Wales, while account is taken of the degree of the accused's mental state prior, during and after the offence, the concept of diminished responsibility is normally used in relation to the classification of the offence (reducing an offence from murder to manslaughter) rather than the mental health aspect.

Germany: The German Penal Code recognises the concept of diminished responsibility, as mentioned in paragraph 21 entitled 'Diminished Capacity'.

Italy: According to the Italian Penal Code, in cases of partial mental impairment, the responsibility of the accused may be diminished. The Code prescribes that anyone who commits a crime by reason of infirmity which greatly reduces her/his capacity of cognition or volition, may receive a reduced penalty with, in some cases, the application of a measure of security (or house custody).

Japan: The Japanese Penal Code states that a crime committed by someone who has insufficient mental capacity (diminished responsibility) is punishable by a mitigated sentence.

Nigeria: No provision is made for diminished responsibility in Nigeria.

Peru: Although the Peruvian Penal Code does not specifically mention diminished responsibility, it refers to it as a condition that requires mitigating sanctions for the subject, as well as the application of security measures as an alternative to sanctions. In addition, whenever some responsibility is proved, the judge must reduce the sanction.

Sweden: Swedish law states that if the offender's ability to control her/his behaviour is diminished because of a mental disorder or for any other reason, this should be regarded as extenuating circumstances.

Thailand: In Thailand, even if the offender is only partially able to appreciate the illegal nature of her/his act, or is only partially able to control her/himself, s/he will be punished for such an offence. The court may, however, inflict a lesser punishment than that provided by the law for such an offence.

Treatment of non-responsible offenders

Canada: Under the Criminal Code of Canada, those found not criminally responsible on account of a mental disorder, are detained in a secure hospital until a review board concludes that they no longer constitute a danger to the public.

Egypt: The Egyptian Criminal Procedure Code states that, if the accused is acquitted of a crime by reason of insanity, the court shall detain the accused in one of the specialised institutions for the mentally-ill until the authorities decide upon her/his release.

England & Wales: In England and Wales, the options for treatment of non-responsible offenders are:

a) an order requiring admission and treatment in hospital;

b) an order giving the right of guardianship to the Social Services;

c) a probation order with conditions requiring social supervision and treatment;

d) absolute discharge.

Germany: The German criminal justice system uses one of the following measures to deal with non-responsible offenders within the 'measures of rehabilitation and security':

a) commitment to a mental health institution;

b) commitment to an institution for the treatment of chemical dependency;

c) commitment to an institution of protective custody;

d) supervision of conduct;

e) withdrawal of driver's license;

f) prohibition to practice a profession.

The Penal Code highlights the principle of proportionality: rehabilitation and security may not be ordered if it is disproportionate to the offender's past crimes and anticipated criminal behaviour, as well as to the amount of danger which s/he poses to society.

Italy: In Italy, the accused who is not responsible for her/his act as a result of total mental impairment, may be admitted to a prison psychiatric hospital if s/he is considered to be a danger to society.

Otherwise, s/he is released from prison and treated voluntarily in the community if the crime committed is not considered to be serious.

Japan: The treatment of mentally-ill offenders at the stage of prosecution and trial in Japan, is as follows. According to the Japanese Penal Code, those accused at the prosecution stage who are deemed to be non-responsible for their actions are not prosecuted and are acquitted at the trial stage. On the other hand, those who are judged to be suffering from diminished responsibility are given mitigated sentences. If the accused is judged to be not responsible due to her/his mental condition, s/he will be treated under the jurisprudence of the medical health system.

In the Japanese medical health system, 3 methods are used for hospitalising mentally-ill offenders: a) voluntary admission; b) hospitalisation for medical protection; and c) compulsory hospitalisation.

With regards to voluntary admission, the 1988 law provides, for the first time, for a category of 'voluntary psychiatric admission'. The new law imposes an obligation on the medical superintendent of a mental hospital to endeavour to admit mentally-disordered persons, if the latter consent to this in writing.

The system of hospitalisation for medical protection provides for the hospitalisation of a mentally-disordered person even without her/his consent, if a person (usually a member of the family or relative of the patient) accepts the responsibility for the patient's protection. In order to reduce the possibility of abuse, collusion or subterfuge in this category, some procedural safeguards have been added:

a) under the new law, the initial examination, which determined whether the person concerned is 'mentally-disordered' and in need of hospitalisation, must be conducted by a certified physician, referred to as a designated physician;

b) under the 1988 law, the evaluation as to whether to prolong the hospitalisation of a patient, shortly after admission, has to be made by a panel of the Prefectural Psychiatric Review Board.

Compulsory hospitalisation can be applied following a request to the Prefectural governor by a member of the general public, seeking the examination, and necessary protection of a person who is, or is suspected of being mentally-disordered; or by a report to the governor from the medical superintendent of a mental hospital, a police officer, a public prosecutor, the head of a probation office or any correctional institution. Upon receipt of this request or report, or on her/his own initiative, the governor must then order the person concerned to be medically examined by a physician certified by the Ministry of Health and Welfare, as stipulated in the new law. If, according to the results of the examination, the person is mentally unfit and likely to cause injury to her/himself or to others unless hospitalised, the governor may commit that person to a Prefectural or designated hospital. The hospitalised patient must then be examined by two or more certified physicians who must both confirm the initial diagnosis.

The 1988 law stipulates that physicians must decide that hospitalisation is necessary when, due to symptoms that are set forth and described in the regulations, the person is deemed likely to attempt suicide, inflict injury upon her/himself, or carry out 'actions posing a threat to the life, body, chastity, reputation, or property, etc., of others or to society, such as murder, injury, assault, problematic sexual behaviour, slander, destruction of property, robbery, intimidation, theft, fraud, arson, playing with fire, etc.'

Nigeria: In Nigeria, the verdict for mentally-ill offenders can be one of the following:

a) unfit to plead or stand trial;

b) not guilty by reason of insanity;

c) guilty but insane.

The offender can either be sent to a psychiatric hospital for treatment or kept in the prison clinic. The duration of the stay in the hospital or prison is always at the state governor's discretion, and may be for life. If there is active therapeutic intervention and the inmate responds positively to treatment and remains well and alert for a reasonable period of time, s/he may be recommended for discharge to her/his relatives who will be required to take full responsibility for her/his continued care.

Peru: According to the Peruvian Penal Code, those offenders regarded as non-responsible for their actions due to their mental condition are exempted from any sanction. If, however, they represent some form of threat to society as a whole, the law authorises the judge to apply security measures, such as commitment to a hospital or specialised out-patient treatment centre, with details on the type of treatment, discharge procedure and the actual details of the case.

Sweden: The Swedish Penal Code envisages a special sanction for mentally-disordered offenders, i.e. commitment to forensic psychiatric care. This sanction is applicable if, by the time of the trial, the offender shows signs of a grave mental disorder and, taking into consideration her/his mental and personal condition, is admitted to an institution for psychiatric care where deprivation of liberty and other measures of compulsion are used.

Thailand: The Thai Criminal Code states that if the court is of the opinion that the release of any person having a deficient mind, mental disease or mental infirmity, who is not punishable, or whose punishment is reduced, will present a danger to the public, the court may order that s/he be recovered in a hospital. The court can also revoke this order at any time. However, the dangerousness should be taken into serious consideration, since, if the court does not decide whether to free the offender or not, the latter might be kept in a mental hospital for treatment on a voluntary basis, or released.

Treatment of borderline cases

Canada: Canadian criminal law does not prescribe any particular procedure for dealing with borderline cases, which are left to the common sense of those administering the law.

Egypt: The legal regulation of borderline cases in Egypt is to inflict a mitigated penalty against the offender.

England & Wales: No specific measure exists in England and Wales to differentiate the salient issues in borderline cases: the extent of the mental disorder is taken into account and the content of medical recommendations weighed before determining the final disposal.

Germany: As a general rule, it can be said that, in Germany, the diagnosis of a borderline personality alone does not say anything about the responsibility or non-responsibility of an offender in relation to a certain offence.

Peru: In Peru, although no records on borderline cases are contained in the national judicial-psychiatric archives of the 'Victor Larco Herrera Hospital', according to the staff of the hospital, the borderline case is responsible for her/his actions.

Sweden: The so-called 'borderline personality' does not receive any special legislative treatment in Sweden.

Thailand: The Criminal Code of Thailand provides no specific definition of each mental illness. In practice, the treatment of borderline cases depends upon the judgement of the court which relies upon the psychiatrist's evaluation.

Psychiatric and psychological examinations to diagnose responsibility

Egypt: In Egypt, the examinations to diagnose responsibility are conducted by a medical expert who is specialised in psychiatric diseases.

England & Wales: In order to diagnose responsibility in England and Wales, a psychiatric and psychological examination is carried out, at the request of the court, by consultant forensic psychiatrists or general psychiatrists, one of whom must be approved under the Mental Health Act of 1983. The patient is visited in prison or hospital, or even at court, and the practitioner submits written or oral evidence.

Italy: In Italy, if a judge considers it appropriate either to establish or rule out responsibility or diminished responsibility, s/he may appoint one or more psychiatrists to make a psychiatric assessment of the subject. The task of the psychiatric expert is to respond to the questions posed by the judge, which generally include at least the following: whether the state of mind of the accused at the time of the offence eliminates, or greatly reduces her/his capacity of cognition and volition; and whether the accused, at the present time, is considered to be a danger to society. To achieve these tasks, the expert must examine the accused and possibly put her/him through specialised physical and psychological tests to observe her/his behaviour. On the basis of the technical knowledge gained by the experts, the judge should then decide whether the accused is responsible for the action or whether the responsibility should be reduced. In theory, the judge has the power to disregard the suggestions made by the experts and decide otherwise. However, since the judge does not have much competence in the psychopathological field, the opinion of the psychiatric expert is usually accepted.

In general, in Italy, the same diagnostic instruments used in clinical psychiatry or psychology are applied during the psychiatric examination to determine the responsibility of the offender, although there are some variations in the methodology or contents of the examination due to the judicial framework. The psychiatric or psychological interview represents the main instrument, and the results thereof are usually completed by psychological tests and standardised methods of a psychiatric examination. A physical and neurological check-up are also included in the examination.

Nigeria: Under the Nigerian legal system, offenders are sent for a comprehensive psychiatric assessment by a qualified psychiatrist, with emphasis on:

a) a detailed history of the offender supplemented by the relatives, or other relevant third persons;

b) circumstances related to the offence provided by the police and any other witnesses.

Peru: According to Peruvian law, non-responsibility due to mental illness cannot be based upon mere possibility, but has to be based upon concrete scientific evidence or a certificate produced by medical experts.

Thailand: In Thailand, the procedure to diagnose responsibility is initiated by obtaining information on the personal background of the offender, as well as her/his criminal record and correspondence, after which a social worker will do the field work. The offender's mental state is then diagnosed and recorded by the psychiatrist in charge and by a nurse, and a psychologist will carry out the psychological test. Laboratory work and a special investigation are also completed. When the information is ready, a clinical meeting is held, headed by the director of the hospital or head of the medical team, in order to discuss and make a final diagnosis, after which the report is sent to the agencies concerned.

Dealing with specific cases in the criminal justice system

Neuroses

England & Wales: In England and Wales, neurosis is a matter for clinical judgement, which means that it can be classified as a mental disorder.

Germany: Under the German Criminal Code, in cases where a criminal act is due to neurosis, a person who is suffering from an illness which causes her/him to be 'incapable of understanding the wrongfulness of her/his conduct or of acting in accordance with this understanding', will not be considered responsible for the offence. If the neurotic disturbance diminishes her/his capability of understanding the wrongfulness of the act, or of acting in accordance, the court may reduce the punishment.

Japan: In Japan, a person suffering from neurosis, a psychosomatic or an adjustment disorder is, in principle, responsible for her/his actions.

Peru: Under the Peruvian legal system, an offender who suffers from neurosis and has a dissociative crisis or consciousness disturbance, may be considered responsible for her/his act, although in a diminished way.

Sweden: Neurosis is classified, under the Swedish system, as a grave mental disorder and neurotics will not usually be imprisoned.

Psychopathic disorder

Canada: While the criminal law makes no special provision for psychopaths, the Supreme Court of Canada has interpreted that the defence of 'mental disorder' would not normally be available to psychopaths.

Egypt: Egyptian Doctrine and Jurisprudence state that a psychopathic disorder is not considered a mental or neurotic illness.

England & Wales: In England and Wales, psychopathic disorder is one of four categories of mental disorders, which means a persistent disorder or disability of mind which results in abnormally aggressive or seriously irresponsible conduct.

Germany: Under the German legal system, a psychopathic development of personality might be characterised by an 'abnormal personality', such as paranoia, hysteria, asthenia, irritability, schizophrenia or anti-social behaviour. Furthermore, it might be manifested by sexual misconduct, sexual perversion, alcoholism and/or drug addiction. Psychopathic disorder is included in the category of 'serious mental abnormality'.

Italy: Under the Italian Criminal Code, offenders with either a psychopathic, neurotic or borderline personality are generally recognised as being responsible for their actions. However, each case has to be examined individually on the basis of the offence and mental condition of the offender.

Japan: In Japan, persons suffering from a personality disorder and psychopaths are, in principle, considered responsible for their actions.

Peru: Peruvian jurisprudence specifies that offenders with abnormal personalities are classified as being responsible for their actions.

226

Sweden: Psychopathic disorder is seldom used, in Sweden, as a diagnosis in the usual conception of a personality disorder, a disorder of character or likewise.

Emotional distress

Canada: Canadian criminal law makes no special provision for emotional distress.

Egypt: Emotional distress is considered as a symptom of a psychological illness in Egypt, and may be described as 'mental infirmity'.

England & Wales: Emotional distress, in England and Wales, is a matter for clinical judgement, which means that it can be classified as a mental disorder.

Germany: In Germany, emotional distress, like affective irritability, fright, over-fatigue or exhaustion, belongs to the category of 'profound interruption of consciousness'.

Italy: The Italian Penal Code states that an emotional passionate state neither excludes nor diminishes responsibility, unless emotional distress is a part of mental infirmity.

Japan: Under the Japanese criminal justice system, since manic-depressives only express this symptom periodically, when they do, they are not considered responsible for their actions. If the symptoms are not apparent, the offenders are considered responsible for their actions.

Sweden: Grave depression, especially if it involves the contemplation of suicide, could be regarded as a grave mental disorder under Swedish legislation.

Irresistible impulse

Canada: Canadian criminal law makes no special provision for irresistible impulse.

Egypt: Egyptian criminal law considers irresistible impulse to be an aspect of mental, neurotic or psychological illness. The final consequence of irresistible impulse is the elimination of freedom and exemption from responsibility.

England & Wales: Legislation in England and Wales considers irresistible impulse is a matter for clinical judgement, which means that irresistible impulse can be classified as a mental disorder.

Germany: The phenomenology of the 'irresistible impulse' belongs to the category of affective disturbances in German law. To this extent, impulsive actions might be sexually or not sexually motivated. From a forensic point of view, these primitive reactions are generally referred to as 'a profound interruption of consciousness'.

Nigeria: As already mentioned earlier, under Nigerian legislation, a person is considered non-responsible if s/he does not have the capacity to understand what s/he is doing, the capacity to control her/her actions, and the capacity to understand the wrongfulness of the act.

Peru: Peruvian forensic psychiatry and jurisprudence have paid particular attention to personality disorders characterised, for example, by impulsiveness and unusual behaviour due to some cerebral syndromes. Most of these cases are considered as diminished responsibility and are valid for a general attenuation of the sentence.

Sweden: Under Swedish legislation, Irresistible impulses of a psychotic character could be regarded as a grave mental disorder.

DANGEROUSNESS

Canada: The Canadian Criminal Code adopts the concept of dangerousness in its criminal justice system.

Egypt: The Egyptian Penal Code does not include a definition for dangerousness.

England & Wales: The concept of dangerousness is also addressed by the Criminal Procedure Act in England and Wales,

Germany: German legislation also adopts the concept of dangerousness.

Italy: The Italian Penal Code adopts the concept of 'social danger'.

Japan: There is no provision in the Japanese Penal Code for the concept of dangerousness.

Nigeria: The concept of dangerousness is not used directly in Nigerian legislation, but it is implied by the frequent question posed by the judge in cases of serious offences. The term 'danger to the public' is not very clear.

Peru: In Peru, although offenders may not be criminally responsible, they can be considered as a danger to society. The Penal Code uses the concept of dangerousness as a factor which determines the judicial application of security measures to the offenders who have committed a crime but are considered non-responsible.

Sweden: In principle, under Swedish legislation, the concept of danger is not used, but in fact it exists with regard to parole. The question of discharge from an institution for forensic psychiatric care is investigated by the county administrative court, focusing on the risk that a mentally-ill offender will relapse into serious crime.

Criteria to determine the concept of dangerousness

Canada: The Canadian Criminal Code deals with dangerous offenders. It provides that in order to impose a dangerous offender status on an offender, an application to that effect (approved by the Attorney General) must be made to the court who may make such an order if it is satisfied that the offence committed is a 'serious personal injury offence' (defined as an offence involving violence against another person or conduct endangering, or likely to endanger the life of another person, or inflicting or likely to inflict severe psychological damage upon another person and for which the offender may be sentenced to imprisonment for 10 years or more, or an offence - or attempt to commit an offence - involving sexual assault as prescribed under the Criminal Code, and the offender constitutes a threat to the life, safety or physical or mental well-being of other persons on the basis of evidence that has been established).

Egypt: The Egyptian Penal Code adopts the concept that the criminal dangerousness of the offender to society is revealed by the circumstances and motives of the offender which, in turn, indicate if there is a serious probability of her/him committing another offence.

England & Wales: In England and Wales, the elements for consideration of dangerousness are:

a) the nature of the offence;

b) the antecedents of the offence;

c) the risk of the offender committing further offences if discharged.

Germany: The criteria to determine the concept of dangerousness are mentioned in the German Penal Code, for the purpose of committing the offender to an institution (either a psychiatric hospital or institution for the treatment of chemical dependency). The precondition for the application of these Articles is that the offender lacks the capacity to comprehend her/his criminal action or suffers from diminished responsibility at the time of committing the unlawful act. Usually, further unlawful acts are foreseen in the future, so the offender is to be considered dangerous.

Italy: A person who has committed a crime is considered to be socially dangerous, when it is very probable that s/he will commit further crimes. The judgement of danger to society expressed in this way in the Italian Penal Code is a predictive, or prognostic judgement, based particularly on the assumption that the offender would commit further crimes. In exercising discretionary powers in the application of the sentence, the judge considers the gravity of the criminal act, but must also take into consideration the capacity of the accused to commit a further crime, which can be inferred from the following elements:

a) the motives to commit a crime and the characteristics of the offender;

b) the offender's criminal and court records and personal history;

c) the current behaviour and attitude towards crime of the offender;

d) the offender's individual, family and social situation.

The judge is assisted by psychiatric experts when making an analysis of the danger to society represented by mentally-ill persons. The experts draw their conclusions from the psycho-sociological aspects of the individual case.

Nigeria: According to Nigerian law, if the patient responds positively to treatment, remains under psychiatric supervision and takes her/his prescribed medication regularly with the co-operation of relatives, the chances of her/his repeating the criminal act is considered to be reduced.

Peru: In the Peruvian Penal Code, the prognosis of future behaviour can be deduced from the likelihood of an offender committing further crimes. In addition, it states that the security measures applied to offenders must be proportionate to their criminal dangerousness. However, the law does not provide a precise definition of the concrete signs of dangerousness. The following are the criteria described in the normative text:

a) a prognosis of dangerousness has to be made which is based on the crime committed and following a psychological evaluation of the offender;

b) while the prognosis of dangerousness is a judicial decision, the court has to rely on the results of the evaluation made by experts.

With regard to security measures, the Penal Code establishes that in-patient treatment should not last longer than the length of the sanction that would have been imposed for the crime. Every 6 months, the medical personnel of the in-patient treatment centre must submit the results of a medical examination to the judges, so as to allow them to decide whether the medical conditions for which the security measures have been applied still persist. However, in practice, due to the lack of space at the special psychiatric hospital for patients recovered by judicial order, the offenders declared to be non-responsible for their actions remain in correctional institutions without any psychiatric treatment. In addition, since there is no actual judicial control for security measures, offenders are likely to remain there for an indefinite period.

Sweden: The question of discharge from the institution for forensic psychiatric care must be investigated by the county administrative court, and focuses on the risk that the mentally-ill offender will relapse into serious crime.

Thailand: In practice, in Thailand, the court looks at the criminal act of the offender and the severity of the illness.

Treatment of dangerous offenders

Egypt: Egyptian legislation prescribes different kinds of measures according to the kind and degree of dangerousness. For example, the legislation determines a number of redressing and emendation measures for juveniles, and for those who are exposed to anti-social behaviour. It determines that insane offenders are to be placed in one of the mental institutions in preparation for treatment, and for habitual offenders to be placed in one of the institutions. Other measures are also applied, such as police control, confiscation and the deprivation of some rights. Security measures are characterised by their unlimited duration, and can be prolonged as long as criminal dangerousness persists.

England & Wales: Crown courts can make restriction orders when directing admission to hospital. The court has to be satisfied that a restriction order is necessary for the protection of the public from serious harm. The Home Secretary may make restriction directions when agreeing to the transfer of sentenced or unsentenced prisoners to hospital. High risk offenders are sent to one of three special hospitals where conditions are of maximum security. These cater for about 1700 detained patients. In addition, there are 13 regional Secure Units providing 650 beds in medium secure conditions, with a further 100 planned. In local hospitals, there is provision for beds for 35 000 mentally-ill patients and 30 mentally-handicapped offenders, including 2 000 beds in locked wards.

Germany: The German Criminal Law provides possibilities to deal with offenders who are determined 'dangerous'. The measures are defined under 'measures of rehabilitation and security' in Articles 63 and 64 of the German Penal Code.

Italy: If the accused is regarded as being incapable of 'cognition' and 'volition' but a danger to society, s/he must be admitted to a prison psychiatric hospital without the provision of any alternative measures adequate to her/his condition and therapeutic needs. There is conflict between what is envisaged by the Penal Code and what is established by the law on 'Voluntary and Compulsory Health Checks and Treatment', which highlights the discrepancy between clinical psychiatry (a need for treatment) and forensic psychiatry (a need for control). This discrepancy creates the inequality between the mentally-ill person who has committed a crime and the mentally-ill person who is not an offender, even though they are both suffering from same mental condition. The psychiatric report, therefore, is an instrument at the service of psychiatric prognosis rather than a means with which to assist the treatment of the mentally-ill person in need of social and health programmes. In this sense, the report gives priority to the aspects of control and social protection rather than to therapeutic aspects. In addition, admission to a prison psychiatric hospital is not regarded as a penalty but as a security measure.

Peru: In Peru, the limited amount of material available from the judicial psychiatric service implies that the therapeutic treatment, which is applied to dangerous non-responsible offenders, is very poor. The judicial psychiatric service focuses more on disciplinary measures and internal order. Through group treatment, the patients are shown the limitation of the psychiatric service and learn norms which they have to follow. On the other hand, those patients who are dangerous but suffer from cerebral organic syndromes are treated by pharmacological medication, which produces positive results.

Thailand: Under legislation in Thailand, the offender is kept in a restricted area of a mental hospital and receives medical care. Psychopaths do not fall into this category and, therefore, behavioural treatment is not applied in these cases.

Psychiatric and psychological examination to diagnose dangerous offenders

England & Wales: The diagnosis of dangerousness is carried out by means of the same examinations described for the diagnosis of responsibility.

Germany: In Germany, once the offender is diagnosed for one reason or another as being non-responsible or suffering from diminished-responsibility, as a result of the psychiatric-psychological examination described earlier, the classification of dangerousness is based on the prognosis of how the mental constitution of the person in question will develop in the future. The criminal justice system demands 'a total evaluation of the offender and her/his offence', this is carried out by means of an intuitive prognosis. This kind of prognosis is based on the knowledge of human nature, professional experience and the individual ethical orientation of the examiner or judge. The clinical or empirical individual prognosis is based on an extensive examination of the subject by means of exploration and observation, including psycho-diagnostic tests. The weighing of the collected data for the prognosis of dangerousness demands, besides psychiatric-psychological qualifications, a great deal of criminological knowledge and experience with offenders, and only those psychologists and psychiatrists who have sufficient criminological experience are allowed to carry out this task.

Italy: Many psychiatrists and forensic psychiatrists in Italy believe that they should not be called upon to make any prognosis since they feel ill-equipped to make such a decision. In reality, although great caution must be exercised in all predictive judgements, it is difficult to imagine anyone else who might be better equipped than the forensic and criminal psychiatrists to undertake such a task. The predictive appraisal of anomalous behaviour originating from, or related to, a mental disorder must be based not only on individual elements, but also on the elements drawn from the offender's individual lifestyle and socio-cultural background. Account is also taken of what are known as 'external indicators': the family and social environment, local psychiatric records, the possibility of the offender becoming reintegrated into the educational or employment system, and the degree of acceptance of her/his return to the community. These external indicators, however, should not be taken into consideration to formulate an opinion on the social danger of the offender, but only to evaluate the level of risk among discharged offenders who are not a danger to society. In the evaluation of the psychiatric social danger, which is the task of the psychiatric expert in the case of confirmed mental impairment, internal indicators must be used, namely, indicators of the individual type of pathology present in the mind.

Peru: According to the clinical practice of the judicial psychiatric service at the Victor Larco Herrera Hospital in Peru, the psychological and psychiatric evaluations to determine whether a patient is dangerous, are also based on the medical diagnosis, crime committed, patient's behaviour in the institution, and her/his family background. The interviews and medical examination seem to be more precise, whereas the psychological tests seem only to be supplemental.

Sweden: Under Swedish legislation, dangerousness is not normally used as a diagnosis.

Thailand: The examinations carried out in Thailand have been described in the above section on psychiatric and psychological examinations to diagnose responsibility.

PSYCHIATRIC EXAMINATIONS

Egypt: Under Egyptian legislation, the psychiatric examination is conducted by a medical expert specialised in mental psychiatric diseases.

England & Wales: A psychiatric examination is carried out to provide forensic information, at the request of the court, to enable the latter to investigate relevant aspects of the case background and decide on an appropriate disposal. The court may alternatively or additionally call for Social Services reports by community psychiatric nurses or approvedsocial workers. Their function is to identify and analyse the behaviour and mental state of the patient, in particular in relation to the offence and previous history, wherever this is relevant.

Germany: A medical expert must be heard if there is a possibility of the accused being committed to a mental health institution, to an institution for the treatment of chemical dependency or to an institution of protective custody. It is permissible, after an expert and the lawyer of the accused have been heard, to commit the accused to a mental health institution if this seems necessary in order to allow the expert to form an opinion on the mental and psychic state of mind of the accused. According to the law, the final decision during the trial rests soley with the court. The Federal Supreme Court names the expert the 'assistant' of the judge. Despite this emphasis on the decision being left with the court, given the professional status and specific knowledge of the experts, they have attained a rather powerful and influential position which is hardly in accordance with the law.

Italy: The task of the psychiatric expert in Italy is to respond to the questions posed by the judge, which generally include at least the following:

a) whether, at the time of the offence, the offender was in a state of mind that eliminated or greatly reduced her/his capacity of 'cognition' and 'volition' due to the infirmity;

b) whether, at the present time, the offender is considered to be a danger to society.

Japan: In Japan, the psychiatric examinations are carried out by designated physicians. In order to qualify for the status of a designated physician, the applicant must possess a rigourous and comprehensive set of educational, training and clinical requirements (at least 3 years' experience in diagnosing and treating mental disorders). Furthermore, in order to maintain this position, the designated physician must continually update his educational background.

As far as the role of the designated physician is concerned, the evaluative physician is only required to examine the offenders subject to a governor's hospitalisation order. The designated physician's duties extend to determining the need to continue the hospitalisation of voluntary patients, and of patients hospitalised under a governor's order. The designated physician must also determine the need for, and type of physical restraints and other restrictions.

Nigeria: In Nigeria, a psychiatrist serves as an expert witness to:

a) determine the fitness of the offender to plead to the charge or otherwise;

b) determine the criminal responsibility of the offender at the time s/he committed the offence;

c) recommend disposal options.

Peru: In Peru, the psychiatric examination can be requested by the judge, defence attorney or a representative of the public minister during any phase of the penal trial. The instructor judge or the court is responsible for demanding an examination, by experts, of the mental condition of the accused, and the experts must then inform the judge or the court of the mental condition of the accused, whether s/he should be sent to hospital or whether s/he is considered to be a danger to the public. The instructor judge will appoint 2 psychiatric experts to carry out the examination. The requirements to become a medical assistant in the psychiatric service are:

a) Peruvian citizenship;

b) a valid title for professional practice within the country;

c) a vocation for the specialisation.

Sweden: In Sweden, a psychiatric examination can be ordered by the court in any criminal case. This is sufficient for the committal of an offender to forensic psychiatric care without special restrictions for discharge. A complete mental examination is in accordance with the Law on Forensic Psychiatric Examinations: special restrictions are compulsory for discharge from forensic psychiatric care.

Thailand: Under Thai legislation, if the court, the police, or the prosecutor suspect that the accused might be suffering from a mental disorder, s/he should be seen by a doctor for evaluation. The doctor may be a medical practitioner or a psychiatrist. The accused might then be admitted to a mental hospital for a certain length of time, or treated as an out-patient.

Criminological examination

Canada: The Canadian Criminal Code empowers the court to order an assessment of the mental condition of the accused if it has reasonable grounds to believe that such evidence is necessary to determine:

a) whether the accused is unfit to stand trial;

b) whether the accused was, at the time of the commission of the alleged offence, suffering from a mental disorder so as to be exempt from criminal responsibility;

c) whether the balance of the mind of the accused was disturbed at the time of commission of the alleged offence, where the accused is a female charged with an offence arising out of the death of her newly-born child;

d) the appropriate disposal to be made where a verdict of not criminally responsible on account of a mental disorder or unfit to stand trial has been rendered in respect of the accused;

e) whether an order should be made to detain the accused in a treatment facility, when the accused has been convicted of the offence.

The Common Law permits expert psychiatric evidence to be given on any matter relevant to the case, but expert opinion evidence may be excluded if the court is satisfied that the matter upon which the expert opinion is expressed, falls within common knowledge and therefore would not be helpful to the judge or jury in seeking the facts.

Egypt: In Egypt, the criminological investigation consists in exploring the offender's personality in its different criminological aspects, in order to collect enough information concerning her/his capacity for responsibility. The conclusion of the criminal investigation is considered an important part in the 'file of the offender's personality'. This file is then presented to the court during the trial.

England & Wales: A criminological examination is not envisaged by legislation in England and Wales.

Germany: The criminological or forensic examination is part of the general psychiatric examination in Germany. Some experts leave this topic until the end of the examination.

Nigeria: No 'so-called criminological examination' is envisaged by Nigerian legislation, but a chemical, i.e. drug-induced abreaction may be used if necessary.

Peru: Although special criminological evaluations are not foreseen for the psychiatric evaluation of the accused, they do in fact appear along with the clinical history and psychological evaluation in the psychiatric report.

Thailand: The criminological examination is not usually used in Thailand.

Sweden: In Sweden, the criminological examination consists of a social investigation including checking to see whether a criminal record exists and an analysis carried out by a social officer.

The use and role of psychiatric/psychological tests in the criminal procedure

Canada: Under Canadian legislation, if the evidence is relevant, and it would be helpful to hear the expert evidence of a psychiatrist or psychologist, this will be accepted in a criminal case.

Egypt: Egyptian legislation does not include provisions for psychiatric and psychological tests.

England & Wales: The court uses the examinations to determine the appropriate disposal and placement of an offender, and are based on the respective contribution of the mental state to criminal behaviour.

Germany: The examination by the psychiatrist is based essentially on the biographical data of the exploration, known as qualitative data. This kind of data aims at assessing the person from a longitudinal section. The examination by the clinical psychologist is based a great deal on the data from psychological tests which are called 'quantitative data' and are considered to be highly objective, at least those that have a standardised form. The gained information represents the personality in a cross-section which should be representative for the longitudinal section. No matter how different these two methods may be, the results they produce must always support one another.

Italy: The expert in Italy must examine the offender by carrying out specialised tests and observing her/his behaviour before reaching the final decision.

Japan: The use and role of psychiatric and/or psychological tests in Japan depends upon the case and the psychiatrist.

Nigeria: No specific psychological test is used in Nigeria, although an electroencephalogram (EEG) is used when necessary.

Thailand: In most of the cases, such psychological tests as the MMPI, the IQ test, the Rorschach Test and Bender Gestalt Test would be performed in evaluating the illness of an offender in the Thailand criminal procedure.

Peru: The psychiatric report in Peru has the systematic structure of a 'psychiatric-clinical history' of the accused. In addition, while the report contains psychological tests as well as other auxiliary examinations such as electroencephalogram, these are considered to be supplementary.

Sweden: In Sweden, the psychological test is usually carried out by a psychologist. It includes an IQ test, a test to discover possible lesions of the brain, and a personality test (e.g. Rorschach). The mental examination report is always signed by the psychiatrist but a complete examination is prepared by a team including a psychiatrist, psychologist, social officer, the offender's special contact person and nursing staff.

The relationship between the judicial decision and the psychiatric examination, especially in the fields of responsibility and dangerousness

Canada: In the Canadian criminal justice system, in criminal cases, decisions on the responsibility and dangerousness of offenders are based on legal, rather than psychiatric criteria. Evidence given by a psychiatrist is, therefore, considered by the court in the context of determining whether the legal criteria are met.

Egypt: In Egypt, although the report of the expert is not obligatory for the court, it is accepted in most of the cases due to its technical character.

England & Wales: As mentioned above, the court takes into consideration the following elements when deciding on the mental condition of an offender:

a) the nature of the offence;

b) the antecedents of the offence;

c) the risk of the offender committing further offences if discharged.

Germany: The final decision in any trial is made by the court. The Federal Supreme Court refers to the expert as an 'assistant' of the judge. The court asks for an expert's opinion in the case of commitment to a mental health institution. It appears that the court agrees with the expert's diagnosis in more than half of the cases.

Italy: In Italy there is no agreement that the psychiatric expert is the most suitable person for formulating a judgement with respect to the responsibility and dangerousness to society of a person. On the other hand, it is generally accepted that the judges should decide whether the accused should be considered responsible, or only partially responsible, and that this decision should be based on the technical knowledge made available to them by the experts. Theoretically speaking, the judge has the power to disregard the suggestions of the psychiatric experts, although s/he obviously has to justify this rejection. However, from a practical point of view, since the judge has no specific preparation to enable her/him to make the right decision in the psychopathological fields, it may be better to rely on the psychiatric experts' reports.

Japan: Under Japanese legislation, the final decision on the mental state of an accused is left to the court, irrespective of the conclusions or recommendations of the psychiatrists.

Nigeria: In the Nigerian criminal justice system, the judicial decision usually defers to expert psychiatric opinion, though different psychiatric experts are usually called to express their views by the defence and the prosecution.

Peru: The psychiatric report has a limited function in the Peruvian penal system. Only if the judge is convinced of the mental illness of the offender, based on the medical report produced by experts, can the accused be sent to a psychiatric hospital. The decision of the court is final.

Sweden: In Sweden too, the court makes the final decision, irrespective of the conclusions or recommendations of the psychiatrists. If the court has doubts concerning the results of the examination or the report sent by an institution, it can turn for advice to the National Board of Health and Welfare. Hitherto, the court has rarely deviated from the conclusions or recommendations of the mental examination or those expressed by the Board.

Thailand: At present, there is no clear distinction between the judicial decision and the psychiatric examination, although most of the medical evidence is accepted by the court. Nevertheless, the judge has the right to provide her/his own verdict, regardless of the medical evidence.

SANCTIONS

Canada: In Canada, two categories of sanctions are envisaged: category 1 deals with the mentally-ill offender who has been convicted and has been sentenced to a term of imprisonment. In this case, the measures applicable, both from a health and a security standpoint, are determined by the prison authorities. As a general rule, however, the offender cannot be given treatment for a medical or psychiatric problem without her/his consent. Category 2 deals with the mentally-ill accused who has been found either unfit to stand trial or not criminally responsible on account of mental disorder. In these cases, the accused is put into a secure hospital rather than a prison. As in the case of Category 1, the general rule is that no treatment can be given without consent, but there is a specific exception with respect to treatment designed to render the accused fit to stand trial. The court may make a treatment order where it is satisfied that (a) without treatment the accused is likely to remain unfit to stand trial; (b) with the prescribed treatment the accused is likely to be rendered fit to stand trial within 60 days; (c) the risk of harm to the accused from the treatment is not disproportionate to the benefit anticipated to be derived from it; and (d) the treatment is the least restrictive and intrusive treatment that could, in the circumstances, be specified to render the accused fit to stand trial. There are also two exceptions to the general rule on involuntary treatment. First, the Common Law permits a doctor to administer treatment without the patient's consent if, without treatment, the patient's life would be in danger. Secondly, persons in either of the above categories may be committed as involuntary patients under the provincial mental health legislation. In some provinces, involuntary patients may be treated without their consent.

Egypt: Egyptian legislation envisages absolutely no punishment for the insane offender, i.e. a person whose illness has prevented her/him from understanding the criminal nature of her/his acts and cannot therefore be held responsible for her/his actions. Mitigated punishment is applied to the partially-insane offender, a person whose illness has only diminished her/his understanding of his crime. If it is proved that the mentally-ill offender, whether insane or partially-insane, represents a threat to society, then measures of security are to be applied. Measures for both irresponsible and partially-responsible offenders, whose danger to society has been proven, consist of placing them in a specialised institution. There are no separate and autonomous institutions for partially-insane offenders, with the exception of one institution that includes different sections. Patients are placed in sections according to the severity of their illness and the degree of their dangerousness. As for the partially-insane offenders, the court has to apply a mitigated sentence, which usually means that the offender spends the duration of his punishment in a ward of the prison hospital which is adapted for mentally-ill offenders.

England & Wales: In England and Wales the following sanctions may be applied:

a) magistrates' and crown courts can order the offender to be detained in hospital. Crown courts can make a restriction order, for a limited or indefinite period of time, which gives the power to grant leave of absence, transfer, discharge or recall to hospital exercisable only with the consent of the Home Secretary;

b) magistrates' and crown courts can place the offender under the guardianship of the local Social Services;

c) magistrates' and crown courts can also make a probation order with treatment as a condition;

d) magistrates' and crown courts can also, of course, decide on discharge, whether absolute or conditional;

e) a crown court can remand an accused person to hospital for treatment instead of prison;

f) the provisions of the Criminal Procedure Insanity and Unfitness to Plead Act of 1991 can be used;

g) the prison medical service can arrange, through the Home Office, the transfer of a prisoner to hospital.

Germany: German Penal Law provides the following measures of rehabilitation and security:

a) commitment to a mental health institution;

b) commitment to an institution for the treatment of chemical dependency;

c) commitment to an institution of protective custody;

d) supervision of conduct;

e) withdrawal of driver's license;

f) prohibition to practice a profession.

The measures are justified by the need of the community for security and by the obligation to resocialise and rehabilitate offenders who are capable of improvement. If the offender is diagnosed as non-responsible, or suffering from diminished responsibility, s/he will not be punished since punishment is associated with guilt, which is only possible in the case of responsibility. Depending on the cause of non-responsibility the patient will be placed in a mental health institution or an institution for the treatment of chemical dependency. In the case of diminished responsibility, the commitment must be adhered to.

Italy: The Italian Penal Code introduced a cumulative system of sanctions and measures of security, such as a house of therapy and custody for partially mentally-ill offenders with diminished responsibility, where therapy is related to diminished responsibility and security is adopted in the case of an offender being a danger to society. On the other hand, a measure of security is only applied to totally mentally-ill offenders who are not criminally responsible for their actions, but who are judged to be a danger to society.

Japan: There are no so-called measures of security for mentally-ill offenders or psychiatric hospitals for criminals in the Japanese criminal justice system.

Nigeria: In Nigeria, the sanction applied to mentally-ill offenders is commitment to prison or confinement in a psychiatric hospital.

Peru: According to the Peruvian Penal Code, the accused who is declared non-responsible for her/his actions is exempt from any sanction. However, measures of security with a minor sanction are applied to those who are declared non-responsible or responsible, when they are determined by the court to be a danger to society. The Penal Code mentions two types of security measures; in-patient and out-patient treatment. In-patient treatment for non-responsible but dangerous offenders, is given at a specialised medical centre or any other adequate facility which can provide both treatment and custody. The duration of the in-patient measure of security will be no longer than that of the period of the prison sentence which would have been applied for the crime committed. Every 6 months, the institutional authorities must submit a medical report to the judge, informing her/him of the condition of the patient. In addition, the new Penal Code adopts a model of a vicarial court for the application of both punitive sanctions and security measures. The law requires that whenever an institutional measure is assigned to those who are responsible or with diminished responsibility, sanctions and measures of security have to be applied before the punitive sanction. The duration of the measure of security will be taken into account for the total period of the sanction. On the other hand, the Peruvian Penal Code does not consider specific regulations strictly related to the execution of security measures. In practice, even though the medical director of the institution, or the medical head of the special service, has to inform the respective judicial authority on a regular basis, the application of security measures is supervised by the psychiatric service. Due to the lack of rules and norms concerning the application of security measures and serious limitations among the medical and correctional facilities, the security measures demanded by the judicial authority are not usually applied in the hospitals or specialised institutions.

Sweden: Apart from being committed to forensic psychiatric care, the Swedish Penal Code provides no special sanctions for mentally-disordered offenders. Apart from a few prisons which have special psychiatric departments for the temporary care of prisoners, there are no so-called hospitals for criminals. All hospitals are administered by the ordinary health service system. Criminal patients who do not have special restrictions will be discharged when the chief psychiatrist reaches the conclusion that the patient no longer suffers from a grave mental disorder, or when her/his mental and personal condition no longer demands that s/he be kept in an institution. If treatment exceeds 4 months, the doctor must apply to the administrative court for the period to be prolonged for 6 months at a time. If the patient has special restrictions, discharge should be decided by the administrative court when there is no longer a risk that the patient, as a result of this mental disorder, might relapse into serious criminality and there is no reason, considering the patient's mental and personal condition, for keeping her/him in the institution.

Thailand: If the offender is considered to be a danger to the public, s/he is kept in a mental institution upon an order from the court, and may be released after a medical report.

Relationship between traditional criminal sanctions and measures of security

England & Wales: It is Home Office policy to encourage co-operation between agencies to ensure that mentally-disordered persons are not prosecuted where this is not required by the public interest. Division policy allows courts to choose alternative options throughout each stage of the criminal justice process. A prison sentence may be appropriate for someone who is currently mentally stable or who has recovered from a mental disorder sufficiently, provided the prison medical service has facilities to meet the patient's needs. However, it is also Home Office policy to transfer mentally-disordered offenders whenever mental illness is of a nature or degree that warrants detention in hospital for medical treatment and, in the cases of psychopathic disorder and mental impairment, such treatment is likely to alleviate or prevent a deterioration of the condition.

Germany: The penal law of Germany is based on the principle of guilt. Therefore, not all the needs of the public for security, in relation to dangerous offences and the healing treatment of mentally-ill offenders, can be satisfied by the institution of a penalty. This fact is the basis for the phenomena of the so-called 'double-track' system, according to which punishment is free from pure prevention. The preventive needs are satisfied by special measures, and not by punishment. An offender who is found responsible may be committed to one or several of the above-mentioned measures, in addition to punishment. With the exception of the committal to an institution of protective custody, the measure shall be carried out prior to the application of the punishment.

Italy: In Italy, as far as diminished responsibility is concerned, a measure of security is added to the traditional sanction which deprives offenders of their freedom. That is, while the offender who is partially responsible for a criminal act is sentenced to imprisonment, a measure of security is also applied if s/he is considered to be dangerous. The main rationale behind this cumulative system, which produces an unreasonable double form of repression, is a belief that the traditional sanction and the new measure of security have different functions; while the former has a retributive function, the latter has a preventive one. However, this idea is now being widely contested due to the reasoning that the traditional sanction also has an important preventive function, except for the use of psychopharmacological treatment.

Peru: Under the Peruvian legislation, the accused who is declared to be non-responsible is exempt from any sanction. However, measures of security are applied to those who are declared non-responsible or partially responsible with a less severe sanction, when they are also declared to be a danger to society by the court. In addition, the new Penal Code adopts a vicarial system for the application of both punitive sanctions and measures of security. The law requires that, whenever an institutional measure is assigned to those who are responsible, or responsible but with diminished responsibility, the measures of security or sanctions have to be applied before the punitive sanction. The duration of the measure of security will be taken into account for the total period of the sanction. However, the judge is allowed to reduce or drop the sanction if the security measure allows for the application of successful treatment.

Role and function of the traditional criminal psychiatric hospitals in the criminal justice system

England & Wales: Although no plans are envisaged, in England and Wales, to change the current three-tier security pattern, the need for an increase in medium security placement has however been recognised. An extension of hostel facilities for patients who are on course for entry into the community is also currently planned.

Germany: In Germany, the commitment to a mental health institution is one of the measures of rehabilitation and security. The characterisation of the measure as one of rehabilitation and security already describes the main function of the traditional criminal psychiatric hospitals. In the best of cases, the offender has the possibility to get better and in the worse s/he will not be cured, but the public may feel safe because s/he is locked up in the 'security' of a psychiatric hospital. The German Penal Code states that committal to a mental health institution is not limited to persons who require treatment or care in the proper medical-psychiatric sense. Since committal serves the purposes of both healing and security, the requirement for treatment or care is not a precondition for the application of this kind of measure.

Italy: In Italy, criminal (forensic) psychiatric hospitals mainly deal with the following cases:

   a) patients who, during trials, are kept in the hospital on a temporary basis as a measure of security;

b) inmates who suffer from a mental illness and are not considered suitable for normal detention due to the illness;

c) inmates who require a measure of security and also suffer from a mental illness;

d) those who are acquitted from prison due to a mental illness, chronic intoxication, or because they are deaf and mute;

e) offenders under 14 years of age;

f) offenders between 14 and 18 years of age who are not guilty due to their incapacity.

The traditional role of measure of security has been increased as a psychiatric sanction. The length of stay in a forensic psychiatric hospital is essentially related to the seriousness of the crime. That is, it is clear that commitment to a forensic psychiatric hospital has a retributive aspect. Originally, forensic psychiatric hospitals were established to perform the two main functions; custody and therapy. Although the custodial function has remained unmodified, the therapeutic function is facing a crisis. This is caused by the 'Basaglia Law', established in 1978, which abolished all psychiatric hospitals in Italy except forensic psychiatric hospitals. The main outcome of this law is that psychiatric treatment has become essentially voluntary. Compulsory treatment is only applied in exceptional cases, which are treated in special sections of normal hospitals. However, since special sections of normal hospitals are not yet well organised in Italy, most individuals considered to be mentally-ill are taken care of by their families with the obvious risks to public security. The role of the forensic psychiatric hospital has not, therefore, focused on custody. The treatment in forensic psychiatric hospitals has, in fact, been similar to that in normal prisons.

Japan: There are no so-called criminal psychiatric hospitals in Japan.

Nigeria: Although there are no criminal psychiatric hospitals in Nigeria, there are a few psychiatric hospitals which may have more secure units for mentally-ill offenders and other certified cases that may attempt to escape. If no psychiatric hospital is available, mentally-ill offenders are kept in prison where they are attended to by a visiting psychiatrist or the prison medical officer.

Peru: In Peru, the presence in prisons of non-responsible mentally-ill offenders was mainly due to the lack of co-ordination between the Ministry of Health and the National Penitentiary. Therefore, in-patient treatment for the mentally-ill who are non-responsible is very restricted, and there is a long waiting list in the prisons to be assigned a bed and some treatment in the psychiatric judicial ward.

Thailand: In Thailand, there is only one hospital which has been set up for forensic psychiatric care, and most forensic psychiatric cases are sent to this hospital for evaluation. Furthermore, this hospital can detain anyone who is considered to be dangerous, although some cases from the provinces can be sent to the conventional mental hospital for treatment.

Role and function of the alternatives to traditional criminal psychiatric hospitals in the criminal justice system

England & Wales: The alternatives to lower security hospitals comprise hostel facilities and flat clusters of single person accommodation. These are normally reserved for conditionally discharged categories who are able to cope in the community. The provision of these places is dependent upon the degree of social service provision available.

Germany: Since the alternative to traditional criminal psychiatric hospitals, namely the commitment to a socio-therapeutic institution, has been dropped by the amendatory act of penal administration in favour of a solution within the punitive administration, no other alternatives are left.

Thailand: The role and function of the alternatives to traditional criminal psychiatric hospitals in the Thai criminal justice system has been described in the last section.

251

REFORMS

The following countries have plans for reform: Canada, Egypt, Italy, Japan, Nigeria, and Sweden.

Aim of the reform

Canada: A major reform was introduced in Canada in February 1992. Its purpose was to modernise and streamline the legislation, and to increase protection of the rights of the mentally-disordered accused, while at the same time assuring the maintenance of adequate protection for the safety of the public.

Egypt: In Egypt, the aim of the project for reform is to formulate new rules concerning mentally-ill offenders which could be in concordance with the most modern theories in law and in medicine.

Italy: In order to understand the reform in the field of mentally-ill offenders, it is necessary to know the most important recent reform of the psychiatric law, i.e., the 'Basaglia Law' of 1978. This law abolished the traditional psychiatric hospitals and attempted to replace them by introducing special sections in normal hospitals for emergency cases. As a result of this law, mentally-ill people are usually cared for by their families with some risk to public security. Therefore, a project which attempts to regulate the problems of mentally-ill offenders was presented to the Senate on 29 September 1983 (withdrawn later). The project proposed to abolish the traditional forensic psychiatric hospitals, as well as the distinction between responsibility and non-responsibility. In addition, it proposed that, while all offenders are considered to be responsible for their acts, they should receive different treatment within the different penitentiaries. In other words, the project attempted to abolish the concept of criminal responsibility and replace it with the concept of dangerousness.

Japan: The main aims of the reform in Japan are to protect the human rights of patients, and to promote community-based social rehabilitation of the mentally-ill.

Nigeria: The aim of the reform in Nigeria is to incorporate the new law into the state of the art in psychiatry and psychiatric practice.

Sweden: The main purposes of the reform in the Swedish criminal justice system are:

 a) to modernise the psychiatric terminology;

 b) to initiate new restrictions for discharge;

 c) to nationalise the mental examination.

Envisaged reform

Canada: The main aims of the major reform of 1992 are to:

 a) modernise the terminology used throughout the legislation;

 b) change the verdict from 'not guilty on account of insanity' to 'not criminally responsible on account of mental disorder';

 c) increase the number of situations in which a psychiatric assessment may be ordered by the court;

 d) provide protection for the accused against the use of statements made by her/him during a court-ordered psychiatric assessment;

 e) clarify the criteria for determining whether an accused is unfit to stand trial on account of mental disorder;

 f) establish a legal authority for the court to order the treatment required to render the accused fit to stand trial;

 g) establish review boards to conduct regular reviews of mentally-disordered accused being held under the authority of the criminal law as being either unfit to stand trial or not criminally responsible;

 h) set out procedural rules to be followed by the review boards and the disposals the boards may make;

i) replace the current system of potentially indefinite detention for those found either unfit to stand trial or not criminally responsible on account of mental disorder with a 'capping' system, so that the mentally-disordered accused cannot be held significantly longer under the authority of the criminal law than if s/he had been convicted of the offence changed;

j) introduce provisions paralleling the Dangerous Offender Provisions which will be applicable to those found not criminally responsible on account of mental disorder;

k) introduce appeal provisions with respect to decisions of review boards;

l) set up a procedure for determining the placement and supervision of 'dual status' offenders who have both an outstanding prison sentence and an order for custody as mentally-disordered accused;

m) create a 'hospital order' scheme, giving the trial judge the power to order that an offender who has just been sentenced by the judge to a term of imprisonment shall serve up to the first 60 days of the sentence in a hospital (if both the hospital and the offender consent to the order);

n) introduce consequential amendments with respect to young offenders and persons tried under military law, to assure that procedures with respect to them are compatible with those applicable to adult offenders under the criminal law.

Egypt: A project for an Egyptian Penal Code was prepared in 1966. This project is a reformulation of the present Code, and therefore contains new rules concerning mentally-ill offenders, their capacity for responsibility, punishment and measures of security.

The present Egyptian Code is of a traditional character and is similar to the French Penal Code of 1810. The Egyptian Penal Code, which was issued in 1937, and its sections, made very few amendments to the rules set out in the previous Code of 1904. At that time, the institution of measures of security and the theory of criminal dangerousness were not yet known and the concept of the half insane was not yet formulated.

Italy: A commission of criminal law professors nominated by the Minister of Justice worked on the reform of the 1930 Penal Code for several years. The commission has completed its work, a Project of 'legge delega', which is being discussed by the Legislative Commission of the Ministry of Justice.

Japan: The main features of the new Mental Health Law are related to hospitalisation procedures and categories, qualification requirements and role of the designated physicians, post admission safeguards, and intermediate community-based social rehabilitation facilities:

As far as hospitalisation procedures and categories (described earlier in the text) are concerned, the main features of the new hospitalisation measures are that they place emphasis on the patients' human rights; and give priority to voluntary hospitalisation among the hospitalisation measures.

As for the qualifications and role of the physicians, the 1988 law clarifies the qualification requirements and role of the physicians who are designated to carry out psychiatric examinations.

In order to improve the protection of the rights of patients, the 1988 Law has introduced a system of post admission safeguards which provide for the submission of regular reports and reviews on the condition and status of patients, a formal system for presenting requests for discharge or improved treatment, and notice of the patients' rights under the new system, to be given to the patient upon hospitalisation. The new law also establishes a psychiatric review board in each Prefecture to act as a special body for receiving and reviewing requests and reports authorised and mandated, respectively, under the new system of safeguards.

The last feature of the new law acknowledges the Ministr++

of Health and Welfare's recognition of the need for intermediate community-based social rehabilitation facilities. The law has charted a fully-formed rehabilitation system, complete with day-care and night-care facilities, group residential facilities, etc. It also authorised the establishment of a variety of rehabilitation facilities: 'Social Reintegration Activities', 'Training Facilities' and 'Sheltered Workshops'.

Sweden: Plans for reform in the Swedish criminal justice system refer to changing the general rules concerning parole. This envisages the entitlement of the offender to parole after serving half of the sentence.

Status of the reform

Canada: All of the above-mentioned reform provisions came into force on 5 February 1992, except for the following:

a) 'Capping' and the new 'dangerous mentally-disordered accused' provisions, which will be brought into force when a reasonable length of time will have elapsed to make any necessary modifications to the mental health legislation;

b) the 'hospital order' provisions' will not take effect nationally until some pilot projects have been conducted to determine likely utilisation rates and costs.

Japan: On 26 September 1987, the New Mental Health Law was promulgated to be effective as of 1 July 1988.

Nigeria: Reform in Nigeria is still at the debate level, with proposals being put forward by various organisations: psychiatrists, criminologists, prison officers and so on.

Sweden: The Swedish legislation concerning mentally-disordered offenders has recently been reformed and the new rules came into force at the beginning of 1992.

CONCLUSIONS AND RECOMMENDATIONS

The analysis of the national reports on mentally-ill offenders makes it possible to distinguish some trends in criminal policy that could prove very important from a legislative point of view. The following considerations reflect some of these trends:

1) as regards the concept of responsibility (or imputability), there is a tendency to emphasise the concept of value, in the sense that not only the abstract capacity of understanding and discernment should be studied, but also the capacity to understand the judicial value of an action and of 'self-determination';

2) often the concept of mental illness tends to include neurosis, pychopathic disorder and what, in general terms, jurisprudence refers to as 'abnormal personality', and also to give judicial value to emotional distress;

3) it is essential to make use of psychological tests to determine illnesses. They should include tests of a biological, psychological, and even sociological nature;

4) the national reports reveal that the concept of dangerousness has remained in most criminal codes and legislations, although empirical data show that it is very difficult to predict criminal behaviour, particularly in the long run. This concept, and its use, might be appropriately replaced by criteria obtained from the results of therapy;

5) as regards sanctions, the vicarial system for measures of security seems to have produced better results than the cumulative one, which only produces a 'duplication' of repression. It might, therefore, be preferable to introduce the vicarial system also in those countries where the cumulative one still exists. It might also be better to introduce a system of new measures of security for mentally-ill offenders rather than to leave their treatment to the health system, for reasons of public order and because criminal procedures would provide more reliable guarantees than

administrative procedures. The most important measure to be taken, however, is the introduction of new types of measures for offenders who are not psychotics, but neurotics and psychopaths. In this field, the experience of the so-called 'socio-therapeutic institutions' in Northern Europe could provide an interesting model for other countries;

6) lastly, as regards the reforms envisaged, the temptation to abolish the distinction between imputability and not-imputability, as has been adopted in Sweden and proposed in Italy, must be resisted. In these countries, the distinction has remained in the field of execution. It would be preferable to take into account the important role of the concept of responsibility as 'orientation' of social behaviour. In future reforms, it would also be important to retain the concept of sanctions especially by stressing the re-socialisation aspect than the traditional sense of custody only.

Publ. No. 1   **Tendencias y necesidades de la investigación criminológica en America Latina.** (1969) 60p. F. Ferracuti, R. Bergalli.

Publ. No. 2   **Manpower and training in the field of social defence.** (1970) 152p. (1)   F. Ferracuti, M. C. Giannini

S.P. No. 1   **Co-ordination of interdisciplinary research in criminology.** (1971) 44p. F. Ferracuti

Publ. No. 3   **Social defence in Uganda: A survey of research.** (1971) 129p.

Publ. No. 4   **Public et justice: Une étude pilote en Tunisie.** (1971) 186p. A. Bouhdiba

S.P. No. 2   **The evaluation and improvement of manpower training programmes in social defence.** (1972) 33p. R. W. Burnham (1)

S.P. No. 3   **Perceptions of deviance: Suggestions for cross-cultural research.** (1972) 84p. G. Newman

S.P. No. 4   **Perception clinique et psychologique de la déviance.** F. Ferracuti and G. Newman
Sexual deviance: A sociological analysis. G. Newman
Aspetti sociali dei comportamenti devianti sessuali. F. Ferracuti and R. Lazzari (1973) 75p.

S.P. No. 5   **Psychoactive drug control: Issues and recommendations.** (1973) 98p. J.J. Moore, C.R.B. Joyce and J. Woodcock (1)

Publ. No. 5   **Migration: Report of the research conference on migration, ethnic minority status and social adaptation, Rome, 13-16 June 1972.** 196p.

Publ. No. 6	A programme for drug use research: Report of the proceedings of a Workshop at Frascati, Italy, 11-15 December 1972. 40p.
S.P. No. 6	Un programma di ricerca sulla droga. Rapporto del seminario di Frascati, Italy, 11-15 dicembre 1972. 93p.
Publ. No. 7	A world directory of criminological institutes. (1974) 152p. B. Kasme (ed.)
Publ. No. 8	Recent contributions to Soviet criminology. (1974) 126p.
Publ. No. 9	Economic crisis and crime: Interim report and materials. (1974) 115p.
Publ. No. 10	Criminological research and decision-making: Studies on the influence of criminological research on criminal policy in The Netherlands and Finland. (1974) 220p.
Publ. No. 11	Evaluation research in criminal justice: Material and proceedings of a research conference convened in the context of the Fifth United Nations Congress for the Prevention of Crime and the Treatment of Offenders. (1976) 321p.
Publ. No. 12	Juvenile justice: An international survey, country reports, related materials and suggestions for future research. (1976) 251p.
Publ. No. 13	The protection of the artistic and archaeological heritage: A view from Italy and India. (1976) 259p
Publ. No. 14	Prison architecture: An international survey of representative closed institutions and analysis of current trends in prison design. (1974) 238p. (2)
Publ. No. 15	Economic crises and crime: Correlations between the state of the economy, deviance and the control of deviance. (1976) 243p.

Publ. No. 16	**Investigating drug abuse: A multinational programme of pilot studies into a non-medical use of drugs.** (1976) 192p. J.J. Moore
Publ. No. 17	**A world directory of criminological institutes.** (2nd edition) (1978) 521p.
Publ. No. 18	**Delay in the administration of criminal justice: India.** (1978) 73p. S.K. Mukherjee and A. Gupta
Publ. No. 19	**Research on drug policy.** (1979) 93p. J.J. Moore and L. Bozzetti
	The effect of Islamic legislation on crime prevention in Saudi Arabia. (1981) 606p. (3)
Publ. No. 20	**A world directory of criminological institutes.** (3rd edition) (1982) 691p.
Publ. No. 21	**Combatting drug abuse.** (1984) 251p. F. Bruno
Publ. No. 22	**Juvenile social maladjustment and human rights in the context of urban development.** (1984) 504p.
Publ. No. 23	**The phenomenology of kidnappings in Sardinia.** (1984) 211p. I.F. Caramazza and U. Leone
Publ. No. 24	**The rôle of the judge in contemporary society.** (1984) 80p. (4)
Publ. No. 25	**Crime and criminal policy: Papers in honour of Manuel López-Rey.** (1985) 747p. P. David (ed.)
Publ. No. 26	**First Joint International Conference on Research in Crime Prevention.** Riyadh, 23-25 January 1984 235p. (5)
Publ. No. 27	**Action-oriented research on youth crime: An international perspective.** (1986) 275p. U. Zvekic (ed.).
Publ. No. 28	**A world directory of criminological institutes.** (4th edition). (1986) 582p. C. Masotti Santoro (ed.).

Publ. No. 29   **Research and international co-operation in criminal justice: Survey on needs and priorities of developing countries.** (1987) 264p. (6) U. Zvekic and A. Mattei.

Publ. No. 30   **Drugs and punishment.** (1988) 146p. (6) D. Cotic.

Publ. No. 31   **Analysing (in)formal mechanisms of crime control: A cross-cultural perspective.** (1988) 343p. (6) M. Findlay and U. Zvekic.

Prison in Africa: Acts of the Seminar for Heads of Penitentiary Administrations of African Countries (1988) 286p.(7)

Publ. No. 32   **The death penalty: A bibliographical research.** (1988) 320p. (6)

Publ. No. 33   **La criminologia en America Latina.** (1990) 288p. (6) L. Aniyar de Castro (ed.).

Publ. No. 35   **A world directory of criminological institutes.** (1990) 661p. (6) C. Masotti Santoro (ed.).

Publ. No. 36   **Essays on crime and development.** (1990) 377p. (6) U. Zvekic (ed.)

Publ. No. 38   **Soviet criminology update.** (1990) 179p. (6) V. N. Kudriavtzav (ed.).

Publ. No. 39   **Diritti umani ed istruzione penale. Corso di formazione sulle tecniche di istruzione ed investigazione.** Castelgandolfo, Italy, 11-22 September 1989 245p.

Publ. No. 40   **Infancia y control penal en America Latina.** (1990) 417p. (9) E. Garcia Méndez and E. Carranza (eds.).

Publ. No. 41   **Toward scientifically based prevention.** (1990) 181p. (6) F. Bruno, M.E. Andreotti and M. Brunetti (eds.).

Publ. No. 42   **Ser niño en America Latina. De las necesidades a los derechos.** (1991) 434p. (10) E. Garcia Mendez and M. del Carmen Bianchi (eds.).

Publ. No. 43   **Compendio per la prevenzione. Vols. I/II/III.** (1991) F. Bruno (ed.).

Publ. No. 44   **Cocaine today: its effects on the individual and society.** (1991) 420p. (11) F. Bruno (ed.).

Publ. No. 45   **Justicia y desarrollo democratico en Italia y America Latina.** (1992) 343p. (6) G. Longo, U. Leone and M. Bonomo (eds.).

Publ. No. 46   **Development and crime. An exploratory study in Yugoslavia.** (1992) 350p. (12) U. Leone, D. Radovanovic and U. Zvekic.

Publ. No. 47   **Criminology in Africa.** (1992) 272p. (6) T. Mushanga (ed.).

Publ. No. 49   **Understanding crime - experiences of crime and crime control.** (1993) 718p. (6) (13) A. Alvazzi del Frate, U. Zvekic and J. J. M. van Dijk (eds.).

                Alternative policing styles: cross-cultural perspectives (1993) 288p. (14) M. Findlay and U. Zvekic.

Publ. No. 50   **Environmental crime, sanctioning strategies and sustainable development** (1993) 420p. (6) (15) A. Alvazzi del Frate and J. Norberry (eds.).

PUBLICATIONS DEFERRED

Publ. No. 34   **Criminology in Latin America.** L. Aniyar de Castro (ed.). 8)

Publ. No. 37   **Prison labour.** (8)

NOTES

(1)   Also published in French and Spanish.

(2)   Available through The Architectural Press, 9 Queen Anne's Gate, London SWH 9BY, England.

(3)   At the request of the Government of The Kingdom of Saudi Arabia, UNSDRI published English, French and Spanish editions of this publication.

(4)   In collaboration with the International Association of Judges.

(5)   In collaboration with the Arab Security Studies and Training Center in Riyadh, The Kingdom of Saudi Arabia.

(6)   Available through United Nations Publications in Geneva (Palais des Nations, CH-1211 Geneva 10, Switzerland) or New York (United Nations Headquarters, Room A3315, New York, N.Y. 10017, U.S.A.).

(7)   In collaboration with the Ministry of Justice of Italy and the International Centre for Sociological, Penal and Penitentiary Studies, Messina, Italy.

(8)   Tentative title.

(9)   Joint UNICRI/ILANUD publication.

(10)   In collaboration with the UNICEF, ILANUD, IIN (Instituto Interamericano del Niño) and DNI (Defensa de los Niños International).

(11)   Also published in Italian.

(12)   Joint UNICRI/IKSI publication.

(13)   Joint UNICRI/Dutch Ministry of Justice/Italian Ministry of the Interior publication.

(14)   Available through Kluwer, Law and Taxation Publisher, P.O. Box 23 7400 GA Deventer, The Netherlands.

(15)   Joint UNICRI/AIC publication.

United Nations Interregional Crime and Justice Research Institute

via Giulia 52, 00186 Rome, Italy
Tel. 6877437 - Fax 6892638